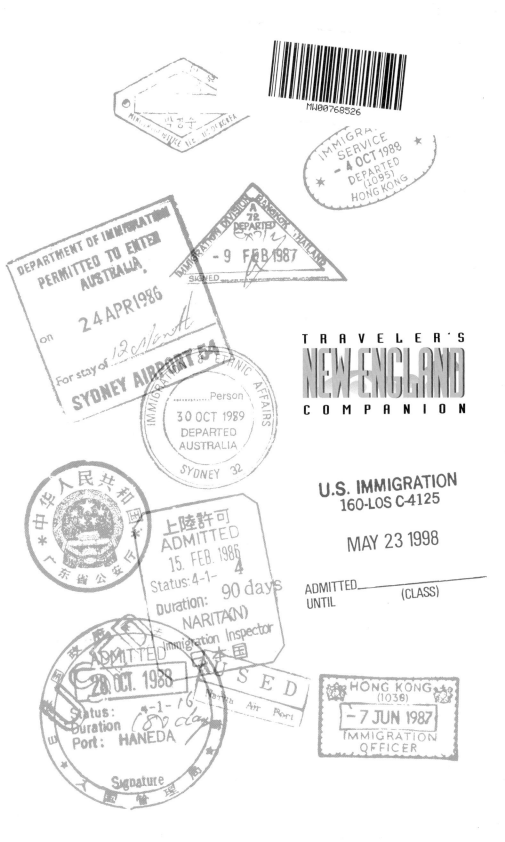

The 1998–1999 Traveler's Companions

ARGENTINA • AUSTRALIA • BALI • CALIFORNIA • CANADA EAST • CANADA WEST • CANADA •
CHINA • COSTA RICA • CUBA • EQUADOR • FLORIDA • HAWAII • HONG KONG • INDIA • INDONESIA •
JAPAN • KENYA • MALAYSIA & SINGAPORE • MEDITERRANEAN FRANCE • MEXICO • NEPAL •
NEW ENGLAND NEW ZEALAND • PERU • PHILIPPINES • PORTUGAL • RUSSIA • SPAIN •
THAILAND • TURKEY • VENEZUELA • VIETNAM, LÁOS AND CAMBODIA

Traveler's NEW ENGLAND Companion
First Published 1998
The Globe Pequot Press
6 Business Park Road, P.O. Box 833,
Old Saybrook, CT 06475-0833
http://www.globe.pequot.com

ISBN: 0 7627 0233 8

By arrangement with Kümmerly+Frey, AG, Switzerland
© 1998 Kümmerly+Frey, AG, Switzerland

Created, edited and produced by
Allan Amsel Publishing, 53 rue Beaudouin,
27700 Les Andelys, France. E-mail: aamsel@aol.com
Editor in Chief: Allan Amsel
Editor: Laura Purdom
Original design concept: Hon Bing-wah
Picture editor and designer: Jane Pinel

Printed by Samhwa Printing Co. Ltd., Seoul, Korea

# T R A V E L E R ' S
# NEW ENGLAND
# C O M P A N I O N

by Lee Daley

Photographed by Robert Holmes

Kümmerly+Frey

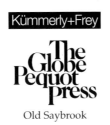

The
Globe
Pequot
Press

Old Saybrook

# Contents

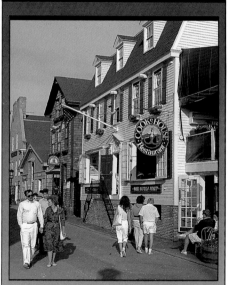

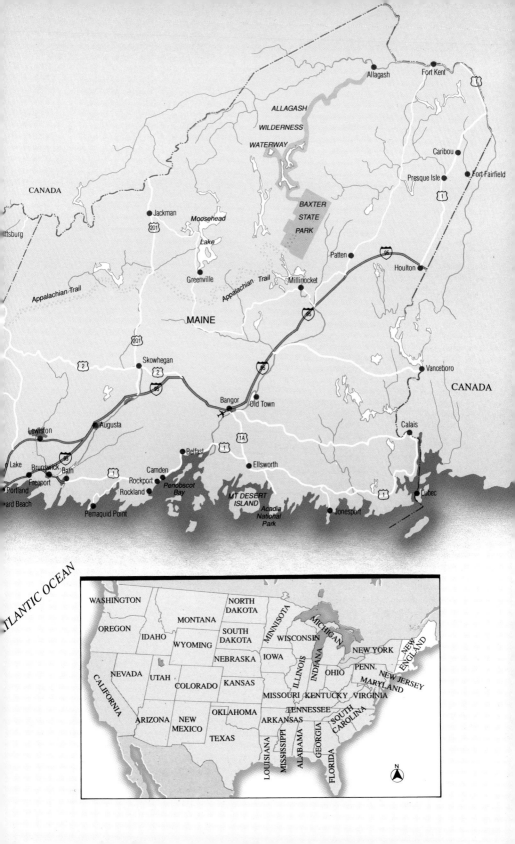

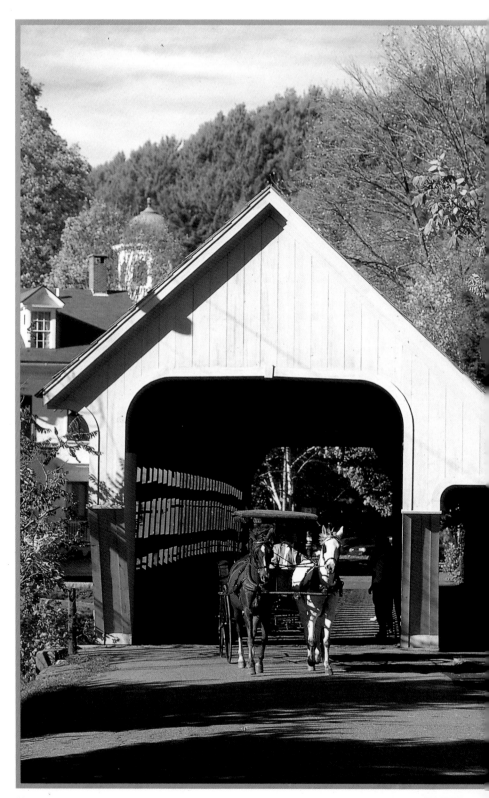

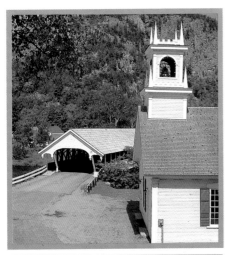

## Catch a Covered Bridge

*BUILT FROM THE 1830S FORWARD, COVERED WOODEN BRIDGES ONCE PROLIFERATED IN NEW ENGLAND, ESPECIALLY IN NEW HAMPSHIRE AND VERMONT.* Often spanning rivers and streams in mountainous regions, they are inevitably inviting and many are called "Kissing Bridges." Photographers collect them, schoolchildren picnic in them, winter sleigh rides and horse-drawn carriages traverse them. And lovers kiss in the privacy of them.

It is thought that bridges were covered to protect the bridge's floor boards from snow and thereby prevent rot. Some say the familiar barn-like walls sheltered skittish horses from taking fright. In early days, travelers who waited out a storm under a bridge's cover could pass the time reading posted handbills touting circus

dates, religious revivals, job openings in lumber factories and cure-all potions. Covered bridges often hosted church suppers and militia meetings.

In **New Hampshire**, the **Cornish–Windsor Bridge**, the nation's longest covered bridge with a 460-ft (140-m) span, crosses the **Connecticut River** in lovely Cornish. A state that also lays claim to possibly the shortest: a 12-ft (three-and-a-half-meter) expanse on a private estate in Alstead.

**Vermont** boasts more than 100 still remaining covered bridges, the most in New England and a testament to America's golden age of craftsmanship. You can cross three covered bridges in the town of **Bennington**, in the southwestern corner of Vermont. All three traverse the Walloomsac River. If you take a side trip to **West Arlington**, you'll see the house where artist Norman Rockwell lived for 10 years. Now called the "Covered Bridge Inn," it's across from the bridge over the Batten Kill River. A shaded green by the bridge makes a pleasant picnic spot. A covered bridge in nearby **Chiselville** spans a deep gorge. Vermont's largest concentration of intact covered bridges is found in the **Waterville–Montgomery** area, just north of the mountain resort town of Stowe. From the neat little village of **Waterville**, Route 109 drops down, twisting back and forth along

OPPOSITE: Woodstock claims Vermont's youngest covered bridge, built in 1969. ABOVE: Union Church and covered bridge over Stark.

the North Branch of the Lamoille River. Rocky ledges and strong currents give the river an exuberant character and six covered bridges afford fine lookouts. Outside of Waterville, in tiny **Belvedere**, are two wooden bridges, the Morgan and the Mill. With any luck, you can catch sight of 12 bridges in a day's time. One, Waterville's Codding or Kissin' Bridge still bears a sign tacked onto it in the 1950s that started a local romantic tradition.

## Linger with Literaries

*IN NEW ENGLAND, WHERE THE LOVE OF BOOKS IS AS NATURAL AS BREATHING, VISITING THE TOWN OF CONCORD IS A RAREFIED EXPERIENCE.* In terms of literary output, few places in America can hold a beeswax candle to **Concord**, Massachusetts. Henry David Thoreau, Nathaniel Hawthorne, Ralph Waldo Emerson and Louisa May Alcott called it home — what's more, all lived here at the same time.

Strolling through town, you can almost feel the presence of the 19th-century writers who resided in its beautiful, but unpretentious, colonial homes. One-hour walking tours, usually given on weekends and holidays, begin in the town center at the **Chamber of Commerce information booth** ☏ (508) 369-3120, Heywood Street. You can walk along the banks of the Concord River to the site of Thoreau's cabin, now a state reservation. Thoreau lived in these woods from 1845 to 1847 and here, he wrote his classic work, *Walden*, in which he advocated a life of simplicity lived in harmony with nature. In *Walden*, Thoreau says, "I went to the woods because I wished to live deliberately, to front only the essential facts of life, and to see if I could not learn what it had to teach and not, when I came to die, discover that I had not lived."

Near Thoreau's former home, you'll see a spring-fed pond where today's Concord kids dive and swim. Rent a canoe at the South Bridge Boat House and paddle the river anytime from April until the first snowfall. A round-trip cruise of about two hours will take you to the famous wooden span of the **Old North Bridge**, site of the firing of "the shot heard round the world," that sparked America's Revolutionary War. All along the river, fine homes line the banks.

Thoreau was a friend of fellow Concordian, Ralph Waldo Emerson. Emerson is best known as the founder of America's Transcendentalist Movement, whose credo professed a belief in the mystical unity of all creation.

Next to the Old North Bridge is the **Old Manse**, where Nathaniel Hawthorne, author of *The Scarlet Letter* and *The House of the Seven Gables*, lived for three years. The home was owned by the Emerson

family for centuries until it was deeded to the National Park Service. It's now a museum, displaying mementos of the Emersons and of the early years of Nathaniel and Sophia Hawthorne's marriage.

The Alcott family moved to Concord in 1857 when Louisa May, author of *Little Women*, was in her mid-20s. Her father, Bronson, was a great friend of Emerson's and a deeply committed Transcendentalist. Although poor, the Alcotts hosted weekly social gatherings at **Orchard House**. The house became the setting for *Little Women*, one of the most widely published children's books ever written. Although Louisa was the youngest member of this lofty literary

group, her work proved most durable. In addition to its literary popularity, the largely autobiographical novel was recently made into a Hollywood film starring Susan Sarandon. Almost all of the structure and furnishings of Orchard House remain in original condition. The Alcott family lived here for 20 years. You'll see the original soapstone sink which Louisa bought for her mother with her first royalty check. Upstairs, several of her sister Mary's sketches, some drawn on the walls, are on display, along with

---

The birth of America's revolution began at the Old North Bridge, Concord, when a minuteman fired "the shot heard 'round the world."

costumes used by the girls when they gave their famous plays.

Stroll through the hillside hush of Sleepy Hollow Cemetery, near the center of town, to **Author's Ridge**, the final resting place of Henry David Thoreau and his family. The Alcotts, the Emersons and the Hawthornes are also buried here. Ralph Waldo Emerson's tombstone is an appropriately natural uncarved rock of native marble.

# Master the Art of Crustacean Cracking

*A CULINARY CHALLENGE WORTH EVERY CRUNCH, CONSUMING THE HOMARUS AMERICANUS, KNOWN MORE COLLOQUIALLY AS THE AMERICAN LOBSTER, IS A REWARDING HANDS-ON EXPERIENCE.* Considered the King of Seafood, **lobsters** are harvested along the entire New England Coast. Every fishing community harbors its own distinct clan of fishermen and women, who "fence" their traditionally defined territories with brightly painted buoys.

The best place to get your lobster fix is where it's harvested. Coastal fishing villages throughout New England sport dining spots ranging from the salty and satisfying harbor shanty to the white-tablecloth eatery overlooking the sea.

One of my favorites is **Barnacle Billy's Seafood Restaurant** in Ogunquit, Maine. (See page 162.) You can work up a true salt's appetite by strolling Marginal Way, a mile-long footpath that begins near downtown Ogunquit, traverses the wild rose-edged cliffs above the Atlantic's rocky coast, and ends steps away from the front door of Barnacle Billy's. Near the entry, you'll select your meal from the listings on the chalkboard menu. Lobster, steamed clams, corn on the cob, garden salad and garlic encrusted rolls are

mainstays. Amble into the waterfront dining room with its view of the marina and cove. You'll sit at a colonial pine table and if it's cool, warm yourself by the crackling fire in one of the two stone fireplaces. If the weather is warm, sun yourself on the outdoor terrace or the upstairs deck overlooking Perkin's Cove boat dock.

Messiness is part of the experience. You'll be given the necessary tools to extract the meat from the lobster's bright red shell — a claw cracker, a small pick or fork for those tiny tight places, a mountain of napkins, a bib, a bowl for the discards, lemon slices and a ramekin of melted butter in which to dip the tender morsels of lobster meat. Lobster cracking and dissecting are skills sharpened with practice. Take your time, enjoy every succulent bite and wash it all down with ice-cold beer or a chilled chardonnay.

# Fall Foliage

*THE PLAIN TRUTH IS THAT IF YOU TRAVEL TO NEW ENGLAND IN THE FALL, YOU'RE IN FOR A SPELL OF PURE MAGIC.* Come mid-September evening's cool dusk brings a sudden snap to the night air. Afternoons, invariably warm and sunny, herald the short, shimmering season of Indian Summer and the beginning of the fall foliage season.

Freshly fallen leaves crunch under foot, shining like jewels in the sharp sunlight. Schoolchildren collect this early crop of scarlet and gold while it is still supple, paste each precious leaf on paper and bring their creations home where parents are known to display them on kitchen walls.

The northern hardwoods — beech, birch and sugar maple — turn golden yellow and orange. The famous red or swamp maple turns yellow and often deep red. Ash produces a reddish-purple that is absolutely brilliant when backed by the light yellow of aspen. Beginning in northern New England, each successive day's drop in temperature inches Mother

OPPOSITE: Litchfield County, Connecticut ablaze with fall colors. Mother Nature paints New England's landscape in brilliant tones each fall.

14　　　　　　　　　　　　　　　　TOP SPOTS

Nature's scotch plaid coverlet farther south, blanketing the countryside in a riot of pumpkin, cranberry, saffron, crimson and ruby.

You'll mark your forays along country roads with stops at farm stands overflowing with fresh harvests of squash, pumpkins, pears and vat-pressed apple cider. Summer corn is past peak, but New England natives purchase Indian corn, usually in three-eared bouquets to hang as seasonal markers on front doors of city apartments and country cottages.

Follow a day of hiking, and leaf-peeping with a mug of local mulled wine sipped before a roaring fire at a neighborly pub or country inn. If you are traveling with children, the little munchkins will want to devour dozens of cinnamon donut holes washed down with apple cider.

Notably, **Mount Washington Valley** in New Hampshire's White Mountains receives worldwide attention each year for its riotous explosion of color. The **White Mountain National Forest** surrounds the Valley while the 28-mile (45-km) **Kancamagus Highway** crisscrosses the forest and with its quaint country villages represents quintessential New England.

Columbus Day weekend traditionally marks the peak of the fall foliage season. Oktoberfest celebrations abound throughout the villages and towns of Massachusetts, New Hampshire and Vermont. Local harvest festivals, countryside pumpkin rides and little theater performances round out the calendar of events.

"Leaf peepers" — volunteers who track and report on the intensity of their community's color quotient — furnish state tourism offices with biweekly reports. For **locations of best fall foliage viewings,** telephone ( (802) 828-3239 in Vermont or the following toll-free numbers ( (800) 262-6660 in New Hampshire; ( (800) 227-6277 in Massachusetts; ( (800) 556-2484 in Rhode Island; ( (800) 252-6863 in Connecticut and ( (800) 533-9595 in Maine.

*TOP SPOTS*

# Cruise the Coast on a Windjammer

*AND YOU'LL FIND YOUR MODERN SOUL RENEWED BY THE BEAUTY OF SEAFARING LIFE THAT FOR CENTURIES HAS LURED SAILORS TO THE SEA.* A flotilla of more than a dozen majestic schooners still plies Maine's rugged central coast, exploring waters they have been sailing for more than 100 years.

These tall-masted beauties are ruggedly constructed, seaworthy vessels, restored with modern day comforts and safety codes in mind. The two and three-masted ships once hauled granite, lumber, fish and lime to ports up and down the Eastern Seaboard. Saved from extinction in the 1930s by Maine artist Frank Swift, they were refitted to carry passengers and bore the new name of windjammers.

Ships vary in length from 20 to 40 m (64 to 132 ft) on deck. Depending on size, each ship sleeps 20 to 44 guests in single, double and triple cabins. The huge sails, in keeping with 19th century tradition, are gaff-rigged. With a shout of "Haul Away!" the captain orders the crew to hoist the sheets and set sail.

Once at sea, wind and tides determine the ship's direction. Scenic harbors, islands and bays are set against a backdrop of granite mountains. Offshore islands with picturesque harbors beckon and most cruises anchor near a different village island each evening.

If eager for exercise, you can practice "schoonerobics" by hoisting and lowering the sails or taking a turn at the wheel. To hone your navigational skills, you can practice plotting a course with the compass and charts that most ships lay out for passengers. Before or after the day's sail, you can swim, go for a run, borrow the ship's rowboat, or explore the local islands on foot. Once under sail, you can stretch out on deck with a good

Tall-masted schooners ply the waters of New England's coast from Rhode Island to Maine.

book, laze in the salt air and sunshine. Overhead the schooner's sails billow in the wind.

While not luxury cruises, most schooners offer home-cooked hearty meals, prepared in the below-deck galley. With fresh baked muffins and blueberry pancakes for breakfast, no one leaves the table hungry. Creamy fish chowder and turkey dinner with all the fixings are other staples of schooner fare. Usually one night is reserved for an on-island lobster bake with fresh lobster and corn in the husk steamed in seaweed over a driftwood fire.

Most of the two- and three-masted schooners are home-based in the salty working ports of Rockland and Camden, Maine, "The Windjammer Capital of the World." Choose one of the newer reproductions or an authentic old schooner, like the *Victory Chimes*, sailing out of Rockland's Penobscot Bay. (See page 171.) Along the route you'll see fishing villages that look almost like they did at the turn of the century when these majestic schooners first set sail. Two-story wooden houses, some topped by a turret called a "widow's walk," line the island streets. The more populated resort towns house shops displaying local crafts.

# Get Spooked at a Haunted House

*OFTEN CALLED "THE BEWITCHING SEAPORT,"* **SALEM**, *MASSACHUSETTS IS FAMOUS BECAUSE OF THE WITCH TRIALS OF 1692.* The spellbinding episode was sparked by a well-meaning Barbadian slave named Tituba, a servant of the Reverend Samuel Parris. Her talent for storytelling, particularly voodoo tales, regaled her charges, Parris' nine-year-old daughter Betty and her 11-year-old cousin, Abigail Williams. The girls soon invited friends to share in the excitement. Hysteria ensued

The courtyard of "Mrs. Jack's" palace, Boston's Isabella Stewart Gardner Museum.

when some of the girls complained of nightmares. Some children would throw themselves on the floor and have fits. When local doctors declared that the girls were witches, people started to believe that the Devil had come to town. The hunt was on and no one was above suspicion.

The **Witch Dungeon Museum** tells the story. You're guaranteed a chill or two as you experience the performance of a Witch trial adapted from the 1692 historical transcripts. Professional actors in repertory reenact the electrifying scene. Another witchy site, the **Salem Witch Museum** in a church-like building, presents a complete look at the witchcraft hysteria. Using life-size figures in sets with a sound track narration and lighting, the museum recreates the drama of the accusers and accused. It's an experience both thought-provoking and timeless in its relevance to present-day issues of human rights and tolerance. The restored **Witch House**, one of the oldest dwellings in the country and home of Jonathan Corwin, judge of the witchcraft court, has been refurbished in the style of the era.

You can buy all sorts of potions and powders at **Crow's Haven Corner** ( (508) 745-8763, 125 Essex Street, a tiny witch shop owned by Laurie Cabot, a present day witch. The shop stocks a spellbinding array of crystal balls, magic wands, moonstones, books — you get the message. The illustrious Ms. Cabot gives readings by appointment.

# Visit a Venetian *Palazzo*

*FROM ITS STAID EXTERIOR, BOSTON'S* **ISABELLA STEWART GARDNER MUSEUM** *GIVES LITTLE HINT OF THE TREASURES IT HOLDS WITHIN.* (See BOSTON, CULTURAL ATTRACTIONS, page 91.)

An exquisite 1903 Venetian *palazzo* crammed with priceless art, it is the legacy of a charismatic heiress, known in her day as "Mrs. Jack." Soon after the flamboyant Isabella Stewart of New York married John Gardner, a

member of Victorian Boston's High society, she became the talk of the Back Bay. Mrs. Gardner scandalized proper contemporaries by posing bare armed in a clinging gown for artist John Singer Sargent and was known to stroll Commonwealth Avenue with her two pet lion cubs on a leash. When her son died at age two, she fled to Europe and immersed herself in the arts. She returned home a new woman, surrounding herself with the most talented artists, writers and musicians of her time. The Gardner home became a fashionable salon, the setting for glittering parties. An astute patron of the arts, she acquired Titian's *Rape of Europa*, Vermeer's *The Concert*, and Rembrandt's *Storm on The Sea of Galilee*.

During the 1890s with an inheritance of two and three-quarter million dollars from her father and a subsequent three million dollars from her merchant husband, Mrs. Gardner set about building **Fenway Court**, her personal concept of a 15th-century *palazzo*. Locals called it "Mrs. Jack's Palace." To this day, the galleries that surround the four-story glass-roofed courtyard remain, as she decreed, unchanged from the original design. At one end of the courtyard, you'll find fountains bubbling while throughout, flowers bloom year round.

Be sure to look upstairs in the gallery filled with mementos, letters and cards from Mrs. Gardner's prolific correspondence with the great and near great of her day. In another of the galleries, "Mrs. Jack's" portrait is on display surrounded by other masterpieces. The museum's eclectic collection includes almost 2,000 priceless objects housed in an urban cultural oasis.

# Meander Through Millionaires' Mansions

*IF YOU WERE NOT TO THE MANOR BORN BUT WOULD LIKE TO HAVE BEEN, THE MANSIONS OF NEWPORT, RHODE ISLAND PROVIDE THE ULTIMATE IN VOYEURISM.*

During Newport's heyday, families such as the Astors, Vanderbilts, and Morgans created a summer society resort unmatched for glitter and opulence. These were "pre-income tax" days when every cent of a dollar went into a man's pocket and the *nouveau riche* were eager to duplicate the palaces and châteaux that had so inspired them on their grand tours of Europe. Now open to the public, America's largest collection of what Europeans would call palaces can keep you enthralled, if not appalled by their ostentation, for days. Although hundreds existed during Newport's Golden Age, only about 70 remain; many of these house private schools and charitable organizations. The **Preservation Society of Newport County** ( (401) 847-1000, 424 Bellevue Avenue, Newport, offers combination admission tickets to many of the mansions.

Tour what many consider to be the most magnificent of the Newport "cottages," Cornelius Vanderbilt's **The Breakers**. The Newport Preservation Society rents — for a grand total of $1 a

year — this Italian Renaissance palace built in 1895. The mansion's 70 rooms are awash in marble, alabaster, gilt, crystal and stained glass. Its Grand Salon was constructed in France and shipped to Newport. Bathtubs have a choice of fresh or salt water.

If you're romantically inclined, you'll love another of the estates, **Rosecliff**, setting for the wooing of Mia Farrow by *The Great Gatsby*. Mrs. J. Hermann Oelrichs, a noted heiress and hostess, commissioned Stanford White to design Rosecliff in the image of the Grand Trianon of Louis XIV in Versailles. The 80 ft by 40 ft (24 m by 12 m) living room doubled as a ballroom and Mrs. Oelrichs is reputed to have spent $25,000 each summer for perfume to rub on the light fixtures. Be sure to notice the appropriately romantic grand staircase built in the shape of a heart.

After visiting one or two of these estates, stroll the five-and-a half-kilometer (three- and-a-half-mile) **Cliff Walk**, a path that overlooks Rhode Island Sound and borders the gardens of several mansions.

Just as the Vanderbilts did, walk the Cliff Walk, bicycle along Ocean Drive, ogle the yachts and revel in all that is Newport.

Newport's Golden Age produced hundreds of "summer cottages". Today about 70 remain; many are open to the public.

# YOUR CHOICE

## The Great Outdoors

New England, with its geographical diversity and four seasons, offers visitors a endless mix of activities on its seacoasts and rivers, forests and mountains. The state of **Connecticut** alone boasts nine state forests and 52 state parks. With a width of less than 40 miles (67 km), **Rhode Island's** 400-mile (645-km) coastline is an embarrassment of riches. Long before cultural events brought world fame to the **Berkshires**, outdoor lovers, including Henry David Thoreau and Herman Melville, explored its mountain peaks and surrounding streams.

**Cape Cod** is much more than miles of white sand beaches and windswept dunes. Bird sanctuaries, cranberry bogs and heavily forested state parks laced with bike paths and hiking trails entice pilgrimages year round. The longest hiking trail on the Cape Cod National Seashore, the **Great Island Trail** in Wellfleet, is only seven miles (11 km) long but it's a challenging passage through pine forest, marsh and foot-grabbing sand. Bird watchers will find lots of opportunity to view migratory birds on Cape Cod, Martha's Vineyard and Nantucket. Countings have recorded more than 300 species, including scores of different songbirds, and huge numbers of shorebirds along the beaches and tidal creeks, in the marshes, and on the mud flats. The **Wellfleet Audubon Sanctuary, North Monomoy Island, Nickerson State**

**Park** and **Barnstable's Great Marsh** all offer fine bird-watching opportunities. Many consider **Nickerson State Park**, on 1,800 acres (728 hectares) of forest in

Brewster, to be one of the best camp sites on the Cape, yet it is only minutes from the ocean and the Cape Cod National Seashore.

**Maine** has 3,500 miles (6,600 km) of shoreline, more than any other Atlantic state, and even more than California. From seaside ambles to back country hiking, Maine offers a trek for everyone. Much of the southern section, between Portland and the border of New Hampshire, has been developed, but north of Portland to the Canadian border the terrain is often

OPPOSITE: New England offers many opportunities for bicyclists to explore the "road less traveled." ABOVE: Angling for a prize catch in New Hampshire's scenic White Mountains.

completely undeveloped and stunningly beautiful. Many small towns add scenic variety.

## HIKING TRAILS

Beginning in southern New England, in Connecticut's Litchfield Hills, a ridge of mountains heads north traveling to the Berkshires in western Massachusetts and the Green Mountains in Vermont. Extending east to New Hampshire's White Mountains and Mount Katahdin in Maine, a network of hiking trails climbs to the summit of Cadillac Mountain in Maine's Acadia National Park. The **Appalachian Trail**, sometimes merging with the Long Trail, stretches south from Maine, through Vermont, New Hampshire, Massachusetts and Connecticut, some 2,000 miles (3,200 km) to its conclusion in Georgia.

Vermont's **Long Trail** begins at Jay's Peak in the Northeast Kingdom and travels south along the Green Mountains to Bennington.

Start your trekking plans by contacting the **Appalachian Mountain Club (AMC)** ✆ (603) 528-8721 TOLL-FREE (800) 262-4455, Box 298, Gorham, NH 03246. The AMC, with more than 60,000 members nationwide, offers guided hut-to-hut adventures from their Pinkham Notch Visitor Center in the White Mountain National Forest. AMC guides lead the hikes, sharing their knowledge of the natural and cultural history of the White Mountains. Even if you plan to hike on your own, you'll find the AMC series of well-organized guide booklets helpful. Outlines and books describe in full the long-distance hiking trails of six states with detailed topographical maps and symbols for shelters, ranger stations, emergency telephones and lookout points along the way. Regional tourist offices provide maps for short local hikes, some quite spectacular, such as the trails in the wilds of Maine's **Baxter State Park**. In most forests and state parks, trails are well marked, posting length, time needed and difficulty of the walk. New Hampshire's **White Mountains** and Maine's **Acadia National Park**, prime outdoor

playgrounds, offer some of the finest trails in the region.

Some of New England's most glorious uplands are in the **White Mountains**. A 94-mile (150-km) driving loop takes in the **Kancamagus Highway**, a lovely wilderness road over **Kancamagus Pass** and continues through **Franconia Notch**, a natural pass between the towering peaks of the Kinsman and Franconia ranges. Here's where you'll see many geological formations including the state symbol, "The Old Man of the Mountain". Driving through this beautiful wilderness, you'll pass a trio of magnificent waterfalls, **Sabbaday Falls**, **Rocky Gorge** and **Lower Falls**. You can swim in the waters of the small beaches near Lower Falls or the pool above Rocky Gorge. A favorite walk is in **Franconia Notch State Park**, through the natural gorge called the **Flume**, whose granite walls extend for 800 ft (244 m). For a token fee, you can enter the gorge's depths and stroll a footbridge through the cleft's dramatic 70-ft- (21-m)-high granite walls. Moss, lichen and other plants grow precariously in niches, while along the path, signs describe how nature carved the gorge.

From the eastern end of the Kancamagus Highway, the **Mount Washington Valley**, generously laced with hiking trails, stretches north. You can drive an alpine toll road to the top of the tallest mountain in the Northeast, the 6,288-ft (2,053-m) **Mount Washington**, which towers over the rest of the Presidential Range. You can also reach the summit on foot using the Appalachian Mountain Club's marked trails or climb aboard the steam-powered locomotive run by the **Mount Washington Cog Railway**. Due to a funnel effect, the mountain bears the full brunt of three continental storm fronts. History records the highest winds ever on its peak at 231 mph (372 kph), where what may seem like a mild breeze down below, becomes a gusty 75-mph (120-kph) howler at the top. **Tuckerman Ravine Trail**, at nearly four and a quarter miles (seven kilometers), is the shortest trail to the top. Several trails climb to the peak where, in spring, more than 60 alpine flower species bloom. Caution is strongly advised and foul weather gear, even on the most seemingly benign days, is strongly recommended.

The state of Maine offers the last vestige of the rugged outdoor experience and lovers of wild natural beauty should make tracks to **Mount Desert Island**. Exposed pink granite peaks crown this hunk of mammoth glacier off the coast of the state's Downeast village of **Bar Harbor**. Thirty-five thousand acres (14,000 hectares) of the island belong to **Acadia National Park (** (207) 288-3338, camping reservations TOLL-FREE **(** (800) 365-2267, Bar Harbor, ME 04609, a forested enclave of mountains, footpaths, hiking trails and carriage roads and New England's only national park. A climb or drive to the 1,530-ft (466-m) peak of **Cadillac Mountain** will put you at the highest point on the eastern seaboard. Make the trek before dawn and you'll be among the first in the nation to greet the new day. A shorter but equally rewarding trail up **Acadia Mountain** on the island's western side affords stupendous views of Somes Sound, the only fjord on the entire east coast.

Rugged types will relish some of the more precipitous of the park's 150 miles (240 km) of hiking trails. A free newspaper, *The Acadia Beaver Log*, calendars tours, guided walks, events and cruises between June and October.

In Vermont, the heady heights of **Green Mountains** have proved irresistible to mountain climbers, skiers and naturalists for centuries. Part of the appeal is the incredible diversity of terrain ranging from rolling foothill trails to dozens of well-marked summits. Many are perfect for an afternoon climb; others cry out for a three-day commitment. Besides the Appalachian Mountain Trail, New England serves up a second treat with the **Long Trail**, a 265-mile- (42-km)-long footpath that hugs the length of the Green Mountains from Massachusetts to Canada. Part of the Long Trail intersects **Mount Mansfield State Forest and Park** as it climbs over 4,393 ft (1,339 m) **Mount Mansfield** through breathtaking **Smuggler's Notch**. Here, around Mount

OPPOSITE: The Mohawk Trail traces an ancient Indian footpath later traversed by stage coaches and covered wagons moving west over the mountains. ABOVE: A timber house on the trail.

Mansfield, you will find some of the best hiking in the state. From nearby **Stowe**, you can ride a gondola close to the summit.

The **Underhill State Park Campground**, scattered around the base of the mountain, is extremely popular. For a brochure listing state maintained campgrounds, contact the **Vermont Department of Forests, Parks and Recreation** ( (802) 241-3655, 108 South Main Street, Waterbury, VT 05676.

# The Open Road

Although small by comparison with the rest of the United States, New England is so topographically and culturally diverse that one could not hope to know it in detail without spending many weeks, if not months, there. Nevertheless, a series of highlights, open road itineraries to discover the best of New England, can give the visitor a marvelous sense of the beauty, complexity and history of this land.

To be sure, your itinerary will naturally be based on your place of entry. The most common entries to New England are by car from New York State, often from the greater New York City area, by plane to Boston or, by car from Canada. If you have only a week in New England, go for the northern half — a day in Boston, then a drive up the coast to Portland. (If it's summer, continue to Sebago Lake State Park.) Turn west toward the White Mountains, and continue westward into southern Vermont, down into the Berkshires of Massachusetts, and back to Boston. If you have two weeks, the northern half is again best. From Boston, drive northward through Newburyport and Portsmouth, continue north along the southern Maine coast, including Portland and as far north as Acadia National Park. Cross Maine into New Hampshire and down to the White Mountains, northwesterly to the Green Mountains and Lake Champlain, then

A magnificent array of fall colors on a quiet roads in northern New England.

down to the Berkshires and back to Boston, with stops, if there's time, in Connecticut's Litchfield Hills and Rhode Island.

The important thing to remember about any New England itinerary is that the destination is never as important as the journey, and that sometimes wandering with no destination is the best journey of all. Depending on your entry, you may want to try one of the following itineraries. In each case, general areas are noted, with detail provided in the text that follows. There are simply too many interesting roads, towns and byways to list them all here, but these three provide a real taste of the flavor of New England.

## CONNECTICUT'S LITCHFIELD HILLS

In a northwest corner of the state, a 60-mile (96-km) circuit tours the highlands of Connecticut passing charming country inns and resorts scattered along lake fronts in the rolling Litchfield Hills. Detour into any town along the route and you're likely to find an historic inn, an art gallery and an antique shop or two.

Just north of **Candlewood Lake**, from the town of **New Milford**, drive north along Route 7. Cross the old covered **Bulls Bridge**, one of only two passable covered bridges left in the state. You'll traverse the bucolic **Housatonic Valley** through natural unspoiled terrain of pine and hardwood, on to the town of **Kent**, an antique maven's delight. Follow the flow of the Housatonic River north along Route 7 to **Kent Falls State Park**, a 275-acre (111-hectare) preserve and a perfect spot for a picnic. In warm weather, cool off in one of the refreshing swimming pools created by water cascading down a natural staircase.

A scenic side trip from here is a short drive on Route 5 to the farming village of **Little Goshen**, the birthplace of America's cheese making industry. The "house that cheese built," a stately brick mansion, stands near the Torrington Country Club. North of **Kent**, still on Route 7, the photogenic **Cornwall** covered bridge spans the river, providing another opportunity to cross a covered bridge.

Follow signs to the storybook town of **Litchfield** via Route 63, where a classic white-steepled Congregational church dominates the village green. Regal white, clapboard houses flank both sides of the village's elm-lined North and South Streets in this state-designated historical district. One of the world's largest collections of works by Ralph Earl, a famous 18th-century portrait painter is on display at the Litchfield Historical Society. America's first law school, a small structure, stands on the grounds of the Tapping Reeve House. The birth places of three illustrious Americans — Harriet Beecher Stow, Ethan Allen and Henry Ward Beecher — are all on North Street.

West from Litchfield, Route 202 passes **Mount Tom State Park**, where a mile-long trail leads to the 1,325-ft (404-m) summit and surrounding views. Snuggled beneath the hills, **Lake Waramaug**, near the junction of Route 45, offers a crescent beach with boating, swimming and camp sites. Near the lake, you can top off your day by taking a wine tour of **Hopkins Vineyard** and raising a glass in their tasting room.

Once back on Route 202, consider a side trip via Route 47 to the **Institute for American Indian Studies** ( (860) 868-0518, a research center and educational museum in the village of Washington. You'll walk through a 17th-century Native American village with a Paleo-Indian campsite, and a life-size longhouse. Some of the Algonquin artifacts are more than 10,000 years old. The museum is open every day April to December, most days January to March. The entire circuit, including side trips to the Indian village, is less than 70 miles (113 km).

## THE BERKSHIRES

In **Western Massachusetts**, less than three hours from New York City and Boston metropolitan areas, the **Berkshire Hills** dominate a landscape of lush countryside filled with cultural and visual delights. Nationally famous for its music, art, architecture and history, the green hills and precipitous granite crests of western

Massachusetts have inspired a host of writers and poets over the years. Herman Melville wrote his epic Moby Dick here; Longfellow, Emerson and Thoreau hiked its trails. As many city dwellers and travelers have discovered, the area is a rewarding destination or detour.

From **Boston**, head west on Interstate 90 (The Mass Pike) and take Exit 1 into **West Stockbridge**, a former railroad town nestled in the Queensboro Pass. Explore West Stockbridge's Main Street shops, markets and parks along the Williamsville River before heading north on Route 41 to visit **Hancock Shaker Village**, a remarkable window onto 19th-century American life with its 20 historic buildings, including a huge, round Shaker barn and working crafts shops.

Back toward West Stockbridge, follow Route 102 to the **Berkshire Botanical Garden**, some 15 acres (six hectares) of intimate landscaped gardens. As you stroll along a woodland trail to the pond garden, you'll pass sculpture exhibits presented by local artists.

Follow Route 102 to Route 183 north to **Lenox**, famed home of **Tanglewood** ( (617) 266-1494 or (413) 637-5165, the summer site of the Boston Symphony Orchestra. (See THE BERKSHIRES, LENOX and TANGLEWOOD, page 140.) Tanglewood's 200-acre (81-hectare) estate is actually one and a half miles west of Lenox. Pack a lunch, arrive early and have a picnic on the lawn outside the 6,000-seat **Music Shed** designed by architect Eero Saarinen. The summer BSO concert series, from June through late August, features performances by some of the world's leading musicians. Lenox, an elegant resort town famous for its 19th-century mansions and its resident writers (Herman Melville, Edith Wharton, Nathaniel Hawthorne), is an excellent base for more in-depth exploration of the Berkshires.

Leaving Tanglewood, continue north on Route 183 to Route 7 toward the city of **Pittsfield**. Here, you may want to visit the

BELOW: One of New England's more photographed sites: "Motif #1," Rockport Harbor.

**Berkshire Museum**, with its outstanding collections of art, history and natural history. From the steps of the museum, look across the town square to the Athenaeum, where the Herman Melville Memorial Room contains works, personal effects, and photographs of the author.

The highest peak in Massachusetts, **Mount Greylock**, looms farther north on Route 7. Drive several miles to the 3,941-ft (1,200-m) summit for spectacular views of the Berkshire panorama. If skies are clear, you will see the Green Mountains of Vermont, New Hampshire's Mount Monadnock, the Adirondacks and Catskills in New York and Mount Everett in the southern Berkshires.

Still motoring north along Route 7, stop in **Williamstown**, one of New England's most beautiful villages, a center for the arts, and home to Williams College and on South Street, the outstanding **Sterling and Francine Clark Art Institute**. More than 30 Renoir paintings make this museum a hidden jewel. Williamstown itself deserves a tour of its own. One of the finest college art museums in the country, the **Williams College Museum of Art** houses some 11,000 works that span the history of art. The neoclassical rotunda of its original structure, an 1846 two-story brick octagon, distinguishes the museum architecturally, and the extensive additions were designed by internationally renowned architect Charles Moor. While on the campus, you may want to visit **Thompson Memorial Chapel** in a modern Gothic building, **Hopkins Observatory** and **Chapin Library**, whose collection includes a repository of rare books.

Route 2 east from Williamstown is called the **Mohawk Trail** and winding west to east is one of the most scenic drives in the Berkshires. The road follows an old trail the Indians of the Five Nations tribe used to traverse the Connecticut and Hudson Valleys. Later, colonial troops used it marching to New York during the French and Indian Wars. Still later, stagecoaches and covered wagons followed the trail. Stop at the marked **observation point** for breathtaking views of mountainous portions of

southern Vermont and northwestern Massachusetts.

As you ascend the trail's **Hoosac Mountain Range** to the **Hairpin Turn**, you'll see vistas of **Mount Greylock**, the **Green Mountains**, and the **Hoosac Valley**. The trail then rises sharply to the **Western Summit**, called Spirit Mountain by Native Americans. Continue through the scenic town of **Florida** to **Whitcomb Summit**, home of the **Elk Memorial** on the highest point of the Mohawk Trail, at 2,200 ft (670 m). Four hundred and 40 yards (400 m) past the peak, **Whitcomb Hill Road** leads to the eastern portal of the **Hoosac Tunnel**. Continue easterly along Route 2 to **Shelbourne Falls**, where you'll see the **Bridge of Flowers**, an old arched trolley bridge transformed into a garden of flowers from spring to fall. Follow signs to **Salmon Falls** to view the **Glacial Potholes** carved out of rock during the Ice Age. The entire Mohawk Trail exposes you to many state parks and forests with swimming and picnic sites.

## CRUISING THE CHAMPLAIN VALLEY

Home to the Holstein and the haystack, the open lands of Vermont's Champlain Valley stretch west to **Lake Champlain** from **Middlebury** and the town of **Brandon** to the south. Vistas of cornfields and apple orchards bear testimony to the region's agricultural heritage. Pint-sized Middlebury's village green, gracious homes and historic inn give it a timeless look. There's nothing pint-sized about the 1,200-acre (485-hectare) **Middlebury College Campus**, just west of town. The college's Summer Language School attracts foreign and American students, whose numbers overflow into adjoining Middlebury, lending a cosmopolitan air to the local scene. You may want to linger a day or more in Middlebury with its fine restaurants and cafés, especially after you review the campus cultural schedule, which usually offers a full fare of plays, dance performances, musical events, films and art exhibits. Check with the **Middlebury Area Chamber of Commerce (** (802) 388-7951, N°2 Court

Square, Middlebury, VT 05753, for lodging and restaurant listings. They can also provide a list of local farms where you can tour dairies, maple sugaring operations and apple orchards. This is a prime area to taste and buy prized Vermont cheeses and honey.

Begin your tour by driving west out of Middlebury via Route 125, and almost immediately turn right at a rotary onto Route 23. You'll see signs for the **University of Vermont (UVM) Morgan Horse Farm** in **Weybridge**. These handsome steeds are the descendants of the bay stallion Justin Morgan, and the first breed of horse developed in America. You can tour the stables housed in a late-1800s slate-roofed barn and observe the Morgans at play as you wander the spacious grounds.

From Middlebury, follow Route 125 west past farmlands and pastoral views made more pristine by the blessed lack of billboards and roadside commerce. Head south on Route 22A, passing through the tiny village of **Bridgport** en route to **Shoreham**, where you'll find an antique shop, country store, crafts and the **Shoreham Inn**, built in 1799. Rumor has it that, back in 1840, packs of wolves prowled the outskirts of town where more than 40,000 sheep grazed. Threatened townspeople were forced to form wolf hunting posses to protect the herds. No such threat exists today in this region where acres of orchards nurture apples galore.

Wind east on Route 73 to a turnoff just before the upcoming town of Orwell. Signs direct you, via a fork in the road, to the ruins of a **Revolutionary War fort**, built in 1776. In and around the ruins, you can hike several miles of narrow, marked trails with scenic outlooks before driving, via Route 73, into **Orwell**. Park in downtown Orwell where you can take another step back in time by entering the interior of **The First National Bank**. Vermont's smallest bank is ensconced in an ornate Victorian Gothic building and you can cash travelers' checks here from one of the tellers who still transact business from behind brass wire cages.

From Orwell, Route 73 travels east, climbing a major ridge, one of the last before the Taconic Mountain Range drapes gently into the Champlain Valley. As you drive through the village of **Sudbury**, notice the Gothic tower looking down on the village from atop the white town hall. Outside Sudbury, the road crests several ridges as it continues east, each ridge affording open vistas of field dotted with silos and barns. Route 73 eventually hugs **Otter Creek**, following its banks before bending away to enter **Brandon**.

Near the Brandon Inn in the center of town is the former home of Stephen A. Douglas, who was born and grew up here. As a young man, Douglas earned his livelihood as a cabinetmaker before moving west to gain fame as an orator, a congressman and a presidential candidate who opposed Abraham Lincoln. Near the Douglas house on Pearl Street is a landmark of Vermont's anti-slavery movement, the home of abolitionist state senator R.V. Marsh, a red brick mansion

National holidays often call for flag displays. This Colonial-style home is located on the Mohawk Trail.

words from Frost's poem ,"A Young Birch," bear witness to the beauty of the scene.

## Sporting Spree

Outdoor New England offers a wealth of sporting options from kayaking its briny seas to rollerblading along the banks of the Charles River. For boating aficionados, New England's 6,130 miles (9,887 km) of shoreline, its thousands of islands, its lovely bays and many harbors all provide unique opportunities for summertime sailing. Bring your own boat if you have one or providing you can attest to your abilities, rent or lease a craft at one of New England's many yacht basins, such as the one at Newport Harbor. Many consider Newport the yachting capital of the world.

Captain Kip Files of Maine's *Victory Chimes Windjammer* tells me his state's mid-coast offers the second finest cruising grounds in the world. When I asked him the whereabouts of the first, he said, "I don't know. I'm still looking for it." (See ROCKLAND, page 171.) **Sail boats** for day trips or longer can be hired in many coastal towns. Besides Maine, the waters around Massachusetts' Cape Ann, the islands of Martha's Vineyard, Nantucket and Block Island, Rhode Island afford sailors superb opportunities.

City sailors set their sights on Boston's Charles River where the **Community Boating Company** ( (617) 512-1038, 21 Embankment Road, has a complete schedule of sailing programs and lessons for adults and children from spring through fall. Another company, **Boston Sailing Center** ( (617) 227-4198, at N°54 Lewis Wharf, provides beginner and advanced instruction year round.

**Bicycling** along the Charles River is wonderfully pleasant via an 18-mile (29-km) bikeway which borders both the Cambridge and Boston sides of the river. If you don't have your own, you can rent a set of wheels from the **Bicycle Workshop** ( (617) 876-6555, 259 Massachusetts Avenue, Cambridge, MA 02142. They'll

modeled after a Greek temple, was a stop on the underground railroad. Before the Civil War, Senator Marsh and members of Brandon's Baptist community banded together to harbor runaway slaves in private homes. The number of slaves sheltered is unknown, but it is known that the Marsh home housed a tunnel, many closets for hiding, and eight secret stairways. For further information, contact **Brandon Area Chamber of Commerce** ( (802) 247-6401, P.O. Box 267, Brandon, VT 05733.

Another side trip from Middlebury, east on Route 125, takes you to the little village of **Ripton** where poet Robert Frost summered in a rustic log cabin. Frost co-founded the Bread Loaf Writers Conference, a summer writer's school, in a former inn here. The state of Vermont designated Frost their official poet laureate in 1961, and in 1983 named this section of the Green Mountain National Forest, "Robert Frost Country." Near his former home, the **Robert Frost Interpretive Trail** meanders through a wooded setting where seven Frost poems are posted at regular intervals. The trail crosses over Beaver Pond into a forest of beeches and birches, where, on a plaque,

*YOUR CHOICE*

even deliver to some hotels. On Cape Cod, bicyclists will also find miles and miles of trails, some paralleling the seashore. Many hotels provide maps showing nearby routes for joggers; some can also be used by bicyclists.

The region's rivers, streams, lakes and ponds afford abundant **freshwater fishing**. Each state publishes guides listing locations and season dates through their fish and game departments. Vermont's Northeast Kingdom boasts lakes stocked with trout and landlocked salmon. Lake Champlain, fishable all year, is one of the few places you can experience the memorable adventure of ice fishing.

Starting in Vermont and flowing north to south along the New Hampshire border before reaching Connecticut, the idyllic Connecticut River harbors innumerable fishing sites for catches of trout, bass and yellow perch.

**Tennis** players who travel to Newport, Rhode Island will want to visit the **Tennis International Hall of Fame** at the Newport Casino, America's most exclusive country club. The very same lawn courts that hosted the first United States Men's Lawn Tennis Tournament are open to the public. (See NEWPORT, page 256.)

*YOUR CHOICE*

**White water rafting** and **canoeing** begin in earnest in spring when seasonal rains swell rivers. Maine's Kennebec River thrills rafters as it courses through an eye-popping 12-mile (19-km) gorge. Many rafting companies along the Kennebec, Penobscot and Dead Rivers supply instruction and all equipment, including boxed lunches. Children eight years or older, accompanied by adults, are allowed on some river rides. **Professional River Runners of Maine** TOLL-FREE ( (800) 325-3911, conducts trips throughout the eastern United States.

**Ski** fever began in New Hampshire's logging camps beck in the 1870s when Scandinavian immigrants brought their native sport to the new land. It spread to the college community in 1914 when Dartmouth University librarian Nathaniel Goodrich descended Vermont's highest peak, Mount Mansfield, in Stowe. Skiing flourished in those early days, without the benefit of gondolas or aerial trams, much less rope tows. Today, it's a multi-million

OPPOSITE: Whiling away an idyllic afternoon in the White Mountains. ABOVE: Guests at the Balsam's Grand Resort Hotel enjoy premier golfing and proximity to Dixville Notch State Park.

dollar industry and one of the region's major attractions.

**Killington**, in Shelburne Center, Vermont, home of the Graduated Length Method which revolutionized the sport, spans seven peaks and is New England's largest ski resort. **Stowe**, Vermont, nestled in a stunning mountain setting is another resort offering extensive downhill and cross-country ski trails. With more than 350 miles (564 km) of well-groomed alpine skiing terrain and 100 miles (160 km) of cross-country trails, there is something for every level or interest. Novices will find many trails on Stowe's Spruce Peak, where the four-mile toll road run is one of the most scenic novice trails to be found.

In Stowe village, on a stormy day, you can choose **indoor skating** at Jackson Arena. Or you can explore the woods on snowshoe with **guided tours** by two Stowe area outfitters, Umiak and Bedside Turners. Another way to enjoy the outdoors is with some of the special activities offered to the public by inns and lodges. Stowehof Inn offers romantic **horse-drawn sleigh** rides for two; the Trapp Family Lodge puts on **wagon rides** for 20. You can **horseback ride** at Edson Hill Manor or take **tennis lessons** from a professional at Topnotch Resort. (See MOUNT MANSFIELD AT STOWE, page 223.)

There are so many inviting resorts and inns offering snow-season recreation that you could spend a lifetime sampling them. The smaller north-country inns of New Hampshire, Maine and Vermont tend to be more notable for tranquillity and cuisine; the bigger and busier resorts offer more activities and amenities. Cozy **Blueberry Hill Inn** ( (802) 247-6735, in Goshen, Vermont, grooms its own ski trails and serves up conviviality along with healthy gourmet meals. The **Trapp Family Lodge** TOLL-FREE ( (800) 826-7000 with its 93 units is smack in the hub of Stowe. Snow making machines at larger resorts assure exhilarating sport from November through May for avid skiers and snowboarders.

The legendary Boston Bruins are memorialized in the New England Sport Museum, Cambridge, Massachusetts.

**SPECTATOR SPORTS**

Want to start an animated conversation with a New Englander, especially a Bostonian? Just mention the Red Sox (baseball), the Bruins (ice hockey), the Celtics (basketball), or the Patriots (football). Fervent sports fans typically quote statistics and rankings of their favorite sports teams at the drop of a mitt.

Watching the **Red Sox** play America's favorite sport from the bleachers in fabled **Fenway Park**, the nation's oldest ballpark, will seat you shoulder to shoulder with rabid baseball loyalists. Past Red Sox rosters contain the names of some of baseball's most legendary players: Babe Ruth, Carl "Yaz" Yastrzemski, Ted Williams, and Roger "The Rocket" Clemens. From early April to late October, you can catch the atmosphere at **Fenway Park** ( (617) 267-1700, at Nº4 Yawkey Way, Boston, MA 02202.

The **Boston Bruins** and the **Celtics** (winners of more NBA championships than any other team) share facilities at the new **Fleet Center** ( (617) 624-1000, 100 Causeway Street, Boston, near North Station. You can tour the team locker rooms and view team memorabilia when games are not taking place.

The **New England Revolution**, New England's new professional soccer team plays at **Foxboro Stadium** ( (508) 543-0250 (ticket information) between April and September.

Intercollegiate sports are usually spirited popular events. Tickets to the **Harvard University football games** can be difficult to obtain, but call ( (617) 495-2211 in season for a schedule of home games.

**BOSTON MARATHON**
Every April on Patriot's Day, world-class runners line up with amateurs for the opening shot of the world's oldest annual marathon, run since 1897. A special fitness event for children, held on Boston Common near the finish line of the race, emphasizes sports participation.

## Backpacking

New England has a wide array of comfortable lodging at reasonable prices but truly inexpensive lodging is hard to find except camping and hosteling. Many young people choose the option of finding a summer job at one of the region's seaside or mountain resorts. While these are usually lower paying positions, they often include lodging, meals and the opportunity to explore a region in depth. Likewise, ski resorts often need temporary help during the winter season.

One way to keep costs down is to plan your itinerary so that you stay in country inns during the week and cities on the weekends. Country resorts often reduce their prices midweek, while city hotels offer package plans for Friday, Saturday and Sunday when business travel is off.

In Boston, a good source for bargain-priced rooms is the **Regional Information Complex for Visitors**, located on the Massachusetts Turnpike at Exit 5. The catch is that the listed hotels usually only offer discount rates for the same day, often with a limit of two or three nights lodging. Rates can be as low as 50 percent

off, though, so if you are flexible, you may get lucky. Other centers are at Logan Airport and train stations, but, in all cases, you must call from the center and tell the reservation clerk the location of the center that you're calling from. Another agency, the **A B & B Agency** ( (617) 720-3540 TOLL-FREE (800) 248-9262, 47 Commercial Wharf, Boston, MA 02110 finds guest rooms in private homes. They list more than 100 choices in Boston, Brookline, Cambridge, some suburbs and Cape Cod. You can even book lodging on a bed and breakfast yacht in Boston Harbor. Ask about their winter specials. **The Massachusetts Office of Travel and Tourism** ( (617) 727-3201, 100 Cambridge Street, Boston, MA 02202, publishes a list of guest houses throughout the state in their free booklet, *Bed and Breakfast Guide*.

There are dozens of campgrounds in New England. Each state's tourism office publishes its own guide to state parks and campgrounds. Some of the most ideal locations are the heavily-wooded White Mountain National Forest campgrounds along the Kancamagus Highway where you can find primitive sites for less than $12. Another state-run campground at Lafayette Place in Franconia Notch State Park has about 100 wooded tent sites in the same price range. In warmer months, demand for these sites is naturally very high so you'll need to arrive early to secure one. In fact, for the weekend, plan to secure your site by Thursday, if possible.

Rough camping without proper equipment, outside designated areas, is discouraged, so if you don't bring your own gear, plan to purchase supplies at one of the excellent outfitters, such as L.L. Bean, in Freeport, Maine. Contact the **White Mountain National Forest headquarters** ( (603) 528-8721 at P.O. Box 638, Laconia, NH 03247. Another good source of information in the White Mountains is the **Lincoln/Woodstock Chamber of Commerce** ( (603) 745-6621 TOLL-FREE (800) 227-4191. The Chamber staffs a large information booth in Lincoln, off Route 93 at Exit 32. Their brochures and maps detail hiking routes in the national forest, trail by trail.

An excellent bargain is the chain of 21 youth hostels in all the states, except Rhode Island, although the most popular ones fill quickly in high season. Massachusetts has eight locations, including a superbly located 220-bed facility near Boston's Back Bay. Most are open year round, except those in Maine, which close during the winter. Besides the usual dormitory accommodations, many hostels also rent private rooms to couples and families, but you need to contact each hostel directly to reserve. For a hosteling map of the United States and a booklet listing addresses and phone numbers of individual hostels, contact **Hosteling International-American Youth Hostels** TOLL-FREE ( (800) 444-6111, 733 15th Street NW, Washington, DC 20005. If you are traveling solo, a youth hostel offers the best value, but with companions sharing the price of a hotel room, the savings of a hostel become less attractive.

Inexpensive accommodation can be found iin the heart of Boston at the **Berkeley Residence Club** ( (617) 482-8850, close to Copley Square and South Station. This 200-room club admits women only. Another great resource is the **Greater Boston YMCA** ( (617) 536-7800 in the Fenway. Lodging, limited to a 10-day stay, includes hot breakfast and maid service. Museums and theater are within walking distance and public transportation stops at the front door.

Families or groups may want to consider the possibility of a home exchange. One clearinghouse sends members an updated list of homes available for vacation exchange. Contact **HomeLink International/Vacation Exchange Club** TOLL-FREE ( (800) 638-3841 FAX (305) 394-1448, P.O. Box 650, Key West, FL 33041.

Getting around New England by public transportation can be economical but, unless you're traveling solo and plan to concentrate your visits on specific areas, you will save money and time by renting a budget-priced car. You'll see much more of the countryside and avail yourself of more economical lodgings with auto

transport, as well. One exception would be for sightseeing in Boston, where, with traffic and limited parking, a car is a hindrance. More important, the **MBTA**, Boston's public transit system (known locally as the "T"), sells visitor passes that provide up to $500 worth of discounts to many attractions. You may purchase a one-, three- or seven-day pass that includes discounts to 15 museums, 10 tours, nine entertainment facilities, six restaurants, eight shops, four dinner theater productions, sail boat and bike rentals. If you're traveling south from Boston to Providence, Hartford or New Haven, you'll find good service via AMTRAK, TOLL-FREE ( (800) 872-7245, which offers special excursion fares, discounts for children and rail passes good for unlimited travel. Several bus lines crisscross the region. **Greyhound Lines** ( (212) 635-0800 TOLL-FREE (800) 231-2222, covers routes between Boston and Worcester, Cape Cod and cities in Connecticut, while **Vermont Transit** ( (802) 864-6811 TOLL-FREE (800) 451-3292, serves the northern tier covering points in Vermont, Maine and New Hampshire.

# Living It Up

THE EXCEPTIONAL HOTELS AND RESTAURANTS
Boston, the Hub of New England, belies its reputation as a staid city when it comes to fine dining and lodging. If seafood is king in this city steeped in tradition, then nouvelle cuisine is queen. Boston's Back Bay, prosperous, cosmopolitan, is one of the city's most vibrant neighborhoods yet it retains an aura of understated opulence and affluence. Gilded lions guard the entry to the **Copley Plaza Hotel**, whose ballroom ushers in the seasonal debutantes' cotillion each June. The 373-room hotel on historic Copley Square offers elegant accommodations. In the **Plaza Dining Room**, Chef David Cardell has created a menu that caters to every taste. Presidents Kennedy and Carter dined here. After dinner, you may want to wander into the Edwardian Plaza

Bar for some mellow jazz. (More detailed information for hotels and restaurants is listed under each city's heading.)

Adjoining nearby Copley Place, **Turner Fisheries Bar & Restaurant** in the **Westin Hotel** serves the freshest seafood; its clam chowder has been elevated to stardom in the city's annual Chowderfest Hall of Fame. Live jazz nightly, with no cover charge, complements the clean modern art decor and handsome oyster bar. Westin's new **Palm Restaurant** has gained renown by serving three- to eight-pound Nova Scotian lobsters. As Boston's tallest hotel, the Westin's spacious rooms and suites afford sweeping river and city views. A skybridge links The Westin to upscale Copley Place, which houses exclusive shops, an 11-screen cinema and in its central atrium, a 60-ft (18-m) travertine and granite water sculpture designed by Dimitri Hadzi. Within the historic **Lenox Hotel, Diamond Jim's Piano Bar** hosts impromptu professionals and amateurs at its all-night sing-alongs. Metropolitan Opera stars have been known to show up and stretch their vocal chords here along with the likes of Tom Selleck and Tony Bennett. The hotel has a long history of catering to musical greats; when Enrico Caruso came to town, he stayed here.

Energy levels don't begin to peak until well past 11 PM at Newbury Street's **Sonsie**, one of the Back Bay's liveliest bistros. Chef Bill Poirier's international cuisine, a Tuscan-inspired dining room, warm-weather outdoor seating and a fashionable upscale clientele all blend to create an eclectic melange that, at Sonsie, really works. For French cuisine, you'll find some of the best at **Aujourd'hui** in the **Four Seasons Hotel**, 200 Boylston Street. If you're in a romantic mood, **Veronique Restaurant** serves innovative dishes in a beautiful room in a faux Tudor castle. The restaurant is in the Longwood Tower building, in Brookline. If you appreciate a prize-winning gourmet soup, you'll want to try one made by Boston's recent winner of the "Best

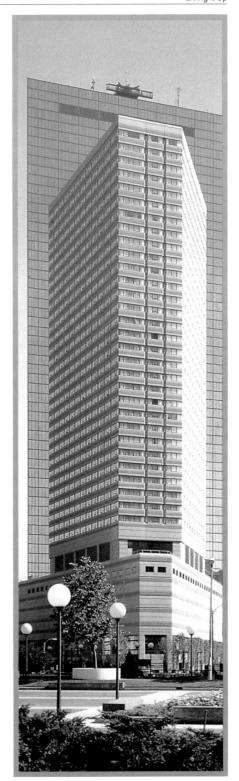

Rooms at The Westin Hotel in Boston's Copley Place afford sweeping city and Charles River views.

Female Chef" Award. Deborah Hughes serves her signature soups — lobster bisque, sweet roasted red pepper soup and rustic tuscan white bean soup — at Cambridge's **Upstairs at The Pudding** ( (617) 864-1933, 10 Holyoke Streets, MA 02138.

Proper Bostonians feel right at home in the elegant surroundings of the **Ritz Carlton Hotel**, especially in one of the rooms with a view of the Public Garden. The decor is traditional European style; fastidiousness is omnipresent down to the wearing of white gloves by the elevator attendants. You can have afternoon tea in the second-floor Ritz Lounge accompanied by the soothing strains of live harp music. On a snowy evening, an hour spent at the cozy Ritz Bar can be a slice of pure magic. It's probably the only downtown hotel where you can sit in front of a crackling fire and enjoy a picture book view of the Public Garden.

The best jazz in the city is across the Charles River at the **Regattabar** in Harvard Square's **Charles Hotel**. Herbie Hancock, Ahmad Jamal, Sonny Rollins and many acclaimed jazz combos have performed at this popular lounge. Hotel guests receive free entry to all shows mid-week and to the late shows on weekends. In the same neighborhood, the original **House of Blues** packs a mean sax and serves New Orleans-style food to music lovers nightly. Cambridge's **House of Blues** in Harvard Square has an intimate living room feel even when it's crowded.

The pleasures of a glass-domed rooftop health spa and the vibrant cultural life of downtown Providence await guests at the luxurious, neoclassically designed **Westin Hotel** ( (401) 598-8000, One West Exchange Street, Providence, RI 02903. You can swim in the hotel's pool. A Tony-award winning theater, **Trinity Repertory Company** and a restaurant scene inspired by the largest culinary school in the world, augment the city's New England charm. Thirty miles (48 km) south of Providence lies **Newport**, the fabled resort city of America's Cup yacht racing and magnificent Gilded Age

mansions. Close to Newport's Cliff Walk, the 12-room **Cliffside Inn** ( (401) 847-1811, 2 Seaview Avenue, RI 02840, an elegant 1880s Victorian home retains the grandeur of the past.

One of the most elegant places in Vermont is the **Inn at Shelburne Farms** ( (802) 985-8498, Harbor Road, Shelburne, VT 05482, a turn-of-the-century mansion with 24 rooms, each furnished in period antiques. Once the family home of William Seward and Lila Vanderbilt Webb, it sits on Saxton's Point overlooking Lake Champlain and the Adirondack mountains. On the property, a 1,000-acre (405-hectare) working farm supplies the inn with fresh produce. The inn and its two dining rooms are open from mid-May to

mid-October. Another wonderful dining experience awaits those traveling in Vermont. The **Inn at Essex** ( (802) 878-1100, 70 Essex Way, near Route 15 in Essex Junction, about 10 miles from downtown Burlington, along with the **New England Culinary Institute** runs the inn's two restaurants, the formal **Butler's** and the more leisurely **Birchtree Café**. Great chefs in training from the institute prepare updated New England style entrees. Call the Inn for both restaurants.

For a dramatic setting, the grandiose **Mount Washington Hotel and Resort** ( (603) 278-6000 TOLL-FREE (800) 258-0330, U.S. 302, Bretton Woods, New Hampshire, a National Historic Landmark, is unbeatable. When it was built in 1902 as

one of America's premier resorts, no expense was spared. Like a legendary fairy tale palace, the gleaming white, twin-towered structure, set against a mountain backdrop, never fails to impress. Its spectacular 2,600-acre (1,053-hectare) property embraces two golf courses, meandering bridle paths, clay tennis courts, pools and play areas. From the hotel's 900-ft- (274-m)-long verandah, the view encompasses the entire Presidential range. An ongoing renovation program has restored much of the resort to its early splendor. A fine dining room, a welcoming lobby with

Guests at the Balsams Grand Resort Hotel enjoy four seasons of activity in the glorious White Mountains.

a working fireplace, and gracious
Victorian-style rooms and suites, make
this grand resort a place where you will
truly feel on top of the world.

Located 60 miles (96 km) north of
Mount Washington, **Balsams Grand
Resort Hotel** ( (603) 255-3400 TOLL-FREE
(800) 255-0600 (out of state) (800) 255-4221
(in New Hampshire) FAX (603) 255-4221,
Dixville Notch, NH 03576, is one of
New England's last *grande dame* hotels.
Situated on 15,000 acres (6,000 hectares)
in the northern mountainous reaches of
New Hampshire, it is just 12 miles (19 km)
from the Canadian border. The small
community of less than 50 voters of
Dixville Notch receives national attention
every four years as they gather in the
Balsams Grand Resort Hotel to cast
the nation's first votes in the country's
presidential elections.

Since 1866 guests have enjoyed the
homely atmosphere, wholesome meals
and nightly entertainment. The Tower
Suite, a Victorian-styled turret with
unobstructed views, is always in demand.
Families find the late night game and
magic shows particularly enjoyable. Golf
courses, pool, tennis, mountain biking,
boating, cross-country and downhill
skiing and children's programs equip
the resort for an invigorating or relaxing
holiday.

Nearby is **Dixville Notch State Park**,
with its waterfall, picnic areas and Table
Rock.

# Family Fun

Vacationing families flock to New
England because it affords activities and
interests for all ages. If you follow the
seasons, you will never run out of things
to do. Beach resorts are ideal summer
vacation sites and remain lovely into
early fall. With 472 miles (761 km) of
coast, New England's rocky shores and
sandy beaches make for many family
activities. Many public beaches are entrance
free or if there is a charge, it is usually
"per car."

**BEACHES**
Once you test the waters, you may want
to choose the Atlantic's southern beaches
for their relatively warmer temperatures
and the lakes and ponds of New Hampshire
and Vermont for their beauty. **Lower Cape
Cod** is a National Seashore stretching
40 miles (64 km) from **Chatham** to
**Provincetown** and a nature lover's
treasure. The cape's 70-mile (113-km)
shoreline boasts an infinite variety of
white-sand beaches and dunes, where
active children can sun, swim and sail.
Hiking paths and biking trails offer

interesting places to stop and swim or climb rocks. For little toddlers, **Falmouth's Old Silver Beach** has an extended crescent of white sand where a sandbar at one end keeps the water shallow. Tidal pools make great spots for minnow fishing. The beach has lifeguards, showers and a snack bar. Another ideal beach for families is one of Cape Cod's most beautiful, **Sandy Neck** off Route A in **West Barnstable**. Younger children can romp over the sand dunes and splash and paddle in the smaller pools that form at low tides. Virtually every Cape Cod town has its own personality and children will find plenty of amusement by exploring the area's miniature golf ranges, playgrounds, museums and picnic sites. (For more information, see CAPE COD).

Families searching for an old-fashioned unsophisticated beach resort will find it at

**Block Island**, 13 miles (eight kilometers) off the Rhode Island coast. Bring just the bare essentials, bathing suits, bikes if you have them, wind breakers for cool nights and a fishing rod. Though the island is only three miles (five kilometers) wide and seven miles (11 km) long, it wraps 200-ft- (60-m)-high bluffs, creamy sand beaches, gentle dunes and rolling surf into an economical kid-sized package. Local kids play summer baseball games two nights a week and visitors ages six to twelve are usually welcome to join. More than 200 species of birds fly over Block Island as they migrate past the Atlantic coast. For more details, contact the **Block Island Chamber of Commerce** TOLL-FREE ( (800) 383-2474, 23 Water Street, Old Harbor, Block Island, RI 02807.

A legion of lakes, rivers and ponds proliferates throughout New England and you are never more than 30 minutes' drive from one. Even swimmin' holes, those memory-evoking ponds where country kids swing out over the water on a rubber tire hung from an overhanging maple, still exist. Ask any local in one of New Hampshire or Vermont's small towns for their favorite location.

**SCHEDULING AND PRE-PLANNING**
Try to schedule visits to museums for days when weather is not ideal for outdoor pursuits. New England has so many museums with children's sections and programs that one needs to avoid the

OPPOSITE TOP: Children enjoy many of the interactive exhibits at the Museum of Science, Cambridge. OPPOSITE BOTTOM: A photographer's delight, the Pemaquid Point Lighthouse is one of many scattered along Maine's central coast. ABOVE: Boylston Street soldier and teddy. RIGHT: Puppetarium.

temptation to overdose the little ones. Provide variety by alternating days spent in the car or on trains with action-oriented activities. It's wise to presume that children's musical tastes will differ from that of their parents. Consider investing in a few cassettes tapes for each child. Plan loosely, build in break time and leave lots of room for spontaneity. Sending the kids to a movie one afternoon while you indulge in an adult pass time is one way to please everyone. A few pre-trip hours spent at your home library can be productive. Look for adventure tales set in New England. For example, if you plan a whale-watching expedition, the family could get in the mood by watching movies like *Free Willy* or reading *Moby Dick*. Amusement parks and aquariums, too, make great outlets for youngsters' energies.

Summer, when cities tend to get muggy, is ideal for beaches. Even so, cities like Boston and Hartford attract families with outdoor concerts, street fairs and parades.

### CITY SIGHTS

In Boston, a free 10-week summer outdoor movie series, called *Friday Flicks* caters to families. Plan a family picnic on Boston's beautiful park along the

Charles River where, at dusk, a giant screen displays a full-length feature film. Another annual summer event brings hundreds of families and kids together for the **Scooper Bowl Festival**, on Boston Common in June, You can taste lots of different flavors in this salute to ice cream. For information, call ℂ (617) 439-7700. The *Kids Love Boston annual guidebook* is a major feature of the *Boston Family Visitor Kit*, which also includes hotel packages and special discount brochures specifically tailored to families planning a weekend or week in Boston. To order, contact the **Greater Boston Convention and Visitors Bureau**, P.O. Box 490, Boston, MA 02199.

One of Boston's oldest walking tour companies offers a special child's-eye view of the Freedom Trail's architecture and history, every Saturday and Sunday, with their specifically designed tour for young walkers of six to 12 years. Contact **Boston by Little Feet Walking Tours** ℂ (617) 367-2345.

### WHALE WATCH CRUISES

The whale watching season begins in spring and extends through October. The entire eastern seaboard presents

BELOW: Fogg Art Museum, Harvard University.
TOP: Boston's Museum of Fine Arts.

prime opportunities for families to experience the sight of these giant mammals' annual migration. Typical sighting cruises last from four to six hours. Several companies offer whale watch cruises from downtown Boston, where you can create your own nautical tour by visiting the **New England Aquarium**, before or after a cruise followed by dinner at the **Chart House Restaurant**, located next to the Aquarium.

## ANIMAL PARKS, AQUARIUMS AND ZOOS

Once poorly rated, the revitalized Franklin Park Zoo, in Boston, is well worth the trek for its world-class **African Tropical Forest ℂ** (617) 442-2002, Franklin Park Road, Boston, MA 02121, opened in 1989. A meandering jungle path takes visitors through a lush three-acre (one-and-a-quarter-hectare) domed habitat where more than 100 birds fly freely through the trees. Lowland gorillas, pygmy hippos, baboons, and spotted leopard inhabit the forest. On Boston's historic waterfront, the **New England Aquarium ℂ** (617) 973-5200, Central Wharf, Boston MA 02110, has a spectacular four-story Giant OceanTank,

populated by hammerhead sharks, huge sea turtles and hundreds of other fish. Two species of penguins are popular. The rockhopper penguin's head feathers resemble a punk hairdo and the jackass penguin acquired its name because it brays like a donkey. Both can be seen in the ground level pools. Sea lion and dolphin shows take place aboard a floating pavilion. The museum also conducts whale-watching excursions.

The **Roger William's Park and Zoo**, a lovely 430-acre (174-hectare) Victorian park, is located just 10 minutes from downtown Providence, Rhode Island. It features formal gardens, paddleboats, picnic areas, a historic cottage and an impressive zoo, where animals from six continents reside in simulations of their natural habitats.

A wonderful outing for children can be had at **Butterfly Place at Papillon Park ℂ** (508)-339-0955, 120 Tyngsboro Road, Westford, MA 01866, where more than 500 butterflies of 24 different species flutter freely in a lush atrium of greenery. The atrium is about 40 miles (65 km) north of Boston and could be included on a drive to southern New Hampshire. (For more information on museums, see BOSTON, HARBORWALK, page 88 and CULTURAL ATTRACTIONS, page 91.)

# Cultural Kicks

New England's cultural riches are so plentiful and pervasive that enjoyment of the arts is really part of everyday life. Each new season heralds annual events and openings at many concert halls and theaters in all six states, with Boston itself being the cultural nucleus. Bostonians like to call their city the "Athens of America" because of its concentration of colleges and universities. A cosmopolitan student population continuously breathes new life into the music scene with performances at two well-known music schools. Both the New England Conservatory of Music and the Berklee College of Music sponsor frequent concerts.

The **Wang Center for the Performing Arts**, in a building restored to its original Roaring Twenties luster, hosts the **Boston Ballet Company** while first-rate live theater can be found at the **Shubert**, **Colonial** and **Wilbur** theaters.

You could spend days enjoying the Boston's **Museum of Fine Arts** vast collections, gallery talks, special lectures and films. Not far from the MFA is the elegant **Isabella Stewart Gardner Museum** where concerts are given on the second floor. (See BOSTON, CULTURAL ATTRACTIONS, page 91.)

Each year more than a million music-lovers attend some 250 concerts performed by the world-famous **Boston Symphony Orchestra** (BSO) at **Symphony Hall**. The **Boston Pops** puts on a series of concerts at the **Esplanade** on the Charles River each summer, where, every Fourth of July, thousands converge, blankets and picnic baskets in tow, for the annual Independence Day Concert, which culminates in an explosion of fireworks over the water. (See page 93.)

During the summer season, the Berkshire Hills resonate with the sounds of music. Theater and dance offerings abound. BSO moves its headquarters to **Tanglewood**. Musicians playing on

original instruments perform at the **Aston Magna Festival** in **Great Barrington**. Operatic arias ring out from the stage of the **Berkshire Opera House** in **Lenox**. The town of Becket celebrates the return of the **Jacob's Pillow Dance Festival**, a 10-week season. So much is offered that you could indulge yourself every night of the week during July and August and still not see it all.

For a calendar of events, contact **The Berkshire Visitor's Bureau** ( (413) 443-9186 TOLL-FREE (800) 237-5747, Berkshire Common, Pittsfield, ME 01201. On Thursdays, the Calendar Section of the *Boston Globe* lists a weekly schedule of cultural events throughout the state.

**Newport** of Rhode Island fills its summer music schedule to the brim with afternoon and evening concerts in the restored mansions along Bellevue Avenue. The world-famous **Newport Jazz Festival** returns each year. At the **Newport Art Association** on Bellevue Avenue, changing exhibits are featured and the **Newport Historical Society** displays collections of Colonial art, and early American glass and furniture. You may even want to visit the historic **Redwood Library** on Bellevue Avenue; among its patrons were writers William and Henry James and Edith Wharton. Obtain a schedule of events from **Newport County Chamber of Commerce** ( (401) 847-1600. (See RHODE ISLAND, NEWPORT, page 256.)

From Benefit Street's "Mile of History" on the east side to festive Federal Hill, Rhode Island's own "Little Italy", the capital city of **Providence** is known and loved for its abundance of historic and cultural attractions. Four centuries of history are alive and well on the streets of Providence, as evidenced by the scores of immaculately preserved Colonial, Federal, Greek Revival and Victorian houses found throughout the city. The Tony Award-winning **Trinity Repertory Company**, the **Rhode Island Philharmonic** and the **Museum of Art/Rhode Island School of Design** offer acclaimed theater, fine arts and orchestral music. Other exciting entertainment options include the seasonal "Broadway" series at the

**Providence Performing Arts Center** and the alternative theater and dance productions at **AS/220**.

**New Haven**, Connecticut, home to Yale University, has earned a reputation as a proving ground for Broadway-bound plays. The university contributes mightily to the city's vibrant arts scene by staging major productions all year at the **Yale Repertory Theater**. Also known for a consistent menu of well-reviewed plays, the **Long Wharf Theater** ( (203) 787-4282, 22 Sargent Drive, rounds out the city's theater scene.

The New England coast, from Rhode Island to Maine, has inspired artists for centuries. Three of New England's most well-known artists, N.C. Andrew and Jamie Wyeth drew inspiration from the stark drama of the Northeastern landscape; while Andrew Wyeth's summer home in Cushing, Maine, is the subject of many of his paintings, including his well-known *Christina's World*. In the nearby city of Rockland, at the **Farnsworth Art Museum**, you can view paintings by all three generations of this premier family of American artists, including *Christina's World*, which the museum owns. Also on exhibit here are many works by artists who summered and studied on the coast. The **New York Ash Can School** is well represented as are the works of many Maine artists, including sculptor Louise Nevelson, a Maine native. (See ROCKLAND, page 171.)

A few miles from Rockland is the tiny and totally charming fishing and shipbuilding village of **Rockport** which was made a Historic District in the 1970s and lists more than 120 registered buildings. **Rockport** has become an artist's center and is home to the **Maine Coast Artists Gallery** in a renovated old livery building. In the center of town, the **Maine Photographic Workshops School** hosts photographers and lecturers from around the world. Look into their workshop gallery where they often mount exhibitions of visiting artists. The restored **Town Hall/Opera House**, at the entrance

Boston's vibrant Quincy Market draws shoppers and diners to its eclectic boutiques and eateries.

to Marine Park, is known for its superior acoustics and sponsors a summer Bay Chamber Concert series, theater, and other cultural events. Another unusual school in town is the **Artisan School**, where visitors are welcome to observe classes in the traditional art of wooden boat construction. (For more about the Maine Photographic Workshops, see SPECIAL INTERESTS, page 57.)

# Shop Till You Drop

Shopping venues in New England run a wide gamut from antique emporiums and country fairs to the world-famous Filene's Basement and the mega-discount outlet. Regional souvenirs are as diverse as silver or pewter ware wrought in designs originated by patriot Paul Revere, and athletic wear emblazoned with the logo of one of Boston's sports teams.

## ANTIQUES

Boston's Newbury Street, the North Shore of Massachusetts, the Berkshire Hills around Great Barrington, New Hampshire's Monadnock region, especially in and around North Conway, and the southern portion of Maine between Kittery and Scarborough all offer lots of places to browse for antiques. Three times a year, more than 2,000 dealers set up shop at the outdoor **Brimfield Antique Fair** in central Massachusetts. If you love antiques, this can be a lot of fun. Miss one of these events in mid-May, July or September and you'll have to console yourself with browsing the antiques shops proliferating along U.S. 20 between Brimfield and Sturbridge. Seasoned antiquers scour bulletin boards and local newspapers for notices of flea markets and country sales in many communities. In central Massachusetts, the **Berkshire County Antique Dealers Association** lists more than 60 members, most of them concentrated along and near Route 7. For a brochure, write to **BCADA**, P.O. Box 95, Sheffield, MA 01257. Another resource for antique dealers' listings is

the **New Hampshire Antique Dealers Association**, P.O. Box 904, Wolfeboro, NH 03894. (See also SHOPPING in TRAVELERS' TIPS, page 272.)

## BOSTON CITY SHOPPING

For a true study in contrasts, balance antique shopping with a day spent in the aisles of **Filene's Basement Store**, 426 Washington Street, Downtown Crossing, a Boston institution for decades, known to locals as "the basement." Many a Brahmin elite and blue collar worker have clothed their families well

and thriftily from the goods offered by this original mother of all markdown emporiums. Since 1947, the annual **Bridal Gown Sale** attracts brides-to-be from all over the world, some arriving as early as two hours before the doors open to line up outside. At the most recent sale, designer and famous-name wedding gowns that would normally retail in other stores for $1,000 to $4,000 were sold for $249. Other excellent buys are found in the giftware, lingerie and luggage departments. Filene's has opened several satellite stores in suburban towns, but the Boston basement remains the best.

In the same neighborhood, the phenomenally successful restoration of the **Fanueil Hall Marketplace** is a festive

World-famous Filene's Basement, a bargain-hunter's mecca.

place to soak up the flavor of local food shops where you can buy bags of bagels fresh from the oven, gargantuan deli sandwiches called "submarines," homemade Italian pizza, steamed lobster, food from every cuisine of the world. Any and all of the hearty fare will fortify your strength and enable you to enjoy the marketplace's eclectic boutique shopping.

In the city's Back Bay, **Newbury Street** rivals New York City's Fifth Avenue with its fashionable couture salons, designer hair stylists, and world-class art galleries. If you're feeling flush, you'll find the best in fine paintings and antiques here. At the lower end of Newbury Street, **Tower Records/Video** bills itself as the largest record store in the known world. Late evenings, the atmosphere can be quite social with midnight closing hours. For used books, browse the well-crammed shelves at **Avenue Victor Hugo Bookshop**, 339 Newbury, where you can pick up a disposable $0.25 romantic novel along with a treasured limited edition. It's the best used bookstore in town. Another Newbury Street landmark store, **Louis of Boston** (men's clothing shop), resides in the former Museum of Natural History building. Their café makes a chic meeting place for lunch.

## OUTLETS

Numerous discount goods outlets offer brand-named items, some off-season or of "seconds" quality, but many pass on significant savings by foregoing the mark up of the merchandiser and selling directly to the public. Several, in restored mills in Maine, are in Freeport and Kittery. In **Freeport**, the renowned **L.L. Bean** store, a purveyor of outdoor clothing and equipment, is open 24 hours daily with a separate overflow store selling slightly damaged or off-season goods. A new **L.L. Bean** factory outlet ( (207) 772-5100, has recently opened in **Portland**, Maine at 542 Congress Street. (See FREEPORT, page 168.) Restored mills in Fall River, Massachusetts, a former 19th century textile center, have found new life as homes for more than 100 factory outlet

stores. The **Worcester Common Outlets**, Worcester, Massachusetts features the largest collection of designer outlets under one roof in New England, with more than 100 famous-brand-name stores, including Barney's of New York. To help plan an expedition to the outlets, purchase a copy of *Factory Outlet Guide to New England*, by A. Miser and A. Pennypincher, published by Globe Pequot Press, available at local bookstores.

## ARTS AND CRAFTS

Country fairs and village stores offer the best opportunity for local crafts purchases. Maine and Vermont potters create beautiful works in both traditional and contemporary designs. In Vermont, look for exquisite quilts, beeswax candles, hand-crafted furniture and blown glass. The **Vermont State Craft Center** at **Frog Hollow** near Middlebury, gathers the best of the works of many artisans and displays it for sale in their retail galleries in Middlebury, Manchester and Burlington. One of the best sources of crafts are country stores in small villages and towns. You'll find very good prices in these small shops whose shelves often spill over with handiwork created by local artisans.

Along the seacoast, in towns like Salem, Newburyport and Marblehead, Massachusetts, you can find antique scrimshaw, delicate carvings done by whalers who whiled away long weeks at sea by etching nautical scenes on whale bones and fashioning them into letter openers, brooches and buttons.

Each year in August, **Sunapee**, New Hampshire hosts the oldest crafts fair in the nation.

You can obtain calendars along with listings of galleries and studios from the **League of New Hampshire Craftsmen**, 205 North Main Street, Concord, NH 03302, the **Maine Crafts Association**, P.O. Box 228, Deer Isle, ME 04627, the **Vermont Crafts Council**, P.O. Box 938, Montpelier, VT 05601.

Smaller art galleries and museum gift shops often offer unusual delights. The **Boston Center for the Arts** (BCA) in

Boston's South End provides studio space for some 60 artists and hosts an annual art and antiques show where you can support the artists' work with the purchase of original pieces. The **Society of Arts and Crafts** at 175 Newbury Street, Boston is a 100-year old cooperative whose artists exhibit hand-tooled leather, weavings, ceramics and furniture for sale.

## Short Breaks

New Englanders know the secret to making the most of their special place. In this region packed with diversions, locals maximize quick escapes with well planned long weekends and day trips. Here are some of my favorite short breaks.

Start by celebrating a spring break on the island of **Nantucket** when millions of daffodils, competing with the gold of native forsythia, burst into bloom. This is a year-round destination but hordes descend on the island in summer so those "in the know" love off-season spring and fall when nature's colors are at their showiest. With its antique houses, cobblestone streets, working windmill and old **lighthouse**, Nantucket harks back to its 17th-century whaling days. The lighthouse overlooks the harbor from Brant Point and for good luck, many visitors toss a coin into the surrounding waters to ensure their return. Boats run to the island year-round from Hyannis on Cape Cod, via the Nantucket Steamship Authority.

Another short break from Hyannis would be to take a 45-minute ferry to **Martha's Vineyard**. Architecture buffs, especially, will have a field day on the Vineyard where they'll see handsome ship captains' houses in **Edgartown**, and a community of several hundred Carpenter Gothic Victorian cottages in **Oak Bluffs**. This island is barely 20 miles long and 10 miles wide (32 km long and 16 km wide) so you can acquaint yourself with its rolling moors, colored cliffs, coves and salt marshes in short order. You can explore the island by car or by bike (bring your own or rent one in Vineyard

Haven). Sloops, schooners and dinghies, some available for day hire, beckon in the harbor.

Connecticut's unspoiled upper shoreline draws weekenders who enjoy its three-century history of seafaring lore beginning with its early days of rigged schooners and clipper ships. When Mamie Eisenhower swung a bottle of champagne over the bow of the *USS Nautilus* in 1954, it was the first nuclear powered ship in the world. Now the submarine is dry docked in **Groton**, next to the Submarine Force Library and Museum. Both are open to the public. You can recapture the early days of America's shipbuilding industry at nearby **Mystic Seaport** where some of the fastest clipper ships in the world were built. You'll want to spend a full day at the Seaport, starting with a tour of one of the more than 50 historic fishing vessels and yachts that fill its waterfront. The *Charles W. Morgan*, a 19th-century wooden whaler, offers hands-on whaling lessons. You can climb all over her, dive into the cramped crew's quarters, and learn how whales were caught. You can even get in the spirit of the sea by joining an impromptu round of chantey singing. (See MYSTIC SEAPORT page 242 and GROTON page 245.)

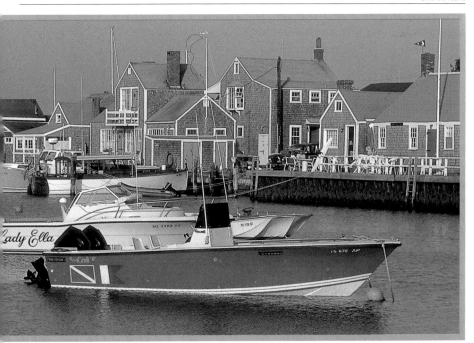

Cape Ann, often called "the other Cape," makes a fine day trip from Boston any time of the year, but my favorite is whale season in spring when, just like clockwork, migrating humpback whales breach the waters within easy eyesight of the whale-watching boats. **Marblehead, Rockport** and **Salem**, the historic towns of Massachusetts' North Shore, are easy short break destinations. Car travel is best but some train transport is available.

Although it's a bit far for a day trip — about 130 miles (210 km) — I've been known to drive myself to **Tanglewood** for a late Sunday afternoon picnic and evening desert accompanied musically by the Boston Symphony Orchestra. Greyhound Bus Company runs several motor coaches a day direct from Boston to nearby **Lenox**.

If mountains inspire you, New Hampshire's southwestern **Mount Monadnock** makes a pleasant drive from Boston. On arrival, a two-hour hike will take you to the top of the 3,165-ft (965-m) pinnacle, a fine spot to enjoy lunch while taking in the five-state view. In winter, you can enjoy the area's network of cross-country ski trails which are marked according to difficulty.

Maine's coastal villages and countless islands can be reached in just a few hours by bus or car from Boston. Although the weather is best in Maine and Vermont in the summer and fall, don't let off-season keep you from exploring the northern states. Each season has its special virtues. A very satisfying short break could be spent in Maine on the midcoast in the port towns of **Camden, Rockport** and **Rockland**, where you could find superb cuisine, fine art at Rockland's Farnsworth Museum and outdoor invigoration with a day cruise on a windjammer. You could stay at one of the lovely bed and breakfast inns in Camden within walking distance of shops and restaurants or opt for the luxury of **Samoset Resort** on the ocean, in Rockport. (See ROCKPORT, page 172.)

The southwestern corner of Vermont is a richly rewarding region for lovers of country inns and art. Prize galleries populate the scenic area around **Manchester**, a town that bills itself as "Manchester and the Mountains." Four ski mountains are nearby so you can literally walk out the front door of your

Seventeenth-century whalers built Nantucket's antique houses and cobblestoned streets. Today's visitors sail, bike and stroll its environs.

lodging and be surrounded by wilderness in minutes. The **Birch Hill Inn** ( (802) 867-4455 TOLL-FREE (800) 372-2761, West Road, Manchester, VT 05254, in Manchester Center, sits on more than 200 acres (80 hectares) and offers mountain views from every room.

The capital city of **Providence**, Rhode Island, renowned for its magnificent architecture and historic landmarks, makes an enticing short break for walkers and garden lovers. Strollers enjoy the new Waterplace, a two-mile riverfront walkway interspersed with park benches and Venice-inspired footbridges that winds its way through the heart of the city to Narragansett Bay. An outdoor amphitheater, on the grounds, presents live shows. Guided walking tours of the city's historic East Side take place year round. Providence's **Trinity Repertory Theater** ( (401) 351-4242, 201 Washington Street, one of the top five repertory companies in the country, offers a full schedule of comedies and classics in two theaters.

A weekend in **Cambridge** can give you a chance to tour the famous universities, browse through dozens of bookstores, mingle with the crowds in the coffee houses, appreciate the fine theater and films offered, and savor fine ethnic cuisine in this fascinating community. Concentrate your sightseeing by staying in Harvard Square, the hub of activity and a constant jumble of perpetual motion. The out-of-town newspaper kiosk, the hodge podge of cafés and sandwich shops, the traffic and crowds can be confusing, but never dull. Amazingly, the square opens directly onto the entry to Harvard Yard, a serene, ivied enclave. Start your tour here by strolling the yard and visiting one of the university's nine museums. The **Fogg Museum** has a collection which includes a staggering 27 works by Rodin. The **Museum of Natural History** is best known for its glass flower collection. Walk along **Brattle Street**, stopping at N°105, the yellow clapboard house where poet Henry Wadsworth Longfellow lived for 45 years. Most of his furnishings and

belongings remain and in the library, you can see several paintings of Minnehaha Falls, the setting of *The Song of Hiawatha*. Another famous poem by Longfellow honors the "village smithy" who lived at 56 Brattle Street in an antique colonial home. The **Blacksmith House's** outdoor café makes a fitting place to linger over coffee or tea while enjoying a book of poetry by one of New England's legendary poets.

Cambridge restaurants mirror the community's cosmopolitan makeup. Inexpensive ethnic eateries vie with pricier formal dining spots. Lodging, too, covers a wide range of accommodations. You can find good bed-and-breakfast possibilities in one of the lovely old homes in a private neighborhood near the Square. Check with the **Cambridge Chamber of Commerce** ( (617) 876-4100, 859 Massachusetts Avenue, Cambridge, MA 02139. The **Charles Hotel** ( (617) 864-1200, One Bennett Street, Cambridge, MA 02138, a sheltered enclave in the heart of the square, provides a restorative retreat after the beehive activity of this academic community. The hotel has a first class spa and indoor pool. You can enjoy live jazz nightly at Regatta Bar, and dine on locally grown, typical New England fare at Henrietta's Kitchen, both part of the hotel. Weekend packages are a good value.

# Festive Flings

New England, all year, is a series of celebrations, many commemorating historical events or the changing of seasons. Summer and fall bring people together in the great outdoors, often gathering to enjoy local food and wine. Country fairs selling handicrafts and local produce often combine down home fun with the excitement of traveling amusement parks to attract families who make a day's outing of it. What follows is a sampling of the hundreds of festivals and gala events, listed by season. Contact each state's visitor and tourism bureau for exact dates and details.

## SPRING

The **New England Spring Flower Show**, one of the nation's oldest and biggest, draws enthusiasts to Boston over a nine-day period, in March. Tastings of beer are likely on March 17, when Irish-Americans celebrate **St. Patrick's Day**. Boston's St. Patrick's Day Parade is one of the nation's most festive. Nantucket celebrates its **Daffodil Festival**, in April, with a parade of antique autos bursting with blooms, gaily decorated shop windows, and a flower show. Throughout March and into April, maple tree tappings give the states of Maine, New Hampshire, Massachusetts and Vermont cause to celebrate with festivals and tastings. In April, on **Patriot's Day**, the **Boston Marathon** begins in Hopkinton and ends with lots of partying in Boston. On the same day, in Lexington and Concord, riders on horseback reenact the **midnight ride of Paul Revere** as crowds of onlookers cheer.

Celebrations of spring get into full swing in May with the annual **Boston Kite Festival** in Franklin Park, the Art Newbury Street in the Back Bay and the **Street Performers' Festival** at Fanueil Hall Marketplace, Mystic Seaport.

In early June there is Burlington's **Discover Jazz Festival** in Vermont. **Memorial Day** weekend signals the official start to the summer season. The holiday commemorates the country's veterans with parades and celebrations over the three-day weekend. On this weekend Connecticut kicks off its **Lobster Weekend**, an old-fashioned lobster bake accompanied by live entertainment.

## SUMMER

The town of Gloucester, Massachusetts honors its deep-sea fishermen each June at the **Festival of St. Peter**, when a flotilla of several hundred vessels participates in a ceremony called the Blessing of the Fleet. Fishermen founded the city almost 400 years ago and generations have enjoyed its bountiful fishing grounds and natural harbor ever since.

Clown on stilts at Independence Day celebration.

Music festivals hit a high note in summer. Berkshire County in Massachusetts hosts two summer-long happenings. At Tanglewood, in Lenox, the **Boston Symphony Orchestra** performs. **Jacob's Pillow Dance Festival** in Lee, the oldest dance festival in the nation, presents jazz, ballet and contemporary dance. Rockport, Maine celebrates its **Annual Downeast Jazz Society Festival**. Jazz moves to Newport, Rhode Island in August alternating with a folk festival. America's most festive holiday, **Independence Day** (July 4), is celebrated on the actual day with parties, parades and fireworks throughout New England. The legendary Boston Pops concert on the Charles River Esplanade culminates in a magnificent fireworks display. **Boston's Harborfest** is six days and nights of seafood, fireworks, performances and more seafood, celebrated the first week of July.

Besides the Tanglewood performances, you'll have the opportunity to attend many other musical festivals. One of the most interesting is the **Mashpee Powwow**, held in July, in Mashpee, Massachusetts. Native Americans come together for three days to honor their heritage with dance competitions, drumming circles, and athletic meets. Also notable in Maine is the **Bar Harbor Festival**, the jazz and classical concerts held for two weeks in late July into August in the mansions at Newport, Rhode Island and the **Great Connecticut Traditional Jazz Festival** in Essex, Connecticut. There's lots happening in Maine during August. Rockland has its annual **Lobster Festival** at the beginning of the month and many towns hold blueberry festivals.

The **Vermont State Fair**, in Rutland, traditionally marks the close of the summer season.

## AUTUMN

**Labor Day** weekend is one of the busiest holiday weekends of the year, so reservations, whenever possible, will avoid disappointments. September heralds the start of the fall foliage season with cooler nights and mild days. Food festivals happen every weekend now that harvest time has arrived. Vermont holds bushels of apple festivals throughout the state. The **Woodstock Apples and Crafts Fair** in early October is one of the best. The month-long **Stratton Arts Festival**, near Manchester, Vermont showcases the work of more than 200 artisans. **Columbus Day**, celebrated the second Monday in October, brings leaf-peepers out in droves. It's a good time to listen to folk music at one of the country concerts held this time of year. The **National Traditional Old-Time Fiddler's Contest** in Barre, Vermont, the **Cajun and Bluegrass Music, Dance and Food Festival** at Stepping Stone Ranch, Escoheag, Rhode Island and the **Rockport Folk Festival** in Rockport, Maine are the top choices for foot stomping and hand clapping.

## WINTER

You can celebrate **Thanksgiving**, the fourth Thursday in November, at Plimouth Plantation where you can partake in a **Pilgrims' procession**, traditional dinner and Thanksgiving service. The month of December is New England's most festive. Once Thanksgiving is over, preparations for **Christmas Day** begin in earnest with tree lightings, carol fests, and candlelight strolls. Boston has two **Christmas tree lighting ceremonies** in December, one on Boston Common and another at the Prudential Center. Earlier in the month, celebrants can attend a **reenactment of**

**the Boston Tea Party** aboard the *Beaver II* in Boston Harbor.

Several mansions in Newport, Rhode Island open for the holidays and for several weeks before Christmas, there are **candlelight tours of Colonial homes**. During the first week of December, Nantucket Island ushers in the season with a **Christmas Shoppers' Stroll**, carol singing, theater performances and craft sales. **First Night**, a nonalcoholic New Year's Eve community festival began in Boston and rapidly spread to scores of towns in New England and elsewhere. Each year, for the price of a First Night Button, families and friends gain entry to a dazzling array of events. Participants, often wearing elaborate costumes or masks, stroll the streets, listening to jazz, observing theater, street puppets, strolling musicians and entertaining visual works of art. The **Boston Festival** begins at 1 PM with a Children and Family Festival, followed by a spectacular participatory street procession to Boston Common for a series of ongoing indoor performances. The night concludes with a midnight fireworks display over Boston Harbor.

Snow festivals and ski/snowboard competitions reach a fever pitch in January and February at ski resorts. Stowe, Vermont holds a **Winter Carnival** and Brookfield, Vermont puts on its annual **Ice Harvest Festival**. Stowe's 10-day **King of Winter Carnival** has a different theme every year, always highlighted by a village-wide ice sculpture exhibition and contest. Sled dog competitions, ski races, and homemade church suppers are some highlights. Other festive events help Vermonters revel in snow season. There's the week-long **Vermont Mozart Festival** in Burlington, a masquerade ball at the **Mad River Valley Winter Carnival** and jazz concerts at the **Brattleboro Winter Carnival**.

# Galloping Gourmets

At the Pilgrims' first Thanksgiving dinner, roast duck and goose, steamed clams, venison, leeks, watercress, wild plums and homemade wines graced the harvest table. In the early 17th century,

OPPOSITE: Carver on Cape Cod, the nation's cranberry capital. Typical village scene in Rhode Island, once know as "the smallest of the forty-eight". ABOVE: A toast to good fellowship, Boston Boat Works.

lobsters were not considered the delicacy they are today; they were so plentiful that colonists fed them to prisoners. From its early roots, New England cuisine has been known for its heartiness but, in the last decade, a culinary renaissance has emerged in this land of baked beans and boiled dinners. For travelers, the dining scene offers outstanding, innovative cuisine coupled with traditional New England fare. You'll find good **seafood** almost everywhere; some say it's the best in the country. Inevitably the coastal areas boast the best variety. Seafood forms the basis of many local dishes. **Chowders,** made with clams, corn or white fish, appear on menus in diners and dining rooms everywhere. Boston's annual clam chowder cook-off is a hotly contested event, with some of the finest regional chefs competing. Restaurants serve lobster boiled, baked and stuffed, as part of a salad or a pie and as the base for lobster bisque.

More **contemporary cuisine** has only recently emerged in the last decade or so as new chefs have challenged the traditions of centuries of New England cooking. One of the first on the forefront of change was James Haller, chef at the Blue Strawberry Restaurant in Portsmouth, New Hampshire. Haller's philosophy was simple. As he says in the introduction to his book, *The Blue Strawberry Cookbook,* "never follow the rules." I love his description of soup: "Soup is like a well-dressed lady. The cream is the woman, the leeks her shoes, the butter her stockings, the wine her petticoat, the main ingredient her dress, and the spices her perfume. Using this analogy, remember that overdressing is cheap, understatement alluring because it offers mystery." At Haller's restaurant, a converted 1797 chandlery, there was no menu card. Few of the courses were named, but each was described in great detail when served. Regular diners never had two courses which tasted completely the same because every course was a creation in itself. Haller reigned as a major innovator of New American cuisine for more than 20 years. The restaurant was recently sold and is now operating under

the name of Lindbergh Crossing, but Haller's brilliant new uses for the area's bounty have left a lasting mark on the culinary front.

Other imaginative chefs working in Boston — Lydia Shire of Biba, Jasper White of Jasper's, Gordon Hamersley of Hamersley's, Bill Poirier of Sonsie's — have also made an impact on the local dining scene by creating novel, contemporary cuisine. The Back Bay, especially Newbury Street, is a hotbed of **chic cafés** and **restaurants**. Sonsie, a three-year-old Newbury Street bistro, manages to attract some of Boston's favorite celebrities. Sonsie's chef Bill Poirier, former sous chef at Biba, and chef at the Charles Hotel, serves up sophisticated but unpretentious menus. He's elevated potato cookery into an art form, with dishes like mashed potato gratin with sun-dried tomatoes, garlic mashed potatoes with shrimp, and an elaborate five-style potato sampler that large parties order to share. Potato fanatics pounce on it as an entree. In the next block, the café at Emporio Armani Express suits those who have room for lobster ravioli after a fitting in the clothing shop next door.

New England's ethnic heritage is dramatically demonstrated in the wide diversity of dining options available. You can buy moon cakes made from rice flour at a baked goods shop in Boston's Chinatown and a few blocks away, in the North End's "Little Italy," indulge yourself in cream-filled Napolitanos and rum cakes.

At inland restaurants and country inns, traditional fare still dominates most menus. **Boston baked beans** are rarely served but **Boston cream pie** and **Indian pudding**, a combination of cornmeal and molasses, are universally popular. **Apple pan dowdy, cornbread, mincemeat pie**, and other favorite old-fashioned dishes are still alive and well. **Corn** lovers, who know enough to eat it shortly after it's picked, eagerly await the first crop of fresh corn in July. Connoisseurs look for the "butter and sugar" variety, a blend of yellow and white kernels. Bright orange **pumpkins** are harvested just before the first frost and are a mainstay of home baked pies. Orchards from Connecticut to Vermont encourage fruit purchases with "Pick Your Own" sales and farm stands display freshly pressed **apple cider** and bushel baskets of crisp apples. New England's apple harvest produces many varieties. Look for Macintosh, Empire, Northern Spy, Cortland and Paula Reds. **Cranberries**, harvested from Cape Cod's bogs, are served in a tart sauce with turkey dinners or pressed into juice. Maine is noted for fresh blueberries, delicious in pies, scones, sauces and toppings for pancakes and waffles.

All those Holsteins in Vermont contribute to the state's production of choice **cheddar cheese** and its famous **Ben and Jerry's ice cream**. Try Vermont **maple syrup** on your morning pancakes. Sold in colorful tins, the syrup packs well for further tastings at home.

Every year, Boston hosts several international **cultural festivals** featuring chefs from around the world. One annual series brings the country's best chefs to **Aujourd'hui**, the award-winning French restaurant at the Four Seasons Hotel. At another, the **Anthony Spinazzola Gala Festival**, you can sample signature dishes from more than 85 of the region's finest restaurants and taste select domestic and international wines from 75 leading wineries. Dates for these events are available from the **Greater Boston Convention and Visitors Bureau** ( (617) 5366-4100

TOLL-FREE (800) 888-5515. P.O. Box 990468, Boston, MA 02199.

Conditions for growing grapes are best in southern New England and some vintners have produced highly drinkable wines by careful exploitation of the region's warmer micro-climates. On Martha's Vineyard, Chicama Vineyards and in Little Compton, Rhode Island, Sakonnet Vineyards produce commendable table wines. (See SPECIAL INTERESTS, page 56.) Fruit wines are another delicacy. At Nashoba Valley Winery, in Concord, Massachusetts, you can taste delightful wines made from pears, peaches and raspberries.

Micro-breweries, too, have sprung up around New England. The Boston Brewing Company was one of the first to popularize the **brew pub** craze by producing Samuel Adam's dark lager. The brewhouse, in the Lenox Hotel at 710 Boylston Street, Boston, serves year-round drafts. Six seasonal offerings add variety. In summer, the brewhouse serves a cherry wheat beer; in late fall Cranberry Lambic is on tap. The beers are reasonably priced and because

The Bull and Finch Pub on Boston's Beacon Hill had a long history as a neighborhood nucleus before adding its "Cheers" moniker.

freshness is the single most important quality of the beer, all kegs are tapped within 48 hours of arrival. The all-malt brewing and Bavarian hops result in a deep golden color, rich malt body and spicy hop character.

## Special Interests

The appeal of the special interest vacation — holiday time used to explore or expand on specific interests — continues to widen as fresh programs and ideas attract newcomers. Where yesterday's travelers saw holiday time as an opportunity to relax and unwind, many travelers today look for ways to expand their horizons by learning a skill, gaining an improved self image or achieving health and fitness goals. New England offers a wide choice of special interest options around which the traveler can plan a vacation with a purpose.

### CULINARY LESSONS, FOOD AND WINE

Enjoying the cuisine of a particular area or culture adds new dimensions to travel and many travelers welcome the chance to learn regional recipes that they can use at home long after a trip is over. Lodging is usually not included with classes but knowledgeable staff members can recommend inns or hotels in the immediate area. The **Silo Cooking School**, in the Litchfield Hills, was founded in 1972 by Ruth Henderson and her husband, New York Pops founder and director Skitch Henderson. They offer more than 70 classes, from March to December, emphasizing ethnic and regional cuisine and wine selection. Classes are held in a converted barn on their 200-acre (81-hectare) property, **Hunt Hill Farms** ( (860) 355-0300 FAX (860) 350-5495, Upland Road, New Milford, CT 06776. Ronnie Fein, author of *The Complete Idiots' Guide to Cooking Basics* emphasizes menu planning and regional cuisine at her **Ronnie Fein School of Creative Cooking** ( (203) 322-7114 FAX (203) 329-3366, 438 Hunting Ridge Road, Stamford, CT 06903. With advance

notice, she can often tailor class schedules to individual itineraries or give private lessons. The **Kushi Institute** ( (413) 623-5741 FAX (413) 623-8827, P.O. Box 7, Becket, MA 01223, in the Berkshires, was founded by Michio Kushi, considered the world's leading macrobiotic teacher, author and counselor. Many international and local guests enjoy the renowned renewal programs at the Institute, a former Franciscan abbey secluded on several hundred acres of woodland and meadows. Wendy Esko and Carry Wolf, two instructors well known in macrobiotic circles, teach classes emphasizing healthy, healing foods. At the institute, you can indulge in other healing services, such as shiatsu massage, morning exercise and personal consultations.

An intense interest in wine and its proper service has inspired the **Master Chef Series** at Sakonnet Vineyards, in the beautiful rolling countryside of coastal **Little Compton**, Rhode Island. Each month, the winery showcases a different regional celebrity chef who conducts a full day demonstration and participation class. Recent guest chefs have included Casey Riley of the Agora Restaurant in the new Westin Resort, Providence and Wayne

Gibson, executive chef of the Castle Hill Inn and Resort, Newport. Should you decide to spend the night in Little Compton, you can arrange advance accommodations at The Roost, the original farm house on the vineyard property. Newly renovated as a bed and breakfast inn with three guest rooms, it offers a relaxing taste of unspoiled rural New England. Contact both at ( (401) 635-8486, P.O. Box 197, Little Compton, RI 02837. In New Hampshire, classes of **A Taste of the Mountains Cooking School** are conducted in an alpine setting at the **Bernerhof Inn** ( (603) 383-9132 TOLL-FREE (800) 548-8007 FAX (603) 383-0809, P.O. Box 240, Glen, NH 03838. The cost of the three-day and weekend classes includes lodging and meals at the inn. The classes focus on preparation of creative, contemporary cuisine and are especially designed for those who prefer a "hands-on" approach to learning. Because the inn is set in the White Mountains of New Hampshire, near Conway, you could easily combine the cooking classes with outdoor activities such as hiking, skiing or golf.

## PHOTOGRAPHY

Rockport, Maine is home to the **Maine Photographic Workshops** ( (207) 236-8581 FAX (207) 235-2588, 2 Central Street, Rockport, ME 04856, founded by writer and photographer David Lyman. The summer program lists nearly 100 one-week workshops and master classes where photographers, filmmakers, and photojournalists of varying backgrounds and skills converge for a week or more of intensive learning and networking. Well-known working photographers such as Bob Krist, Sam Abell, Sarah Leen and Mary Ellen Mark are among the many instructors. Workshops for beginner, amateur and advanced photographers may be taken individually or in sequence. Meals are served on location in a warm family-style atmosphere and the school can arrange housing near the campus. While Rockport's remoteness lends itself to concentration, it's accessible from

OPPOSITE: Fresh maple syrup — a ubiquitous ingredient in regional cuisine. BELOW: The Evolution Spa at Equinox Spa Resort specializes in European-style therapies.

Route 1, the tourist route along the Maine coast. The nearby village of Camden offers wonderful dining, shopping, boating and theater. Also in Maine, the **Ogunquit Photography School** ( (207) 646-705, P.O. Box 2234, Ogunquit, ME 03907, conducts a series of four- and five-day on-site workshops from May to October. Workshops are limited to 12 students and are tailored to the needs of the group. Some more popular topics include color photography, the development of personal vision, travel, outdoor and nature photography. Traveling workshops take students to other parts of New England.

### ART AND CRAFTS

Each summer, the **Wooden Boat School of Maine** ( (207) 359-4651 FAX (207) 359-8920, P.O. Box 78, Naskeag Road, Brooklin, ME 04616, teaches the craft of boat building and related classes in woodworking. A location photographer teaches students the art of marine photography.

### NATURE STUDIES

The **Massachusetts Audubon Society** ( (508) 349-2615 FAX (508) 349-2632, Wellfleet Bay Wildlife Sanctuary, P.O. Box 236, South Wellfleet, MA 02663.

conducts a host of programs year-round at the wildlife sanctuary on Cape Cod. The Audubon sanctuary, in a 700-acre (300-hectare) preserve of pine woods with fresh water ponds and salt marshes, is the setting for guided hikes, bird watches and other outdoor studies. In August, two-day to one-week courses in writing, art and nature photography emphasize nature and the outdoor experience. Shared accommodations are available on site.

### HEALTH SPAS

The **Evolution Spa** ( (802) 362-4700 TOLL-FREE (800) 362-4787 FAX (802) 362-4861 at the historic Equinox Resort, Route 7A, Manchester Village, VT 05254, specializes in European-style therapies, offering guests thalasso soaks, herbal wraps and Swedish saunas. Three- and seven-night package plans focus on medical, nutritional, and beauty services. You'll have the services of a personal weight trainer in the fully equipped workout center along with a well-designed spa menu and loads of distractions on the grounds — Hiking trails, downhill and cross-country skiing, horseback riding, bicycling, canoeing, horse-drawn carriage rides and antique shopping in the village.

Pampering is the byword at the **Norwich Inn Spa & Villa** ( (860) 886-2401 TOLL-FREE (800) 275-4772 FAX (860) 886-4492, 607 West Thames Street, Norwich, CT 06360, a 1920s country inn high on a bluff near Connecticut's Thames River. The spa philosophy is one of luxurious nurturing, offering a full range of restorative and beauty treatments. You can limit your visit to a day or try one of the inn's two-to five-day packages. In the area are the Mystic Seaport Maritime Museum, and the Eugene O'Neill Theater Center.

## TAKING A TOUR

For those on a limited schedule, a tour can often maximize a destination's highlights. Letting professionals make the arrangements allows for more actual travel time. Specialty tours, too, allow travelers with specific interests or hobbies to mix with like-minded enthusiasts. Because of an agency's ability to obtain group pricing from airlines and hotels, the arrangements they make can often be more comprehensive and less expensive than if you spend time making them on your own. Unless otherwise noted, information on all of the following tours can be obtained from the **Greater Boston**

**Convention and Visitors Bureau** ( (617) 536-4100 TOLL-FREE (800) 888-5515, P.O. Box 990468, Prudential Tower, Boston, MA 02199, which lists literally hundreds of tours throughout New England. Within 30 miles of Boston, there are more than 100 tour options for walking, hiking, canoeing and bird watching.

**Tourco**, noted for their New England expertise and personal service, caters to leisure and adventure travelers. Skiers can join their group ski tours to major resorts such as Sugarloaf, Waterville Valley and Killington. Two tours — the week-long New England Autumn Splendor and the two-week New England/Niagara Falls Tour — show visitors much of the region.

**Tour Guides of New England** has introduced noteworthy new tours. One, "Boston: the Garden City," is a full day excursion focusing on the beautiful gardens of Boston and its famed landscape architects. Highlighted are the Public Garden, the glass flowers at Harvard's Botanical Gardens, the Frederick Law Olmsted Estate, and the Arnold Arboretum.

OPPOSITE: Each year, thousand flock to Concord's Old North Bridge and the homes of Thoreau, Alcott and Emerson. ABOVE: Bar Harbor's shoreline on Maine's craggy coast.

Themed tours by **Ego Trips**, a new Boston-based company focus on summer music and theater, New England fall foliage, and outlet shopping. They offer an exclusive "RV/Motorhome Tour of the National Parks and Recreation Areas of New England."

A **Student's Boston** is a multi-day group tour package of Greater Boston based on experiential learning. Students take part in activities such as a typical Thanksgiving dinner, attending a professional sporting event, and visiting some of the area's top colleges and universities.

Because Boston has the distinction of being the sixth largest Jewish community in the country and has set many precedents for Jewish people, **Dale Myerow Associates** ( (617) 592-3284, has devised a fascinating **Jewish Boston Tour** for groups by arrangement. The tour includes a number of important existing landmarks and vestiges such as the original immigrant neighborhoods of the West End and the North End, the Vilna Shul, a synagogue on Beacon Hill, and the new Holocaust Memorial that shows how the Jewish people in Boston established their roots and contributed to the richness and culture of Boston today.

An art historian leads a specially arranged visit to "Three Contemporary Artists and Their Studios" through **Boston By Design**. Participants meet an artist who was once a Hollywood bad guy, an artist who is represented at the Whitney and the Guggenheim, and a printmaker.

Year-round the **Old Town Trolley Tour Company** ( (617) 269-7150, conducts 100-minute narrated sightseeing tours of Boson's major highlights with options of disembarking and reboarding. The company also has a new escorted Brew Pub Tour which visits three of Boston's most popular brew pubs. Samples of the micro-brews created by each pub are served with complimentary hors d'œuvres at each stop. The **Boston Duck Tour** ( (617) 723-DUCK, is a wildly popular ride taking passengers through the streets of Boston and into the Charles River aboard a brightly colored World War II amphibious vehicle. For non-English speaking travelers, **Discover Boston Multilingual Trolley Tours** offers a city tour in French, German, Spanish, Italian or Japanese.

**Boston By Foot** guides lead the Beacon Hill Sunset Stroll past the golden-domed State House, elegant row homes of red brick and hidden gardens, as they embellish the walk with tales of famous residents and visitors, past and present.

**Cape Ann Whale Watch (** (508) 283-5110, offers lighthouse tours and nature cruises besides their regularly scheduled whale watch cruises out of Gloucester, Massachusetts. **Old Ipswich Tours**, based in Ipswich, Massachusetts, conducts custom jaunts which specialize in history, family, nature/environmental and student tours of the North Shore. Also, near Ipswich, a company called **Tours of Cranes Islands** takes passengers aboard the *Osprey* for a trip across the Castle Neck River to visit the 650-acre (263-hectare) Crane Wildlife Refuge. Lovers of lighthouses will enjoy a nautical excursion by **Captain John Boats** TOLL-FREE **(** (800) 242-2469, of Plymouth, Massachusetts. An expert recounts stories of six of lighthouses and the keepers who operated them. The **New Bedford, Massachusetts Office of Tourism (** (508) 979-1763, emphasizes another nautical themes by offering walking tours of the Historic District of this "whaling city" written about by Herman Melville. Look into their self-guided *Dock Walks*, focusing on schooners, lightships and the Waterfront Park.

**American Express (** (617) 723-8400, One Court Street, Boston, MA 02108, provides many useful traveler services for the New England region, including arrangements for city tours, auto rentals and package plans.

OPPOSITE: Trinity Church reflected in the gleaming facade of John Hancock Tower, Copley Square, Boston. RIGHT: Pemaquid Point on Maine's central coast.

# Welcome to New England

## A PLACE APART

There are so many reasons to visit New England that no book can enumerate them all. It is truly a place apart, an often-beautiful land of lakes, seashores, mountains, river valleys, villages, towns and bustling cities. Not only the best of America's past, it is also much of the cultural, educational and technological promise of its coming centuries. In a nation bereft of a long historical tradition, New England keeps a way of life, architecture and culture linked to America's earliest days and to the Europe which preceded them.

Composed of six states, including five of the original thirteen colonies, New England is so steeped in the history and culture of the United States it is difficult to imagine an America without New England. Although geographically small when compared to the rest of the nation, New England has had perhaps the strongest impact of any region on the country as a whole.

Named "New" England by the early explorer Sir John Smith, it is the New World's strongest link, historically and culturally, to the Old. Yet it is also profoundly American, from its colonial villages, farmsteads and elegant Victorian city streets to the bold commercial vigor of its modern skylines. And if New England is the land where American liberty was born, it has also nurtured this liberty with its continuing commitment to education and culture, expressed today in a concentration of many of the nation's best colleges, universities, museums, theaters and concert halls.

But these are not the best reasons to come to New England. The best reasons are countless and include the multicolored splendor of the autumn hills, the crystalline purity of the northern lakes, the salty smell of the sea, the beauty of villages couched in emerald pastures and peaceful river valleys, the glitter of trout streams emerging from spring snow, the towering granite peaks, the vast forests of spruce and pine, the taste of America as once it truly was.

## A LAND FOR ALL SEASONS

And New England is a land for all seasons. In winter the earth lies beneath a blanket of white; woodsmoke rises from the chimneys; skaters flit across the frozen ponds while on the lakes fishermen huddle in their huts and drop their lines through holes in the deep ice. Children sled on steep back streets and country slopes; the hills are alive with skiers; snowshoers and cross-country skiers wander back-country

trails through forests whose silence is broken only by the occasional chatter of a chickadee.

Spring, the rebirth of life, is magical in New England. After months of cold, the warm March winds melt the snow and in April the buds burst forth, transforming the gaunt gray branches to brilliant green. The geese, ducks and first songbirds begin to return; children follow the thawing trout streams and early blossoms paint the apple orchards.

Summer brings hot days and the lakes fill with swimmers, water skiers and boaters. Fishermen cast and troll for trout, lake salmon, pickerel, bass and other game fish. The ocean bays are a kaleidoscope of sails and spinnakers; surf and sandy beaches glimmer in the warm sun. Rafters, kayakers and canoers ride the rivers and hikers wander the peaks, hills and forests.

Ocean fog OPPOSITE and rolling hills ABOVE characterize New England's scenic charm.

But it is fall that is the glory of New England. From north to south the woodlands blaze with countless shades of scarlet, crimson, vermilion, yellow, gold and orange; as the leaves fall the white birches and tan beeches and oaks stand out against the darker firs, spruce, tamaracks and pines. Hunters go forth to seek deer, pheasant, moose and other prey to stock their larders. The rural air has a scent of apples and coming snow and families draw closer round the hearth, conscious of the ending of the year.

## PEAKS, BAYS AND RIVERS

New England occupies an area of only 66,672 sq miles (172,680 sq km) in the northeast corner of the United States, bordered by New York to the south and west, by Quebec and New Brunswick to the north and by the Atlantic Ocean to the east. In size it is somewhat smaller than Great Britain, less than half the size of California and slightly larger than Michigan or Illinois.

Maine is the only New England state which was not part of the original thirteen colonies, because it was part of Massachusetts until 1820. At 33,265 sq miles (86,156 sq km) Maine is also half the total area of New England and more than three times the size of Vermont, New Hampshire, or Massachusetts and nearly six times the size of Connecticut.

At 1,212 sq miles (3,139 sq km), Rhode Island is New England's and the nation's, smallest state.

The Appalachian chain dominates much of western New England, from Mt. Katahdin in northern Maine down through Maine's Rangely Mountains and the White Mountains of Maine and New Hampshire. Further west, the lower, forested Green Mountains span the entire length of Vermont and continue into Massachusetts as the Berkshires and on across Connecticut to join the Taconic Mountains of New York.

Like New England's mountains, its rivers run primarily north to south, swinging east to meet the sea at wide, island-filled bays from Maine's Bar Harbor to Connecticut's shores of Long Island Sound. Many of New England's rivers keep their native American names — the Merrimac, Penobscot, Kennebec and the 400-mile (644-km) Connecticut, which runs almost the entire length of western New England, separating Vermont from New Hampshire and bisecting Massachusetts and Connecticut to reach Long Island Sound.

Because eras of glaciation have given it relatively poor, rocky soil, New England has never been an agricultural center, although its sheep-raising industry was a significant national resource in the nineteenth century and Maine's potatoes remain the nation's best. Endowed with a magnificent coastline and hundreds of bays and harbors, New England first derived its prosperity from ship building and fisheries. In the nineteenth century, New England's textile, leather and other manufacturing became the nation's most predominant. In recent years, electronics, computer and data communications technologies, weaponry, banking and a growing tourist industry have become major aspects of New England's commercial vitality.

## THE NEW ENGLANDERS

New Englanders have learned to live with the various stereotypes which have been assigned to them — the shrewd Connecticut Yankee, the imperturbable Boston Brahmin, or the terse and taciturn inhabitant of Maine, New Hampshire, or Vermont. These characterizations, once more valid, have become blurred over the years by the mixing of Irish, Italian, Polish and other European genes. The beliefs and traditions that these immigrants added to a population traditionally English and ethically Puritan brought a welcome infusion of renewed vigor and broader cultural tolerance.

New Hampshire's White Mountains display an array of vivid fall colors OPPOSITE.

The population of the six New England states is unevenly distributed. A majority inhabits the southern half of the region, in cities such as Boston, Providence and Hartford, swelling their hubs and sprawling suburbs to house almost three-quarters of New England's 13 million inhabitants.

In the three northern states, the cities and towns are smaller with greater distances between them and there remain large areas of wilderness, particularly in Maine.

from one horizon to the other. Fish were so plentiful in the streams they could be literally scooped out by hand or net. The forests were filled with animals that are now legend: caribou, wolf, eastern buffalo and panther.

But the Europeans, with their conviction that anyone not a Christian was a "devil," had little interest in or respect for New England's inhabitants, or for its wildlife. The environment took a back seat to buccaneering. Whenever possible, the colonists cheated the Indians out of title to

The original settlers of New England's wilderness were the Algonquin Indians, whose ancestors came to the region in southward migrations from the Bering Strait about 12,000 to 15,000 years ago. These people hardly modified the land in which they lived, finding adequate sustenance in the forests, lakes, rivers and ocean. Some tribes also grew pumpkins, beans, corn and other vegetables.

As human migration from Europe turned from trickle to torrent between the seventeenth and twentieth centuries, the ecological diversity and bounty of the land was diminished and in many areas totally destroyed. Once flocks of geese truly darkened the sky, covering it in a solid cloud

their lands by devious and meaningless agreements; when the Indians refused such stratagems, the colonists simply overwhelmed them with their firepower, leaving smallpox and alcohol to further reduce their numbers. Today, the names for lakes and rivers, for islands and mountains, are almost all that connects New England with its tribal past.

By the late seventeenth century, the English Puritans had established a theocracy that imposed upon their new world and was to impose upon their descendants, a prevailing sense of order, discipline and frugality. These qualities were to remain strong in the New England Yankee temperament until the spiritual earnestness that had accompanied them diminished in the eighteenth century. Under the influence of the practical elements of the Puritan ethic, fleets of merchant and fishing ships, including slavers and privateers, expanded and brought increasing prosperity to New England and with it the accumulation of wealth.

This wealth and the independence derived from it, caused bitter resentment toward the "mother country" when England arbitrarily imposed a number of trade edicts and taxes upon this, her most affluent North American possession.

textile mills that rose beside New England's rivers, bringing with them their own language and customs. Portuguese fishermen augmented the region's fishing fleets, Italians came to labor on construction sites and formed a "little Italy" of their own in many a New England town. The Jews came, so did the Poles, the Russians and the Swedes, all forming distinctive communities where, for a time, their cultural heritages could be celebrated and preserved. Although they have long since been absorbed into the mainstream of New England life, their ways and

In angry response, the colonists rose up in successful rebellion, drove the British into the sea and formed a new nation. This fledgling nation, born in New England and Virginia and the Carolinas, moved ever westward, its numbers increased by a steady flow of immigrants from across the sea. By the late 1840s, after worsening English repressions and "the great hunger" in Ireland, the Irish came to New England in great numbers. In time, their political and oratory skills gave them a stronghold on local governments, particularly in Massachusetts, where they have continued to exercise an active role.

French Canadians, too, emigrated from neighboring Canada to work in the many

the ways of those who came before them together create the human pageant that is now New England.

ABOVE and OPPOSITE: Faces of today's New Englanders display a warmth and friendliness at odds with the taciturn reputation of their forebears.

# Eastern Massa-chusetts, Boston and Cape Cod

## THE HEART OF NEW ENGLAND

The geographical "middle" of New England, Massachusetts is an irregular rectangle of 8,257 sq miles (21,385 sq km) bordering Rhode Island and Connecticut in the south and Vermont and New Hampshire in the north.

In the west, the rolling and at times massive, Berkshire Hills are one of the nation's loveliest mountain regions. The Connecticut River flows from north to south across the western middle of the state, its wide channel and tree-bordered banks offering tranquillity and beautiful vistas. The Massachusetts coast offers a variety of natural beauty to those who love the sea. Though not as impressive as Maine's, it is best exemplified by the sand dunes, beaches and cranberry bogs of Cape Cod. The offshore islands, Nantucket and Martha's Vineyard, have a unique charm that draws many thousands of visitors each year.

But it is to the Massachusetts villages and towns, with their superb colonial architecture and to modern and historic Boston, that the visitor is drawn.

### GENERAL INFORMATION

The **Massachusetts Office of Travel and Tourism** ( (617) 727-3201 TOLL-FREE (800) 447-6277 FAX (617) 727-6525, 13th floor, 100 Cambridge Street, Boston, MA 02202, provides a free travel kit that can be useful in planning a vacation in its historic cities or picturesque countryside. For travel information, call TOLL-FREE (800) 624-MASS.

## BACKGROUND

Long before Europeans reached the shores of Massachusetts, a variety of Indian tribes, belonging mostly to the Algonquin federation, peopled the land. They first welcomed these strange, white-skinned people, sheltered them from the cold winter and fed them in times of hunger. But it soon became

Boston's State House was designed by noted architect Charles Bullfinch and completed in 1795 on land that originally belonged to John Hancock.

clear that these European guests did not intend to go home, would not respond with friendship in kind, but rather intended to take over the Indian lands, betray and enslave the tribes and force them to accept this strange religion which insisted that humans had crucified the Great Spirit. Courageous and independent, the Indian tribes one by one chose annihilation in war over serfdom, or died pitiably by the thousands from diseases introduced by the new immigrants.

### THE FIRST EUROPEANS

Someday, archaeologists and historians may discover incontrovertible proof that Scandinavian or other European explorers reached New England well before Columbus came to the New World. Some now claim it was the Viking, Eric the Red, or his son, Leif Ericsson, who was the first European to reach Cape Cod. Records do show that the English explorer John Cabot visited the Massachusetts coast in 1497, only five years after Columbus discovered the New World. Yet it was well over a century before there were any permanent settlements here.

### PILGRIMS AND PURITANS

Four days before Christmas, 1620, a shipload of pilgrims from Southampton, England, weighed anchor off what is now Plymouth. They had left England on September 15, intending to go to Jamestown, but had first reached land at Cape Cod on November 19. Before disembarking at what they were to call Plymouth Rock, they drew up a charter which they termed the Mayflower Compact. This document established a temporary government based on the principle of the will of the majority; as such it set the stage for the American Revolution and the writing of the Constitution of the United States 150 years thereafter. Little could these first settlers have imagined that by the end of the century nearly 100,000 men, women and children would have crossed the ocean from England to settle in the Massachusetts wilderness.

In 1630, a second settlement, based on theocratic principles, was founded at Massachusetts Bay by John Winthrop and his hard-working, God-fearing Puritans. It was in this spirit that "the good town of Boston" was established — a town which quickly became, as the city remains today, the hub of New England business, cultural and intellectual life.

## THE SEEDS OF REVOLUTION

In subsequent years, British mismanagement of its American possessions created mistrust and anger in the colonies. Nowhere was this more notable than in Massachusetts. A stubborn king and a politically unwise Parliament burdened the colonies with unreasonable taxes. The Acts of Trade required that the colonies trade only with England and its markets. The Tea Act, the Stamp Act, the Townshend Acts and the Intolerable Acts — all were perceived in the colonies as either oppressive or punitive and created reactions of increasing defiance. "No taxation without representation" became the rallying cry that carried the colonists to revolution.

By 1775, under the uncompromising leadership of Bostonians like Samuel Adams, James Otis and John Hancock, Massachusetts had become a catalyst uniting the 13 colonies. Their speeches provoked protests that eventually exploded into action and bloody revolution. Indeed, "the shot heard 'round the world" and the first battle of the revolution took place on Massachusetts soil.

On April 19, 1775, British soldiers fired on the minutemen, as the patriot soldiers were termed, on the green in Lexington, Massachusetts — the first time mutual hostility became open warfare. Two months later on June 17, the Battle of Bunker Hill was fought, actually not on the hill for which it was named but on nearby Breed's Hill. In this battle, the colonial militia were defeated by British regulars. Nonetheless it fired the fighting spirit of the Continental soldier and the determination of the colonists to sustain revolution until independence was achieved.

As a consequence of this revolution a new nation was born in 1776, a nation that was to name itself the United States. Its cornerstone was laid in Massachusetts.

OPPOSITE: A replica of the *Mayflower*, the clipper that brought the pilgrims to Plymouth in 1620, is anchored in Plymouth harbor.

## THE MARITIME MERCHANTS

Although Massachusetts experienced some political problems after the Revolution, it survived economically by exploiting the seas. Fishing, whaling and the China trade made fortunes for daring seafarers and enterprising merchants. Those fortunes stood the state in good stead when the 19th century saw a decline in the maritime economy. Fortunes brought home to Boston in the sleek hulls of sailing ships were, during the industrial revolution, wisely invested in new industrial endeavors, notably textile manufacture. Textiles were to become the state's economic backbone as mill towns were quickly built along Massachusetts rivers. By 1850 the city of Lowell was a world leader in textile production.

## THE TWENTIETH CENTURY

When, in the early years of the 20th century, cheap labor in the southern states and abroad began to draw the textile industry away from New England, Massachusetts sought out new sources of income. By mid-century, the state regained economic stability in electronic and related industries — the high-tech revolution.

Since its earliest beginnings, Massachusetts has been the cultural and intellectual center of New England. In politics and government, its statesmen, once pre-eminent in the struggle for independence, became active thereafter in the affairs of the new nation. For more than two hundred years Massachusetts statesmen have continued to exert creative leadership in the nation's subsequent existence, as recently as the Presidency of John F. Kennedy and the Presidential campaigns of Robert Kennedy and Michael Dukakis.

Massachusetts is the home of more institutions of higher learning than any other state in the Union. Among them are two of the world's most prestigious universities — Harvard University and the Massachusetts Institute of Technology (MIT), as well as five of the nation's most academically outstanding colleges — Williams, Amherst, Smith, Mount Holyoke and Wellesley.

Throughout the years Massachusetts has retained, in some measure, the ethical standards that characterized its beginnings: a capacity for independent thinking, a strong moral sense, a consistent faith in the power of education, a capacity for hard work and a commitment to frugality.

## BOSTON

It is easy to fall in love with Boston. Beautiful and sophisticated, it represents an almost

through famous neighborhoods — elegant Beacon Hill, fashionable Back Bay and historic North End.

Boston's nearly three million citizens, if one includes the city's outlying suburbs, is half the population of the state. They are a mix of blue bloods and blue collars, of sixth generation "Brahmins" and first generation Irish, the wealthy and the disadvantaged, the gentry and the homeless.

Over the centuries, Boston has provided more than its share of scholars, writers and

perfect marriage of historic preservation and economic revitalization. The union has created a marvelous skyline of contrasts. Tall skyscrapers and the imposing modern Government Center alternate with the steeple of the Old North Church, the clock tower of the Customs House and other historic landmarks.

## BACKGROUND

The city, founded by the Puritans in 1630, is inextricably associated with America's first role as a British colony. It remains proud of its part in the struggle for independence. Narrow streets, much as they were in colonial times, twist and turn haphazardly

statesmen, men and women who have profoundly influenced the life of the nation. Indeed, Boston could be said to combine in its history and people the classic elements of America's heritage and its promise for the future.

### Shawmut Peninsula

John Winthrop and his Puritans are said to have "stolen" much of the Shawmut Peninsula from hermit preacher Reverend William Blackstone to establish the city of Boston. The city owed much of its rapid growth to its fine deep water harbor and its fishing and merchant fleet that, by the 18th century, was the third largest in the English-speaking world.

Settlers in ever-increasing numbers came to Boston, making it the hub of trade and commerce in the English colonies and the most prosperous city in the English colonial empire. However, when the Crown and Parliament grew greedy and imposed upon the colonies a series of oppressive taxes and trade regulations, Boston led the break from the Mother Country.

## Cradle of Independence

Years before the Revolution, the Massachusetts House of Representatives denied the right of Parliament to tax the colonies without representation and it was Boston's revolutionaries whose speeches at meeting after meeting rallied their compatriots to unite against British oppression.

In March, 1770, one such group gathered outside the Old State House loudly protesting British tax policies. British soldiers fired into the crowd, killing five people. News of the "Boston Massacre" spread through New England, everywhere fanning hotter and hotter the flames of rebellion.

In meetings at Faneuil Hall and the Old Meeting House, Sam Otis and Samuel Adams continued to call for independence. One meeting, in December, 1773, led to the "Boston Tea Party," when about 90 colonists disguised as Indians boarded English ships by night in Boston Harbor and dumped more than three hundred chests of tea into the sea. In retaliation, the English closed the harbor and, in May, 1774, sent troops to occupy the city, forcing Boston's citizens to house the hated British soldiers in their homes.

The festering anger and resentment came to a head on April 18, 1775, when Paul Revere traveled to Lexington on his famous "Midnight Ride" to warn patriot leaders that British troops were on their way to nearby Concord to confiscate arms stored there by colonists. Bloody skirmishes the next day at Lexington Green and later at Concord gave the colonial militia its baptism by fire and marked the beginning of the Revolution.

George Washington, formerly a colonel of the Virginia militia, assumed general command of the Continental forces at Cambridge in July, 1775. He proved to be a brilliant soldier and politician. In less than a year he had wrested Boston from British control. The city continued free for the remaining years of the Revolution and, thereafter, exercised a major role in the affairs of the new nation.

From the time of the Revolution and well into the 19th century, Boston's ships sailed the seas of the world reaping great riches. Wealthy merchants transformed Beacon Hill and Back Bay into showplaces, featuring splendid mansions and elegant townhouses. The city became known as the "Athens of

America" and the "Boston Brahmin," a symbol of the ultimate in human culture and refinement.

## The Immigrant Wave

When, in the middle of the 19th century, Boston's maritime eminence began to fade, a manufacturing economy gradually took its place. In the same period, new waves of European immigrants reached the shores of America. Thousands of Polish, Irish and Italian workers came to Boston, as well as to other New England cities, eager to begin life anew and to find work in this burgeoning industrial economy. With the rapid influx of people of different customs and nationalities, Boston's population tended to become segregated. Enclaves of Irish or Poles or Italians grew up in older neighborhoods while the "proper" Bostonians kept to themselves in their own enclaves on Beacon Hill and Back Bay.

OPPOSITE and ABOVE: Boston's Fourth of July festivities.

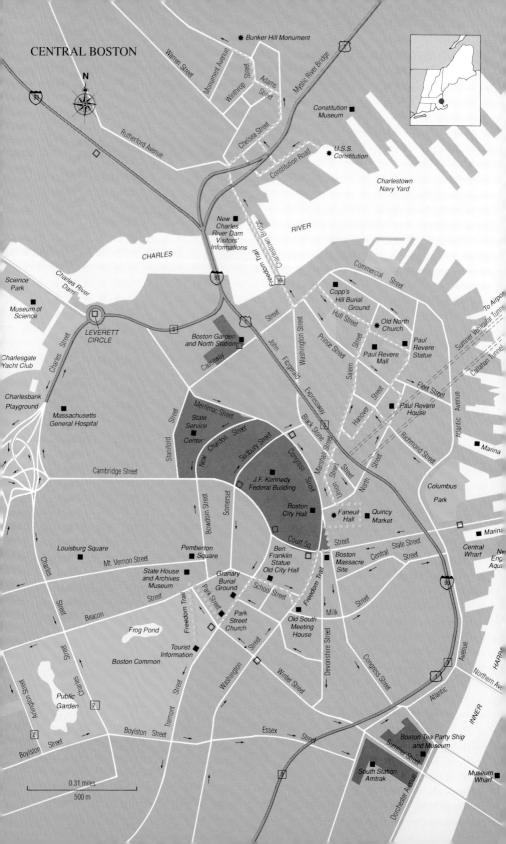

# CENTRAL BOSTON

N

★ Bunker Hill Monument

Warren Street

Monument Avenue

Winthrop Street

Adams Street

Chelsea Street

Mystic River Bridge

Rutherford Avenue

Constitution Museum

Constitution Road

★ U.S.S. Constitution

Charlestown Navy Yard

New Charles River Dam Visitors' Informations

Charlestown Bridge

Freedom Trail

CHARLES RIVER

Science Park

Charles River Dam

LEVERETT CIRCLE

Museum of Science

Charlesgate Yacht Club

Charles Street

Charlesbank Playground

Massachusetts General Hospital

Boston Garden and North Station

Causeway

Commercial Street

Copp's Hill Bunal Ground

Hull Street

Old North Church

Paul Revere Statue

Prince Street

Salem Street

Paul Revere Mall

Fleet Street

Paul Revere House

Hanover Street

Richmond Street

Sumner Vehicular Tunnel

Callahan Tunnel

To Airport

Marina

Columbus Park

Merrimac Street

State Service Center

New Chardon Street

Sudbury Street

Staniford Street

Cambridge Street

John Fitzgerald Expressway

Washington Street

Black Stone Street

Marshall Street

North Street

Congress Street

J.F. Kennedy Federal Building

Boston City Hall

★ Faneuil Hall

Quincy Market

Marina

Central Wharf

New England Aqua

Bowdoin Street

Somerset Street

Louisburg Square

Mt. Vernon Street

Pemberton Square

Court Sq.

Ben Franklin Statue Old City Hall

Boston Massacre Site

State Street

Central Street

State House and Archives Museum

Park Street

Beacon Street

Charles Street

Granary Burial Ground

School Street

Freedom Trail

Park Street Church

Old South Meeting House

Milk Street

Devonshire Street

Congress Street

Frog Pond

Tourist Information

Boston Common

Washington Street

Winter Street

Public Garden

Arlington Street

Charles Street

Boylston Street

Essex Street

Boston Tea Party Ship and Museum

Summer Street

South Station Amtrak

Museum Wharf

Atlantic Avenue

Northern Avenue

Dorchester Avenue

INNER HARBOR

0.31 miles

500 m

## Decline and Revival

By the end of the 19th century, Boston and all of Massachusetts lost much of their manufacturing base to southern states, which could offer cheaper labor and lower taxes. The city's decline continued well into the 20th century. In the 1960s, the area's incredible reserve of "brain power" at Harvard and MIT attracted high technology industries and research and development, which in turn fueled an urban revolution. Under the leadership of MIT-alumnus and architect I. M. Pei, Boston began to regain part of its former splendor. Expansive skyscrapers, government centers and office complexes mingled with the historic buildings to create a "new" Boston look — one of urban sophistication infused with the charm of an earlier era.

Today Boston is one of America's most livable cities. It remains the financial, commercial, intellectual and cultural hub of New England. The cobbled streets twist and turn, while an emerald necklace of parks and greenbelts (designed last century by the renowned landscape architect Frederick Law Olmstead) encircles the city. Ethnic neighborhoods break up any tendency toward urban sprawl, with each enclave having its own distinct appeal.

---

### GENERAL INFORMATION

The **Greater Boston Convention and Visitors Bureau** ( (617) 536-4100 FAX (617) 424-7664, Prudential Plaza, P.O. Box 990468, Boston, MA 02199, can send you its free planning guide in advance of your trip. You can also pick-up a copy at the **Prudential Visitor Center** in the Prudential Center Plaza, open daily from 8:30 AM to 5 PM, or at the **Boston Commons Visitor Information Center** at Tremont and Winter Streets, also open daily, from 8 AM to 5 PM. In the downtown historic center, the **National Park Service**, which manages the Freedom Trail, keeps its Visitor Center at 15 State Street open from 9 AM to 5 PM.

---

### TOURING BOSTON

Boston is a city to be explored on foot. Its two historic trails — the Freedom Trail and the Black Heritage Trail will lead you in the

footsteps of the people who built America. The Freedom Trail, a three-mile (five-kilometer) walking tour has been laid out by the National Park Service. It winds through the city and across the river into Charlestown, passing along its route 16 major historic sites and buildings related to the Revolutionary era. It also goes through the varied neighborhoods that characterize the city: the Italian North End, the "Old Boston" section of Beacon Hill and the Irish community in Charlestown. Do not worry about getting lost; signposts and a red line painted on the

sidewalk point you in the right direction. It takes about half a day to see all the sights if you are in a hurry; allow an entire day for a leisurely stroll. The Black Heritage Trail explores the history of Boston's 19th century African American community.

To start your Freedom Trail or Black Heritage Trail tour, go to the information kiosk by the Boston Common on Tremont Street, a few steps down from the Park Street "T" station. This is an area with souvenir vendors hawking Boston memorabilia and food carts offering hot dogs, ice cream and sweets. Inside the kiosk you can pick up a map of either or both of the Trails, along with information about the city's other attractions.

### The Freedom Trail

For the Freedom Trail follow the **red line** into the **Boston Common**. This handsome 45-acre (18-hectare) city green was purchased for $150 by the Puritan city fathers in 1634

---

Swan boats for rent at the pond in Boston's Public Gardens.

as a militia "trayning field" and for the "feeding of Cattell" [sic]. Under law, the Common can still be used for these purposes.

The Common has always been the pride of the city, even though in the beginning it was used for public hangings and punishments. In fact, the Puritans had a pillory built here to make an example of transgressors; the first to be pilloried was the carpenter who built it, who was accused of charging too much money for his work.

During the Battle of Bunker Hill, the British used the Common as an encamp-

harbor beacon that once topped this hill and gave the neighborhood its name. The archives here contain valuable historic documents, including the original Charter of the Massachusetts Bay Colony.

Across the street from the Common is the lovely **Park Street Church**, its tall steeple a familiar Boston landmark since it was built in 1809. Abolitionist William Lloyd Garrison gave his first anti-slavery speech here in 1829.

Next to the church is the **Old Granary Burying Ground**, so-named for the 17th-

ment and embarked for Charlestown from its grounds. Today, the Common is filled with hilly knolls and winding paths, statues and gurgling fountains. Noontime office workers often stroll through the park to enjoy the open space; in summer, outdoor concerts are held here. Sadly, however, like most urban open spaces in the United States, the Common is decidedly less appealing at night; even in daytime panhandlers and drunks are a common sight and you should, needless to say, be on guard against pickpockets.

You can follow the Trail across Beacon Street to the "new" **State House**, designed by Charles Bulfinch and completed in 1795 on land that originally belonged to John Hancock. Its golden dome gleams like the

century granary that used to stand here. Established in 1660, it contains the graves of several notable Americans, including John Hancock, who signed the Declaration of Independence; the Revolutionary leader and orator Samuel Adams; the revolutionary Paul Revere; Peter Faneuil, who gave the city Faneuil Hall; and the victims of the Boston Massacre. Also interred here is Mary ("Mother") Goose, who concocted nursery rhymes to entertain her grandchildren.

Farther along the Trail at Tremont and School Streets is **King's Chapel**, completed in 1754; it was the first Anglican church in New England. In pre-Revolutionary times, the church was graced with gifts of silver and vestments from Queen Anne and King

George III. The old cemetery next to the church contains the graves of John Winthrop, the first Puritan governor of the colony and Elizabeth Pain, a 17th-century woman accused of adultery and said to have inspired Nathaniel Hawthorne to write his classic novel, *The Scarlet Letter*. Also on School Street is the statue of **Benjamin Franklin**, the first portrait statue erected in Boston and the **Old Corner Bookstore**, a red brick house dating to 1712 that was the center of literary Boston in the 19th century. Noted authors, including Hawthorne, Longfellow and Emerson, gathered here to discuss their craft.

The **Old South Meeting House**, built in 1729, was the largest building in colonial Boston. It frequently hosted town meetings, especially in the years leading to the Revolution, when men such as Samuel Adams and John Hancock rallied the townspeople against the British. One of those meetings (held December 16, 1773), called to discuss the new British tea tax, led to the famous Boston Tea Party.

The **Old State House**, at Washington, Court and State Streets, is located in the heart of downtown Boston, overshadowed by the towering steel and glass behemoths of **Government Center**. Built in 1713, the Old State House was the seat of colonial government and public life. In 1761, James Otis railed against unfair British regulations, prompting John Adams later to write, "then and there, the child Independence was born." And on July 18, 1776, from the east balcony, the Declaration of Independence was first proclaimed to the citizens of Boston.

A circle of cobblestones in the street just outside the Old State House marks the site of the **Boston Massacre**. Paul Revere's famed engraving helped to make the Massacre a key event in the growing popular resistance to British rule.

Follow the red line into **Dock Square**, with its boutiques, food stands, markets and bricked plaza. Also located here are **Faneuil Hall** and **Quincy Market**.

It is ironic that the Hall known as the "Cradle of Liberty" — because its second-floor meeting house hosted several important (and vociferous) protests against British colonial policies — was donated to the city in 1742 by Dutch slave trader Peter Faneuil.

The first floor of the Hall has always been a market; however, stalls that once offered fresh meat, vegetables and dairy products to colonial Bostonians have been transformed into modern boutique stands and food booths catering to tourists.

Note the grasshopper weather vane atop the hall dome; for over two centuries it has been the symbol of Faneuil Hall. Fashioned in 1742 and a fine example of colonial artistry, it was inspired by similar weather vanes on the Royal Exchange building in London and is the only part of the

original Faneuil Hall which remains totally unmodified.

The Freedom Trail passes next through riotous **Haymarket Square**, a sprawling open-air food market with booths offering everything from fresh meats to hand-polished fruits and vegetables. Use the pedestrian underpass to cross Fitzgerald Expressway. This brings you to the **North End**, Boston's famed Italian neighborhood.

The North End, not Back Bay, is the city's oldest neighborhood. In fact, until the 19th century, this section of narrow, twisting streets was about all there was to Boston.

Faneuil Hall OPPOSITE and Paul Revere's House ABOVE are preserved as memorials to America's fight for independence.

When landfill and reclamation projects created new city dwellings, wealthy Boston families moved out of the crowded North End and waves of immigrants moved in.

Today, it is a colorful area with its streetside restaurants featuring noontime plates of homemade pasta, sausage and pizza. It also contains two of the most revered historic shrines along the Freedom Trail.

If **Paul Revere** were alive today, he would still have a **home** in Boston. That home, in North Square, is where the Revere family lived from 1770 to 1800. The clap-

board building was built in 1680 by a wealthy merchant on the site of Puritan minister Increase Mather's home, which was destroyed by fire in 1676. In its time a fashionable townhouse, it is today the oldest wooden house in Boston.

While living here, Revere produced his famous Boston Massacre engraving, took part in the Boston Tea Party, secretly carried important revolutionary dispatches to Philadelphia and participated in numerous other radical causes.

On April 18, 1775, Revere left his house, slipped out of the city in a rowboat, borrowed a horse in Charlestown and rode to Lexington to warn revolutionaries there that the British were marching from Boston to seize munitions hidden in Concord.

The interior of the house has been restored and many Revere artifacts — including some of his exquisite silversmith work, his old rocking chair and saddlebags — are displayed.

"One if by land and two if by sea" is a phrase familiar to all American schoolchil-

dren. It was the signal to be given from the **Old North Church** (at the foot of Hull Street near the end of Paul Revere Mall) to warn revolutionaries of a British invasion aimed at Lexington and Concord. In April 1775, a church sexton hung two lanterns from the steeple's highest windows to indicate British troop movements.

The 190-ft (58-m) white steeple has been a city landmark since the church — the oldest in Boston — was built in 1723. Inside the church, pew 54 once belonged to Paul Revere's son and was occupied several times by Revere himself. The church bells were cast in Gloucester, England, the first made for Britain's North American empire; they sound now only on Sunday mornings before services.

Up Hull Street is **Copp's Hill Burying Ground**. The earliest graves here date from 1660 and include those of Increase, Cotton and Samuel Mather, important figures in early Boston history. One of the more interesting graves is that of the revolutionary Daniel Malcolm, who defiantly requested that "he be buried 10 feet deep, safe from British Musket Balls." He got his wish, but six years later, British soldiers got the last laugh when they used his tombstone for target practice. Today you can still see the marks on the stone.

Copp's Hill was also the site of a British cannon, which was trained on Bunker Hill across the Charles River during the battle. You can see the same view of Bunker Hill that British General Burgoyne had when he directed cannon fire at the entrenched revolutionaries.

Here you cross the Charlestown Bridge and then either walk up Monument Avenue to Bunker Hill, or keep to the waterfront along Constitution Avenue to visit the *Constitution*, the Navy's oldest fighting ship.

A 221-ft (67-m) white granite obelisk stands as a memorial to the men who fought at the Battle of Bunker Hill. The **Bunker Hill monument** is actually on Breed's Hill, where the misnamed clash took place on June 17, 1775. About 1,200 Americans and 3,000 British troops took part in the battle. The first English attack failed and British troops twice required reinforcements.

The revolutionaries eventually were forced to withdraw; colonial General Prescott ordered a retreat only after all ammunition had been used. The toll: for the Americans, 140 killed, 271 wounded, 30 captured; for the British, 226 killed, 828 wounded.

Even though the revolutionaries were defeated, the Battle of Bunker Hill proved to the revolutionaries that they measured up well in battle against the British regulars. Said General Washington of the clash: "I am content. The liberties of the country are safe."

The monument's observation tower offers a panoramic view of Boston, the harbor, its islands and the USS Constitution; its spiral staircase has 294 steps leading to the top, with no elevator. An excellent audiovisual presentation explaining the battle in detail, as well as the events leading up to it, can be seen at the **Bunker Hill Pavilion** on Hoosac Pier, just off Constitution Avenue.

Along the harbor front is the **Charlestown Navy Yard**, one of the first naval shipyards in the nation and the last stop on the Freedom Trail.

A tour of the yard's exhibits spans nearly 200 years of maritime history. At the **Visitor Information Center**, you can view a 10-minute slide show and receive information on guided walking tours.

Beginning in 1800, the yard built, serviced and supplied ships for the Navy. Workers swarmed over the dry docks, rope walks and shipways cluttered with maritime equipment. The yard reached peak operation during World War II, when it employed more than 50,000 men and women who built and repaired a record number of vessels.

Attractions include Pier 1 (one of the 11 original wharves that serviced ships), the 1833 dry dock (one of the first of its kind in the country), the Maritime Society Museum and the Commandant's House.

But the centerpiece of the yard is the magnificent **USS Constitution** ( (617) 426-1812, the oldest commissioned warship in the Navy, (admission free; open daily from 9:30 AM to 3:30 PM). The foundations of the United States Navy were established by Congress in 1794 upon authorization of six new frigates. One of these was the USS Constitution, a 44-gun warship built at the nearby Hartt's Shipyard and launched in 1797.

She sailed against the Barbary pirates, fought the British in the war of 1812 and engaged in 40 sea battles without a loss. When a British sailor saw shots bounce off the USS Constitution's planking, he shouted, "Her sides are made of iron!" Thus the ship gained its renowned nickname, "Old Ironsides."

The USS Constitution is still a commissioned warship; members of its present crew take visitors on tours of the spar deck with its huge cannons that fire 32 lb (15 kg) shells, the gun deck with its 30 24-lb- (11-kg)-long

guns, the captain's quarters below decks and the berthing deck where the crew slept in hammocks. At the rear is the ship's wheel, which required the strength of four men to control. Sailors also climbed the ropes to the "fighting tops" positioned on each mast to fire on enemy ships.

### The Black Heritage Trail

This trail consists of 14 sites all located in the Beacon Hill area, including the **African American Meeting House**, the oldest Black church edifice still standing in the United States; and the **Robert Gould Shaw and**

OPPOSITE and ABOVE: Clapboard and red-brick houses, typical of Boston's Colonial architecture, are much admired for their style.

**54th Regiment Memorial** which pays
tribute to the Civil War Union Army's first
black regiment. Robert Gould Shaw, a
young white officer from a prominent
Boston family, volunteered for its command. The **Smith Court Residences** are five
residential structures typical of the homes
occupied by Black Bostonians in the
19th century. William C. Nell, America's
first published black historian, boarded in
Nº 3 from 1851 to 1865. Nell was also a community activist and a leader in the struggle
to integrate Boston's public schools before
the Civil War. Homes on the Black Heritage
Trail are not open to the public, being private
residences; but, you can enter the African
Meeting House and another site, the **Abiel
Smith School**.

**Beacon Hill**
The Beacon Hill neighborhood, with its
narrow gas-lit streets, elegant townhouses
and tall shade trees, is like a city-within-a-
city with turn-of-the-century splendor. This
has not always been the case. In the late
17th-century, the Trimount neighborhood
(Beacon Hill's old name) was a wild no-
man's land referred to by some Bostonians
as Mt. Whoredom. But when the State
House was built here in 1798, many of the
city's wealthiest families rushed to commission State House architect Charles Bulfinch
to design Federal mansions and elegant
bow-fronted Greek Revival row houses.
Beacon Hill had arrived and it remains one
of the most desirable districts in which to
live.

Today, a walk along the bumpy sidewalks of Beacon Hill is reminiscent of a more elegant, peaceful era. It is a splendid oasis of fine period architecture and tranquil surroundings yet within a stone's throw of busy downtown Boston.

Start your tour at the Common on **Beacon Street**. Numbers 39 and 40 are Bulfinch-designed twin mansions that house the Women's City Club of Boston; guided tours of the homes' elegant Greek Revival interiors are by appointment only. Also note the Beacon Hill "purple glass" in the windows, caused when sunlight reacted with impurities in the imported English glass, turning it a distinctive purple color.

Go north on Spruce, past old servants' houses, to **Mount Vernon Street**. This is

*Eastern Massachusetts, Boston and Cape Cod*

arguably the most beautiful street on "the Hill," as locals now call it. The **Nichols House Museum**, another 1804 Bulfinch design, is typical of Beacon Hill's architecture from its golden era. It is one of the few private homes on the Hill open to visitors and is lavishly furnished in period decor.

Just off Mt. Vernon is **Louisburg Square**. Its ornate homes frame the elegant green, creating the ultimate in traditional Boston-style charm; a home in this idyllic enclave remains the dream of many Bostonians. Louisa May Alcott, author of *Little Women*, lived here, as did novelist William Dean Howells. One of Howells' books, *The Rise of Silas Lapham*, relates the life of Boston's wealthy in the mid-nineteen hundreds.

Christmas is a great time to visit Beacon Hill, when strolling carolers are a holiday tradition. With its 19th-century ambiance, you almost expect Whittier or Longfellow to pop up on the green.

Other Beacon Hill streets of interest to visitors are narrow, cobblestoned **Acorn Street** and, for its coffee houses, galleries and chic shops, **Charles Street**.

If you prefer a guided tour to simply wandering around, **Boston By Foot** ℂ (617) 367-2345, offers one-and-a-half hour walking tours of the Hill, as well as walks along the Freedom Trail and through historic Copley Square.

### Back Bay and Copley Square

Back Bay's wide Commonwealth Avenue is fashioned after the grand boulevards of Paris, while the streets are lined with beautiful Victorian brownstone row houses. Since the 1870s, a Back Bay address has been a coveted status symbol.

**Copley Square** is the heart of Back Bay and displays some of Boston's best 19th- and 20th-century architecture.

The 1877 **Trinity Church**, designed by Henry Hobson Richardson, is a magnificent Romanesque design some consider the best church architecture in America. Inspired by the great cathedrals of France and Spain, it is massive in scale. Inside, the intricate

During the summer, Bostonians are drawn to the city's many parks and pedestrian walkways.

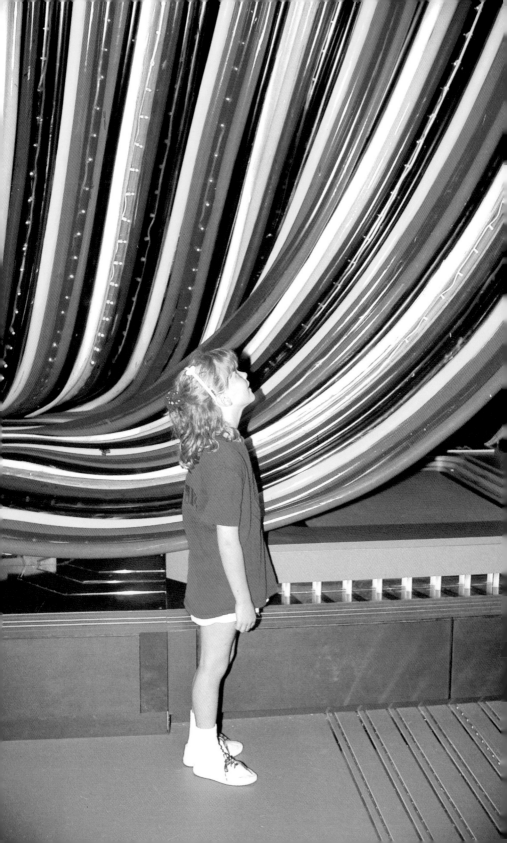

details include rich wall murals, carvings and friezes.

Across Dartmouth Street is the **Boston Public Library**, the world's oldest free library. The Library, with its collection of six million books, is approached through an elegant central courtyard with a fountain and a spectacular entry fashioned after a Greek temple and graced with a grand Siena marble staircase. The library is enriched by murals, bronzes and paintings by some of the world's most renowned artists and is a tranquil retreat from the bustle of Boston.

Cross St. James Avenue to reach the **John Hancock Tower**, a striking, glass-covered 60-story skyscraper designed by I.M. Pei. New England's tallest building, it is the corporate headquarters of the John Hancock Mutual Life Insurance Company. It acts as a giant mirror, reflecting the Back Bay cityscape in its tall glass walls. It has long been plagued by the not insignificant problem of its glass sheets falling off; this however, seems to have been completely remedied in recent years.

One of the best ways to see Boston is from the Tower's 60th-floor **observatory** ( (617) 247-1976. High-speed elevators carry visitors 740 ft (226 m) from the street to the observatory in about 30 seconds, from where they can see a panorama embracing the gold-domed State House, the gracious townhouses of Beacon Hill, Boston Harbor's islands, Cambridge, the North and South shores and the distant White Mountains of southern New Hampshire. Observatory exhibits include "Boston 1775," a light and sound show about Revolutionary Boston.

Down Stuart Street is **Copley Place**, a $500 million shopping and eating emporium. Along Huntington Avenue are the 14acre (five-and-a-half-hectare) grounds of the **Christian Science Center**, world headquarters for the Church of Christ, Science and the *Christian Science Monitor*, a highly respected national daily newspaper. The landscape at the Christian Science complex is dominated by the 1894 Romanesque-style Mother Church — one of Boston's architectural gems — made of gleaming white New Hampshire granite. A domed extension combining Renaissance and Byzantine architectural concepts was added in 1906. The organ is one of the largest in the world with a total of 13,595 pipes! After a look around this fine building, follow the signs back out on the plaza to the "Mapparium", located inside the church's publishing offices. This giant antique glass globe is a unique experience. Visitors walk across a bridge and find themselves, literally, at the center of the earth, gazing out at the world. Besides being lovely, it's a great place to marvel at the political fortunes of the planet. See how many defunct countries you can locate.

Backtrack to reach the **Prudential Center**, another corporate insurance headquarters skyscraper with its own 50th-floor Skywalk, an observation tower from which 360-degree views of the city with accompanying historical commentary can be enjoyed. Sunset is the best time to visit.

**The Leather District**

The Leather District was once the center of Boston's shoe industry. Today the factories and warehouses have disappeared to be replaced by high rise office buildings and a contingent of art galleries that, in the heyday of this district's revival, rivaled Newbury Street. The number of galleries has diminished somewhat, but there are still many worth seeing. And they're free. The galleries cluster around South Street which runs parallel to Atlantic Avenue right next to South Station — the city's major Amtrak and bus depot. The galleries can usually provide you with a guide — a printed map to all the galleries in the area — to get you started. Combine a walk around this district with a tour of Boston's Chinatown, just a few blocks to the west. Look for the red and gold pagoda gate.

**Government Center**

Rising in the middle of the city like a fortress of poured-concrete, steel and glass is Government Center, an urban renewal program designed by I.M. Pei that transformed 60 acres (24 hectares) of tattoo parlors and pornography stores which only 30 years ago dominated the squalid Scollay Square district,

OPPOSITE: Boston's Computer Museum captivates visitors of all ages.

into some of the most imposing buildings in Boston and created a new focus for the city. The district's centerpiece is the new **City Hall**, designed by Kallman, McKinell and Knowles. It is a massive inverted pyramid resting on a plaza of brick resembling "an Aztec temple on a brick desert."

Surrounding the Hall are several modern buildings that add to the district's futuristic feel: the tall twin towers of the **John F. Kennedy Office Building**, the **Center Plaza Building** with its contours that curve to the slope of Beacon Hill and the **State Service**

**Center**, whose sharp architectural lines cut the horizon northwest of the Hall.

In fact, the only historic 19th-century building that survived Government Center's transformation is the **Sears Crescent**, notable for the huge 200 gallon (900 liter) steaming tea pot that hangs from one corner of the building to mark the site of what was the largest tea store in Boston.

The district's display of modern architecture is on a grand scale and its huge open spaces a welcoming oasis from the crowded city neighborhoods.

### The Harborwalk

Harborwalk is a two-mile (three-kilometer) trail that loops around Boston's historic waterfront, providing a bird's-eye view of the wharves, boats and islands. It begins at the National Park Service Visitor Center (on State Street near the Old State House) and ends at the Boston Tea Party Ship and Mu-

seum. Along the way are some interesting historic and commercial buildings, as well as sights and sounds of maritime Boston. Highlights include:

The **Boston Children's Museum** ( (617) 426-8855, 300 Congress Street (admission $7; $1 on Friday 5 PM to 9 PM, reductions for children and senior citizens; open every day but Monday, 10 AM to 5 PM, Friday until 9 PM), on Museum Wharf across the Fort Point Channel, has been called "the country's best museum for kids." Its varied displays, exhibits and special events are guaranteed to entertain children of all ages. Toddlers jump over steps and slide down platforms in Playspace; older kids climb like monkeys from platform to platform within a futuristic sculpture; and teens can even try out the latest dance steps at the Clubhouse. There are replicas of an Indian wigwam, a country street, a two-story Japanese house and a television studio equipped with viewing monitors.

The **New England Aquarium** ( (617) 973-5200, Central Wharf, off Atlantic Avenue (admission $8.50 with reductions for children and senior citizens; open Monday, Wednesday and Friday, 9 AM to 5 PM), contains a four-story ocean coral reef glass tank filled with sharks, turtles and more than 600 other sea creatures. Dolphin and sea lion shows are offered daily on the *Discovery*. One of its newest exhibits, "Wired for Sound," demonstrates just how noisy the underwater world can be. From here you can board whale-watching cruises on the wharf, which head to Stellwagen Bank, one of the East Coast's prime whale habitats.

The **Computer Museum** ( (617) 423-6758, Museum Wharf (admission $7, half-price Sunday 3 to 5 PM, with reductions for children, students and senior citizens; open every day except Monday, 10 AM to 5 PM, Friday until 9 PM), features state-of-the-art computer technology in interactive displays. You can play games, create art, write music — in fact almost anything is possible here, including a computer that not only talks, but can carry on a "conversation."

Another pleasant option is the **Boston Tea Party Ship and Museum** ( (617) 338-1773, near South Station at Congress Street Bridge (admission $6.50 with reductions for

ABOVE: In downtown Boston, American history is at your fingertips. OPPOSITE: The John Fitzgerald Kennedy Memorial Library and Museum.

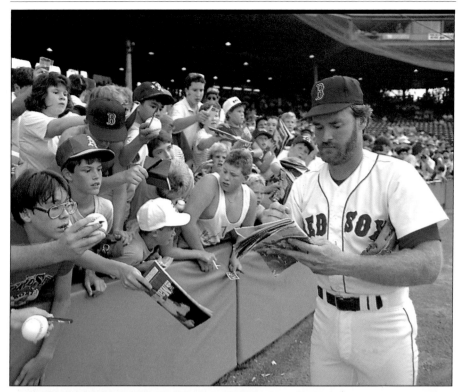

children, students and seniors; open daily 9 AM to dusk). It is a full-scale replica of the British brigantine *Beaver* and costumed guides relate the history of the 1773 Boston Tea Party. Museum artifacts include a tea chest reputed to be among those tossed into the water on that fateful night.

## CULTURAL ATTRACTIONS

### Museums

The best known of Boston's museums is the **Museum of Fine Arts** ℂ (617) 267-9300, 465 Huntington Avenue (admission $8 adults, free admission Wednesday, 4 to 9:45 PM., free to children under 16, open Tuesday to Saturday, 10 AM to 5 PM, Wednesday 10 AM to 10 PM). It was originally the beneficiary of artifacts gathered by Boston's wealthy Brahmins as they traveled the world in the 19th century; those objects still form the centerpieces of its varied collections.

It is today considered one of the world's great museums. The handsome 1909 Greek temple-style building contains more than 200 galleries. The Oriental collection is one of the most remarkable in the country, with Buddhist paintings and sculptures, some dating to the 12th century, dominating the Japanese displays; ceramics, including objects from the Han dynasty (third century), highlight the Chinese section.

The Egyptian artifacts are largely the bounty of a 40-year Middle East expedition sponsored by the Museum and Harvard University. It is reputed to be the finest collection of 4,000-year-old antiquities outside Cairo.

The European galleries display a large selection of Monets; in the American collection are Gilbert Stuart's portraits of George and Martha Washington. Twentieth-century art is displayed in the museum's new glass-roofed wing.

Just a short walk away is the **Isabella Stewart Gardner Museum** ℂ (617) 566-1401, 280 The Fenway (admission $7 with reductions for children, students and seniors; open Wednesday to Sunday, noon to 5 PM, Tuesday noon to 6:30 PM), a Venetian-style palazzo which houses the personal collections of an eccentric 19th-century millionaire. Isabella Stewart Gardner commis-

sioned agents to travel the world in search of fine art and they purchased six million dollars worth which included Matisses, Whistlers and Titian's *Rape of Europa*, painted for Philip II of Spain. Other treasures include beautiful tapestries, centuries-old mosaics and sculpture. Its courtyard, with Venetian-style windows and balconies, flowering plants and trees framing a Roman floor mosaic from Livia that dates to the second century, is a delight.

The **John F. Kennedy Memorial Library and Museum** ℂ (617) 929-4523, Columbia Point, off Morrissey Boulevard (admission $6 for adults, $4 for seniors and students, free for those under age 16; open daily from 9 AM to 5 PM), is another of architect I.M. Pei's designs and some consider the sleek concrete and glass structure to be one of his best.

Nine exhibit halls, filled with family and presidential memorabilia encircle a central room containing the president's desk as it was on November 22, 1963 when President Kennedy was assassinated during a motorcade ride through the streets of Dallas. A 35-minute film chronicles his life and times. Other displays feature artifacts from his PT-109 days and the Cuban missile crisis. A eight-story gray glass contemplation pavilion contains only an American flag, a bench and a Kennedy quotation engraved on the wall.

Another **Kennedy** museum is his **birthplace** ℂ (617) 566-7937, in suburban Brookline. The house has been restored to the way it looked in 1917, the year Kennedy was born and offers audio guided tours narrated by his mother, Rose Kennedy.

The **Museum of Science** and the **Charles Hayden Planetarium** ℂ (617) 723-2500, Science Park, along the Charles River (admission $7.50 adults, $5 for children and seniors; open Tuesday to Sunday, 9 AM to 5 PM, Friday 9 AM to 9 PM), are hands-on delights and feature a life-sized model of an Apollo space capsule, a 20-ft (six-meter) plastic tyrannosaurus rex and a "lightning-making" machine.

---

OPPOSITE TOP: Boston's Red Sox baseball team has an avid local following. OPPOSITE BOTTOM: Food stands and boutiques line Quincy Market.

**Fenway Park** is also a museum of sorts. Located just off Brookline Avenue, in Back Bay, it is home to the Boston Red Sox, the city's major league baseball team. Fenway is also one of the oldest, most charming and intimate of baseball stadiums, which brings the fans so close to the action that they can almost reach out and touch the players.

**Music and Theater**
The world-famous **Boston Symphony Orchestra** performs in **Symphony Hall** ( (617) 266-1492, Massachusetts Avenue and the **Boston Pops** performs outdoors at the **Hatch Memorial Shell** on the Charles River Esplanade during the summer, as does the **Boston Ballet Company**. Theaters and performing arts centers are found throughout the city. The **Wang Center for the Performing Arts** ( (617) 482-9393, 268 Tremont Street, a 3,800-seat theater offers Broadway musicals, ballet and opera performances. It is home to the **Boston Ballet** and hosts visiting dance companies including the **Alvin Ailey American Dance Theatre** and the **Bolshoi Ballet Academy**. In Boston's theatre district, you will find live performances at, among others, the **Wilbur Theatre** (617) 423-4008, 246 Tremont Street; the nearby **Colonial Theatre** ( (617) 426-9366, 106 Boylston Street at Tremont and the **Shubert Theatre** ( (617) 426-4520, 265 Tremont Street.

At the BosTix kiosks you can get **half-priced day-of-the-show tickets** to music, theatre and dance performances throughout the city. BosTix has two downtown locations: BosTix Faneuil Hall Marketplace is found along the Freedom Trail — a short walk from the Government Center, Haymarket and State Street "T" stops. The booth is adjacent to The Limited and Houlihan's Restaurant with the nearest parking at 75 State Street or the Government Center Garage near Haymarket. BosTix Copley Square is adjacent to Trinity Church, the Boston Public Library and the John Hancock Tower. The kiosk is on the corner of Boylston and Dartmouth Streets near the Copley and Back Bay "T" stops with the closest parking at 200 Berkeley Street (entrance on Clarendon Street). Both kiosks are open Tuesday through Saturday 10 AM to 6 PM, Sunday 11 AM to 4 PM. They are generally, closed

Mondays, but the Copley Square location is open on Mondays during summer and fall. Half-price tickets go on sale at 11 AM. Bring cash; BosTix does not take credit cards or checks.

**SHOPPING**

If you were born to shop, get your wallet out, because Boston has it all. **Back Bay** is one of the leading shopping districts; its **Newbury Street** is the city's equivalent to New York's Fifth Avenue with its ultra-chic boutiques, clothiers and galleries. Brooks Brothers, Divino, Louis, Martini Carl, Settebello and Parachute offer the latest fashions from designers such as Kendo and Armani. Also down the street is Burberry's, makers of the renowned British trench coat that helps to keep Bostonians warm during their often-bitter winters.

**Copley Place**, a new $500 million shopping and dining palace, showcases the international fashions of Gucci, Louis Vuitton, Jaegar and plenty of others. New England's only Neiman-Marcus department store offers a Texas-sized selection of high-quality merchandise. And if you are in the mood for something gold, try Tiffany's. Just down the block is the **Prudential Center**, for Saks Fifth Avenue and Lord and Taylor.

**Downtown Crossing** is unquestionably the city's most popular shopping area for all walks of Boston society. **Macy's** has newly arrived on the scene, bringing trendy and classic designs for both men and women, not to mention a fine selection of upscale housewares. Then there is **Filene's**, a sophisticated fashion emporium whose basement sales are a Boston tradition. All sorts of designer items are sold here at bargain-basement prices, with prices further slashed at regular intervals until the remaining merchandise is sold or finally donated to charity.

Beacon Hill's **Charles Street** is the neighborhood's commercial center. Its many art galleries, antique stores and coffee houses make it an interesting place for browsing.

Sightseeing buses tour elegant downtown Boston.

Finally, **Bloomingdales**, of New York City fame, is located in nearby Newton, Massachusetts, just west of Boston.

## WHERE TO STAY

As in most major American cities, Boston hotels tend to be expensive and many cost over $200 for a double. However, Boston does offer value for the price. By shopping around you can frequently book a weekend package that includes a room on Friday and Saturday night for about two thirds the weekday rate. These often vary with the season, but don't hesitate to ask about weekend rates when you call for reservations. You can find yourself in Boston without a room if the Red Sox are playing or during graduation time at the numerous colleges in and around the city.

### Super Luxury Hotels

For elegant old-style Boston hospitality, you cannot beat the **Wyndham Copley Plaza Hotel** ( (617) 267-5300 TOLL-FREE (800) 996-3426 FAX (617 247-6681, 138 St. James Avenue; the **Ritz-Carlton** ( (617) 536-5700 TOLL-FREE (800) 241-3333 FAX (617) 536-1335, Arlington and Newbury Street; and the **Omni Parker House** ( (617) 227-8600 TOLL-FREE (800) 843-6664 FAX (617) 742-5729, 60 School Street.

A skybridge links Boston's tallest hotel — the **Westin Hotel at Copley Place** ( (617) 262-9600 TOLL-FREE (800) 228-3000 FAX (617) 424-7483, 10 Huntington Avenue — to the upscale shopping at Copley Place. A very classy luxury hotel, decorated with murals by N.C. Wyeth (the father of Andrew, is **Le Hotel Meridien Boston** ( (617) 451-1900 TOLL-FREE (800) 543-4300 FAX (617) 423-2844, 250 Franklin Street, now owned by Air France. Another superb hotel is the new **Four Seasons** ( (617) 338-4400 TOLL-FREE (800) 332-3442 FAX (617) 423-0154, 200 Boylston Street.

In this same category is the European-style **Bostonian Hotel** ( (617) 523-3600 TOLL-FREE (800) 343-0922 FAX (617) 523-2454, Faneuil Hall Marketplace, Dock Square which is centrally located near Faneuil Hall, Government Center and the Haymarket. Children under 12 stay free. Expect to pay over $220 for a double at the above hotels.

### Expensive

On the waterfront is the ultra-modern **Marriott Long Wharf** ( (617) 227-0800 TOLL-FREE (800) 228-9290 FAX (617) 227-2867, 296 State Street. Similarly priced at the high end of expensive are **Back Bay Hilton Hotel** ( (617) 236-1100 FAX (617) 267-8893, 40 Dalton Street; and **Swissotel Boston** ( (617) 451-2600 TOLL-FREE (800) 992-0124 FAX (617) 451-2198, 1 Avenue de Lafayette. Located near the Prudential Center is the **Lenox Hotel** ( (617) 536-5300 TOLL-FREE (800) 225-7676 FAX (617) 236-0351, 710 Boylston Street. If you are attracted to large-scale hotels, there is the **Marriott at Copley Place** ( (617) 236-5800 TOLL-FREE (800) 228-9290 FAX (617) 236-5885, 110 Huntington Avenue. The **Holiday Inn Select—Government Center** ( (617) 742-7630 TOLL-FREE (800) 238-8000 FAX (617) 742-4192, 2 Blossom Street, Boston, is attractive for families as children under 18 stay free.

### Moderate to Inexpensive

Howard Johnson's operates two establishments in the city that are among the best of the moderately priced hotels: **Howard Johnson Lodge Fenway** ( (617) 267-8300 TOLL-FREE (800) 654-2000 FAX (617) 267-2763, 1271 Boylston Street; and **Howard Johnson's Hotel Kenmore Square** ( (617) 267-3100 TOLL-FREE (800) 654-2000 FAX (617) 424-1045 575 Commonwealth Avenue. If you are flying out early in the morning or arriving late at night, the **Holiday Inn — Boston Airport** ( (617) 569-5250 FAX (617) 567-3725, 225 McClellan Highway, is a good standby. The **Milner Hotel** ( (617) 426-6220 TOLL-FREE (800) 453-1731 FAX (617) 350-0360, 78 South Charles Street (moderate), is a quaint brownstone in the heart of Boston. A continental breakfast is included in the price of a room. It's centrally located and within walking distance of theaters, restaurants, colleges, and nightclubs. All rooms have private baths, air conditioners, and cable television.

It may be necessary to leave the center of the city to find budget accommodations. **Brookline** is a pleasant suburb well-connected to downtown by the MBTA Green line and offers two good values: **Beacon Street Guest House** ( (617) 232-0292 TOLL-FREE

(800) 872-7211 FAX (617) 734-5815, 1047 Beacon Street, Brookline, is listed in the National Register for Historic Places. It has small rooms with semi-private baths as well as large rooms with private baths (moderate to inexpensive). **Brookline Manor Guest House (** (617) 232-0003 TOLL-FREE (800) 535-5325 FAX (617) 734-5815, 32 Centre Street, Brookline, is a four-storied Victorian guesthouse on a tree lined residential avenue. Rooms are available with private or shared baths (moderate to inexpensive).

With so few inexpensive rooms in Boston, a good alternative for budget lodging are the many bed and breakfast establishments where a double room will cost between $45 and $90. You can book a bed and breakfast through the **Bed and Breakfast Associates Bay Colony, Inc. (** (617) 449-5302 FAX (617) 449-5958, P.O. Box 57166, Babson Park Branch, Boston, MA 02157.

## EATING OUT

In Boston you can find a bit of everything when it comes to cuisine, but no one should visit New England without tasting its seafood specialties — creamy clam chowder, fresh lobster, fish chowder, fried or steamed clams and fried cod. These are served at several of the moderately priced restaurants listed below. Reservations are advised for evening meals at all restaurants.

It may come as a disappointment, but you will be hard-pressed to find the famous Boston baked beans in a restaurant. Once the staple of the New Englander's diet, this wholesome, tasty dish is now considered low-brow and uncouth. Also sadly absent from the menus is the traditional New England boiled dinner — a joint of ham boiled for hours with cabbage, carrots, onions, turnips and potatoes.

### Expensive

Most of the top-of-the-line restaurants in Boston specialize in European fare except for the **Hampshire House (** (617) 227-9600, 84 Beacon Street. It was known for its fine cuisine long before its Bull & Finch Pub, which inspired the television series, *Cheers*, thrust it into the national spotlight. Here you can dine on New England clam chowder

and lobster, or steaks and chicken prepared with a French or Italian twist. **Turner Fisheries (** (617) 424-7425, within the Westin Hotel, Copley Place, is renowned for fresh seafood — the restaurant's clam chowder has been elevated to the citywide Chowderfest Hall of Fame. Here, you can dine until 11:30 PM; the lounge features jazz nightly until 1 AM.

For French cuisine, Boston has several restaurants from which you can choose. **Another Season (** (617) 367-0880, on Beacon Hill (97 Mount Vernon Street) has a week-

day (Monday to Thursday) fixed price, four-course menu that is moderately priced. Downtown at **Maison Robert (** (617) 227-3370, 45 School Street, weather permitting, you can lunch or dine outside. Here you can also order New England food, such as a New England lobster in champagne sauce. **Aujourd'hui (** (617) 451-1392, in the Four Seasons Hotel, 200 Boylston Street, and **Le Marquis de Lafayette (** (617) 451-2600, in the Lafayette Hotel, 1 Avenue de Lafayette, also serve French-style meals.

For a change of pace, **Café Budapest (** (617) 266-1979, in the Copley Square Hotel, 47 Huntington Avenue, serves, as its name

ABOVE: Downtown dining out of doors.

suggests, Hungarian dishes. **Jasper** ( (617) 523-1126, 240 Commercial Street, prepares superb Continental meals in an elegant ambiance. **Sonsie** ( (617) 351-2500, 327 Newbury Street, a stylish bistro, offers *al fresco* dining at their sidewalk tables or elegant dining inside with a creative, eclectic menu and lively atmosphere.

## Moderate

Along the waterfront are the best seafood restaurants. Recommended are **Anthony's Pier Four Restaurant** ( (617) 423-6363, 140 Northern Avenue and **Jimmy's Harborside Restaurant** ( (617) 423-1000, 242 Northern Avenue. Nearby is **Ye Olde Union House** ( (617) 227-2750, 41 Union Street.

Famous for its "fresh" lobster stew, **Durgin Park Market Dining Room** ( (617) 227-2038, 340 Faneuil Hall Marketplace, also claims to have been established "before you were born." As no reservations are accepted here, it is wise to arrive early on weekends.

In Boston, you can also find excellent Italian restaurants. **Cricket's** ( (617) 720-5570, Faneuil Hall Marketplace and **Davio's Ristorante and Café** ( (617) 262-4810, 269 Newbury Street, are highly recommended.

For good food served with elegance at a reasonable price, there is the **Café Plaza** ( (617) 267-5300, in the Plaza Hotel, 138 St. James Avenue.

**Samuel Adams Brewhouse** ( (617) 522-9080, in the Lenox Hotel, 716 Boylston Street, serves wholesome sandwiches and soups, in a convivial atmosphere.

The North End is packed with great places to eat. Try **The Daily Catch** ( (617) 523-8567, 323 Hanover Street, for wonderful seafood; or **Joe Tecce's** ( (617) 742-6210, 61 North Washington Street, for a memorable Italian meal.

## Inexpensive

Like its hotels, Boston's restaurants are pricey. However, many of the above establishments serve a lower price luncheon menu and the thrifty traveler, who wants to sample the "high life" of Boston, would do well to eat a late lunch and a light dinner.

For lighter meals, Boston abounds with establishments serving Italian sandwiches and pizzas. The Italian sandwich, originally a long hard roll filled with salami, tomato, lettuce, onions, black olives and topped with olive oil, now comes in a wide variety of fillings. Some have even become so "yuppie" as to include bean sprouts. An Italian sandwich is a meal in a bun. Along the same line are meatball and Italian sausage sandwiches, which are filling and tasty.

There are plenty of interesting, inexpensive eateries in the Leather District, but the **Blue Diner** (617) 695-0087, 150 Kneeland Street, got there first. It's one of only a handful of authentic railroad diner car restaurants in Boston proper. The Blue Diner, however, does not serve the traditional hash-house grub and it is decidedly more expensive than the average New England diner. Still, at $6 to $14 for an entrée, it's a good cheap meal. It is a wildly popular place, especially for Sunday brunch when you should try the challah French toast. The Blue Diner is open seven days a week, 24 hours a day and reservations are strongly suggested.

If you are in the Leather district for a gallery tour and the Blue Diner is crowded (see page 87), walk over to nearby Chinatown and into any **Vietnamese** restaurant for a cheap, filling and delicious bowl of *bun* or noodle soup ($3 to $5).

Oozing European atmosphere, with a touch of Boston rambunctiousness, **Jacob Wirth** ( (617) 338-8586 FAX (617) 338-0866, 33–37 Stuart Street, is a Boston landmark, convenient to the Theater District, and a must for the visitor. The food is German–American (moderate to inexpensive), there is frequent live music and a piano bar on Friday night. It's open Sunday to Monday noon to 8 PM, Tuesday to Thursday 11:30 AM to 11 PM, Friday and Saturday noon to 12 AM.

In the North End, **Pizzeria Regina** ( (617) 227-0765, 11 1/2 Thatcher Street, is the real thing; and **The European** ( (617) 523-5694, 218 Hanover Street, is cannoli and cappuccino heaven.

## GETTING AROUND

Motorists should be aware that much of Boston's street plan was laid out by wandering cows in the late 1600s. It can be confusing to find your way from point A to point B, and maddening to try to park your vehicle when you get there. The MBTA or "T" is Boston's subway system and is really the best way to get around downtown. It's not super efficient, (after all, parts of it are the oldest subway in the world) but it beats battling Boston traffic. After around midnight, when the "T" closes, taxis are readily available.

The system for getting around on the "T" is not difficult to grasp if you remember that all lines (with the exception of the Blue Line) run via Park Street Station on Tremont Street in downtown Boston. Train directions are based on the concept of "in bound" to Park

Street station or "out bound" — traveling away from Park Street Station. The Red Line runs from Quincy south of Boston, through Park Street Station downtown and on to Harvard Square in Cambridge, and Somerville. The Blue Line takes you to and from Logan Airport. The Green Line is more complicated with four branches, but essentially runs east to west from East Cambridge and the North End through Park Street station downtown and onward into the western suburbs of Brookline, Allston, and Brighton. Finally, the Orange Line runs from Charlestown to Roxbury also via Park Street Station.

A ride on the "T" costs $.85; and tokens can be purchased at the stations. If you plan to ride for several days, the **Boston Passport**

may be a good value for you. It also keeps you out of the queue for tokens. Prices are: $5 for a one-day, $9 for a three-day, and $18 for a seven-day Passport. Passports are sold at North Station, South Station, and Back Bay Station; at Airport, Government Center, Harvard Square, and Riverside MBTA stations; at visitor information centers on Boston Common, in Quincy Market, and at several hotels and newsstands.

For MBTA inquiries, dial ( (617) 222-3200.

## DRIVING AND PARKING

If you must drive in Boston, be warned that a massive 10-year construction program known as the "Big Dig" or, officially, the Central Artery/Third Harbor Tunnel Project is well under way. A third tunnel is being built under Boston Harbor and the rusting eyesore of Boston's Central Artery (the major north-south roadway through Boston) is being "depressed" — reconstructed underground. The upshot — until 2002 — is that Boston traffic, road conditions and parking are liable to all sorts of disruptions. However, the contractors are doing an admirable job of keeping construction areas livable and passable and the disruptions should not be an additional deterrent to driving in the Hub. (Boston drivers should perhaps, but that's another story.) For up-to-date information on general snarls or Big Dig restricted roads, detours and access, call SmarTravler ( (617) 374-1234 or dial up their web page: http://www.smartravler.com/bos/. You can also get daily traffic reports from TV and radio. An on-the-spot reporter in a hovering helicopter will tell you all about it. In any case, do not underestimate the importance of being *au courant* on Boston traffic conditions.

## CAMBRIDGE

If Boston were Paris — Cambridge, across the Charles River to the north, would be the Left Bank. A vibrant mix of students, artists, immigrants and factory workers — this small but densely populated industrial city

ABOVE: Street chess challenger in Cambridge.

is also home to two of the world's most prestigious universities: the Massachusetts Institute of Technology and Harvard University.

## THE LIVELY SQUARES

Cambridge is defined largely by the individual character of its city squares. There are five major squares, all served by the T (with the exception of Inman). They are, from east to west: Kendall, Central, Inman, Harvard (see below) and Porter. **Kendall Square** is where you'll find the Massachusetts Insti-

tute of Technology (see page 99). Formerly nothing more than MIT and it's attendant factories, the streets around Kendall Square are now quite gentrified — though not residential. There are many good and inexpensive restaurants in the area as well as live music venues and movie theaters. **Central Square** is a slice of the world — a gritty but lively street life characterizes this area — and it is not to be missed if you're interested in cutting-edge music, ethnic food and contemporary art. Naturally, international cooking is the order of the day with an especially good selection of Indian cuisine. You'll also find Eritrean, Portuguese, and Haitian Creole cooking — among many others. A quiet residential area, **Inman Square** is less accessible but interesting for it's Rosie's Bakery, at the crossroads of Inman, Hampshire and Cambridge Streets, where you can "have" a "chocolate orgasm" and sample many other famously delicious bakery

ABOVE: Phoning home from Harvard Square. OPPOSITE: The Colonial buildings of Harvard University dominate Cambridge.

treats. There are also several interesting shops in the area, including an award-winning toy store, **Sandy & Son** ( (617) 491-6290, 1360 Cambridge Street. **Porter Square** is both a high-priced residential area and a shopping district. Here you'll find dozens of good restaurants in all price-categories, many interesting clothing shops, and even a strip mall shopping plaza with a Dunkin' Donuts when you get tired of paying $2 for your morning coffee. Best of all in this area are the small boutiques that line Massachusetts Avenue as it runs south towards Harvard Square. Joie de Vivre ( (617) 864-8188, at $N^o$ 1792, is my favorite. It's always packed with unusual gift items and has a great selection of art postcards.

### Shopping in Harvard Square

The intellectual, if not geographical, heart of Cambridge and destination for thousands of travelers from throughout the world, Harvard Square is, well inevitable. Much gentrified over the years, the individually owned coffee shops, music clubs and burger joints that formerly had pride of place here, have been forced to make way for the Gap, Starbucks and a host of ATMs (automatic teller machines). Enjoy the world-class shopping, have a café latte, soak up the atmosphere, but remember — a few jewels of the old Harvard Square still exist.

"The square" — as it is known locally — is still a Mecca for book lovers: **Wordsworth Bookstore**, 30 Brattle Street, is a remarkable place for paperbacks (including foreign editions in English). They seem to have it all and every paperback is discounted 10 percent. Best of all, Wordsworth is open 363 days a year and late into the evening. (Monday to Saturday from 9 AM to 11:15 PM and Sunday 10 AM to 10:15 PM.) **Schoenhof's Foreign Books**, 76A Mt. Auburn Street is a comprehensive foreign language bookstore with everything from language learning tapes to reference to literature in 280 languages. **Grollier**, 6 Plympton Street, is the poetry place — a charming and well-stocked hole-in-the-wall that could very well inspire a line or two. The **Harvard Coop**, Harvard square, runs the official Harvard bookstore, and is also the place for all your Harvardiana needs from T-shirts to umbrellas, to baby clothes with the Harvard emblem. You may not have a diploma with "Harvard" emblazoned on it, but you *can* have a pair of boxer shorts.

## WHAT TO SEE

Don't leave Cambridge without a brief walk through its historic district. Your first stop should be the **Cambridge Discovery Booth**, Harvard Square, where you can pick-up information and maps of Cambridge, as well as public transportation schedules. The handsome **Common** was the encampment site

Tours of the campus are offered daily. Two of the most interesting buildings are the triangular-roofed **Kresge Auditorium** and the moated **MIT Chapel**, both designed by Eero Saarinen.

### Harvard University

Continue down Massachusetts Avenue and you will head directly into **Harvard Yard**. This is the heart of **Harvard University**, the oldest college in the United States, established in 1636 to train young men for the ministry. Six American presidents graduated from

for George Washington's colonial army for nearly a year. **Brattle Street** is notable for "Tory Row," named for homes built by wealthy British sympathizers during the Revolution. (Most of the houses date back to the 19th century.) Also on Brattle is the house of Maine poet Henry Wadsworth Longfellow, who lived here for nearly 50 years. The 1759 structure was also Washington's army headquarters during the British attack on Boston.

### Massachusetts Institute of Technology

MIT, situated along the Charles River just off the bridge, is world-famous for its research in science and engineering and for the Nobel laureates among its numbers.

Harvard and its alumni include countless statesmen and renowned thinkers in every field and from every corner of the world.

The **Harvard Information Center** ☎ (617) 495-1573, 1350 Massachusetts Avenue, provides maps and materials outlining the campus highlights; guided tours are offered from June through September.

Harvard itself, with more than 400 buildings, resembles a small village rather than a typical campus. **Massachusetts Hall** is the oldest building on the campus, dating to 1720; its handsome red brick walls adorned with ivy provided the architectural inspiration for other buildings on the grounds. During the Revolution, the Hall headquartered colonial troops.

Nearby are **Harvard Hall** (1776) and the very English Holden Chapel (1744), complete with its own coat of arms. But **University Hall**, a white granite building completed in 1815 from a Charles Bulfinch design, is one of the most striking structures on campus. In front of the building is Daniel Chester French's statue of university namesake John Harvard, a 17th-century minister who willed a large sum of money to the fledgling college. (The model for the work was not actually Harvard at all, but rather a 19th-century student whom Chester thought fit the ideal of what John Harvard should have looked like.)

The many-columned **Widener Memorial Library**, was built in memory of a victim of the sinking of the Titanic. It contains more than 10 million volumes in its collections.

Do not overlook Harvard's fine museums. The works of Van Gogh, Renoir and Picasso can be found at the **Fogg Art Museum**; in the **Sackler Museum**, just across the street, is one of the world's finest collections of Chinese jade; German Expressionists dominate at the **Busch-Reisinger Museum**.

Other interesting displays include the **Peabody Museum of Archaeology and Ethnology** (North American Indians, with relics from Lewis and Clark's 1803 explorations) and the **Botanical Garden's** German glass-blown flowers, depicting nearly 800 different species of flowering plants. However, the **Museum of Comparative Zoology** has the most fascinating collections, including a 225-million-year-old egg, a six-million-year-old turtle shell, the 25,000-year-old Harvard Mastodon (found in New Jersey), a 180-million-year-old dinosaur and a genuine giant sea monster.

## WHERE TO STAY

Cambridge hotel rates tend to be high and reservations will be essential during graduation season (mid-May to early June) and college registration (late August and early September).

### Luxury and Expensive
For ultra-modern, luxury lodging in either Boston or Cambridge, try the riverside **Hyatt Regency Cambridge** ( (617) 492-1234

TOLL-FREE (800) 233-1234 FAX (617) 491-6906, 575 Memorial Drive. Patterned after the Hyatt Regency in San Francisco, it has a glass elevator that carries you to the revolving Spinnaker Restaurant (see below), which serves Italian meals.

For night life without having to leave the hotel, you can stay at the **Charles Hotel in Harvard Square** ( (617) 864-1200 TOLL-FREE (800) 882-1818 FAX (617) 864-5715, One Bennett Street, whose **Regattabar** is one of the top jazz clubs in Boston.

Of equal quality and price are **Marriott Boston-Cambridge** ( (617) 494-6600 TOLL-FREE (800) 228-9290 FAX (617) 494-0036, Kendall Square and **Royal Sonesta Hotel** ( (617) 491-3600 TOLL-FREE (800) 343-7170 FAX (617) 661-5956, 5 Cambridge Parkway.

### Moderate
**Howard Johnson's Motel** ( (617) 492-7777 TOLL-FREE (800) 654-2000 FAX (617) 492-6038, 777 Memorial Driv and **Susse Chalet Inn Cambridge** ( (617) 661-7800 TOLL-FREE (800) 258-1980 FAX (617) 868-8153, at 211 Concord Turnpike, Cambridge 02148, are reliable.

## EATING OUT

Cambridge, like Boston, has fine dining establishments, but the Cambridge coffeehouses, which serve food along with coffee, tea and hot drinks, have a style of their own. They abound in the university area and rise and fall in popularity with the whims of the college crowd. Ice cream parlors are popular here. Hit Harvard Square on a hot summer's day for the best ice cream treats in Boston or Cambridge.

### Expensive to Moderate
**Rialto** ( (617) 661-5050, in the Charles Hotel, One Bennett Street, serves a fine selection of Mediterranean cuisines in a rich, welcoming dining room. **Henrietta's Table** ( (617) 661-5005), also in the Charles Hotel, specializes in Yankee specialty foods and is more modestly priced. **Panache** ( (617) 492-9500, 798 Main Street, serves excellent lobster as well as the best lamb in the area. At **Upstairs at the Hasty Pudding** ( (617) 864-1933, 10 Holyoke Street, you can get a fixed-price three-course English or French dinner. The

Spinnaker Restaurant ✆ (617) 492-1234, atop the Hyatt Regency, 575 Memorial Drive, serves Italian cuisine.

House of Blues ✆ (617) 491-2583, 96 Winthrop Street, is the place for ribs and casual dining. The "all blue" decor features lots of musical memorabilia, with live entertainment nightly and a Sunday Gospel Brunch.

**Inexpensive**

For a taste of the old Harvard Square, turn the corner down John F. Kennedy Street from the center of the square and find the **Tasty**. This may be the world's smallest café. Three stools snuggle up to a linoleum counter and a chef cooks up greasy burgers here in an atmosphere from a different era. **Mr. and Mrs. Bartley's** (from the square walk east on Massachusetts Avenue for three blocks) serves up the best burgers in town as well as unusual twists on New England favorites such as a turkey sandwich with stuffing, gravy and cranberry sauce (recommended). The atmosphere is friendly with diners sitting elbow to elbow. The lime rickies — sweet soda fountain drinks made with fresh limes — at Mr. and Mrs. Bartley's are without a doubt the best in New England. After a long ramble in the square, get a large rickie and walk down toward the Charles River away from the hubbub of Harvard Square.

| SOMERVILLE |
| --- |

With the gentrification of Cambridge, artists studios (if not galleries) these days tend to cluster around the less trendy Somerville. Two "T" stops north of Harvard Square is Somerville's **Davis Square** where a third University, Tufts, turns out more of the intellectual stock of New England. Davis Square may be one of the more interesting places on Boston's "Left Bank". It is in the thralls of transformation from a working class enclave to a popular artist and student hang out.

## WHAT TO SEE

Davis Square is where you'll find the lively **Someday Café** — one of the few coffee shops left in the area where you can bring a book and sit for hours. Right next door is the grand

old **Somerville Theatre**, now a cinema where you can see a second-run film any day of the week for $2. Children will love **Sprouts Theatre** ✆ (617) 628-9575, 255 Elm Street, at the Boston Baked Theatre, an intimate space in the basement of an unlikely office building. Sprouts has a regular and excellent line up of children's shows — inventive take-offs on fairy tales and fables — that can be counted on to entertain the grown ups as well. The actors are professionals. The children sit on the floor directly in line with the proscenium and participate in the action. There are one-hour shows every Saturday at 1 PM and Sunday at 1 and 3 PM.

## EATING OUT

When you say "Davis Square" to many Massachusetts residents, the first thing that comes to mind is **Red Bones**. (This place is so famous it doesn't even have an address. Just head for Davis Square and Elm Street and ask the first person you pass for directions.) Slow-cooked Memphis-style barbecue is the specialty. This inexpensive and very informal restaurant is not to be missed. The barbecue is out-of-this-world, and the beer is cold and plentiful. Or try the catfish and a mason jar full of homemade iced tea or lemonade. Celebrity-spotting need not be confined to Harvard Square either: Steve Tyler from the band Aerosmith is a Red Bones regular.

If Red Bones is crowded, wander down to the **Rosebud Diner** ✆ (617) 666-6015, 381 Summer Street, where you can eat very good, inexpensive food in a spot-and-polish restored railway car. Try the "Rosebud" sandwich — delicious chicken cutlet on a bun with "homefries".

| LEXINGTON AND CONCORD |
| --- |

## BACKGROUND

"Bloody Butchery by the British Troops" screamed the headlines of the *Salem Gazette*, describing the fight that took place between 77 colonial militiamen and 700 regular British troops on April 19, 1775. These were the "shots heard 'round the world."

Word of the battles at Lexington Green and at Concord bridge back along the 20-mile (32-km) road to Boston spread quickly through the American colonies, uniting the colonists in a resolve to fight for their independence. What had begun as a struggle between English authorities determined to enforce the will of Parliament and the people of Massachusetts, who were just as determined to retain their rights as English citizens, soon escalated into a war for independence which lasted more than eight years. By 1775, Britain's oppressive economic policies had transformed America into a powder keg of discontent.

The English government suggested that General Thomas Gage, governor of Massachusetts and commander of the British forces, jail revolutionary rabble-rousers like Sam Adams and John Hancock. But Gage knew where such actions would lead and decided on what he thought was a less inflammatory engagement: to seize the revolutionaries' arms supplies stored in Concord. His mission's success depended on secrecy to ensure little resistance by the townspeople. Despite his precautions, Boston's revolutionaries knew of Gage's plan before his troops left the city and sent Paul Revere and William Dawes to Lexington with news of the advancing soldiers.

In Lexington, revolutionaries gathered at Buckman's Tavern on the Common to await the arrival of the British troops. When the 77 minutemen saw the Redcoats, they formed two long lines. Militia Captain John Parker exhorted his men, "Stand your ground. Don't fire unless fired upon. But if they mean to have a war, let it begin here!"

Soon British officer Major John Pitcairn ordered the patriots to disband; in the face of more than 700 British regulars, there wasn't much else they could do. As the militiamen slowly obeyed, a shot rang out, no one knows from which side. Then British troops, many of them inexperienced in actual combat, began firing wildly at the revolutionaries, ignoring their commanders' orders to stop. When it was over, eight Americans lay dead and the first battle of the Revolution had taken place.

The British continued to Concord where they searched all buildings for arms; what they found they burned or tossed into ponds. When the revolutionaries saw smoke coming from Concord, they thought the British were burning the town and advanced to attack them at Concord's North Bridge. "Fire, fellow soldiers, for God's sake, fire!" yelled revolutionary Major Buttrick of Concord. Having been joined by minutemen from the surrounding countryside, the militia soon outnumbered the English by four to one.

The battle raged on. The British were driven into retreat along the road back to Boston, where they were attacked constantly. One British officer said it "seemed as if there was a musket behind every tree." Some of the heaviest fighting took place at Menotomy, with more than 5,000 troops on both sides. Eventually, the British reinforcements arrived to save Gage's troops from annihilation and they retreated to Bunker Hill in Boston.

The final toll: for the British, 73 dead, 173 wounded, 26 missing; for the revolutionaries, 49 dead, 40 wounded, five missing. Now England knew that the American rebellion ran deeper than dissatisfaction over taxes; the American people were prepared to fight for their freedom.

## WHAT TO SEE

**Lexington** — a short drive west of Boston — is a good place to begin your "Revolution" tour. Often called the "cradle of American liberty," nearly 100,000 visitors a year trek **Battle Green** where troops and patriots fought. The battle line is marked by a sculpture of the *Minuteman*.

On the Green is the **Buckman Tavern**, where revolutionary militia gathered before the battle. The tavern's old front door has a bullet hole made by a British musket ball during the fight. Inside, you will find the original seven-feet- (two-meter)-wide tap room, along with many other historic artifacts.

The 17th-century **Hancock-Clarke House** is where Paul Revere and William Dawes warned Sam Adams and John Hancock of the British advance. The nearby **Munro House** served as British headquarters and a field hospital for troops after the battle. Other historic sites are detailed in walking tour maps available at the **Lexington Historical Society** ( (617) 861-0928, on the Common.

From Lexington, you can follow the battle road down Massachusetts Avenue. At the **Fiske House** site, intense close-quarter fighting took place; it also marks the boundary of **Minuteman National Historic Park**, which encompasses the battlegrounds.

Your first stop in the park should be at the Battle Road Visitor Center (Route 2A), where a film and maps portray the skirmish. During summer months, reenactments of the battle are sponsored by the National Park Service. Up the road is the **Paul Revere Capture Site**, where Revere was taken by British troops when he, William Dawes and Dr. Samuel Prescott were surprised by an English patrol as they rode on from Lexington to Concord to warn of the British advance. The captured Revere later escaped, Dawes fled back to Lexington, but Prescott eluded the British to carry word of their march to Concord.

Continuing west is **Bloody Angles**, so-called for two sharp turns in the road which provided ambush points for the militia. Eight British soldiers were killed here during their retreat. Just before reaching Concord is **Meriam House**, which gave cover to minutemen as they fired on fleeing British troops crossing a narrow bridge.

Finally, Concord's **North Bridge** is where the American revolutionaries first fired a volley against British soldiers. It is difficult to believe that these beautiful surroundings could have been host to such bloody undertakings. You can walk the battle route and even cross over the North Bridge itself. Daniel Chester French's statue, the *Minuteman*, stands here, a memorial to the citizen-soldiers of 1775 who led the fight for freedom. You get a panoramic overview of the battleground from the **North Bridge Visitor Center** ( (617) 369-6993.

In the nearby town of Lincoln, you will find the highly-respected **DeCordova Museum and Sculpture Park** (617) 259-8355, 51 Sandy Pond Road. Hours are Tuesday to Sunday from 12 noon to 5 PM and on selected Monday holidays. Admission is $6 for adults, $4 for seniors, students and children under 12, and free for children under six. The Museum Sculpture Park is open year round during daylight hours and admission is free.

## WHERE TO STAY

In Concord it is possible to stay in Henry David Thoreau's former home, now the **Colonial Inn** ( (508) 369-9200 TOLL-FREE (800) 370-9200 FAX (508) 369-2170, 48 Monument Square (moderate to expensive). It has a good restaurant with seafood, continental specialties, home-baked breads and pastries.

Another alternative is the **Best Western at Historic Concord** ( 508-369-6100 TOLL-FREE (800) 528-1234 FAX (508) 371-1656, 740 Elm Street, Concord, MA 01742 (moderate).

## THE WORCESTER AREA

### WORCESTER

Industrial Worcester is the second largest city in Massachusetts. Situated 50 miles (80 km) west of Boston, it is not a major tourist destination, but the **Worcester Art Museum** ( (508) 799-4406, 55 Salisbury Street (admission $5 for adults $3 for seniors and children age 12 to 18, free for those under 12; open year-round except Monday), houses one of the finest collections of art and antiquities in New England.

One of the museum's displays is that of the priceless artifacts from Antioch, dating from the second to the 6th century AD. The collection resides in Worcester because the museum sponsored a series of Syrian excavations in the 1930s which unearthed these ancient treasures.

For serious history buffs, the **American Antiquarian Society** ( (508) 755-5221, Salisbury Street and Park Avenue, admission free, open Monday to Friday from 9 AM to 5 PM, closed holidays, has the largest collection of source materials covering the nation's first 250 years of history. This collection includes copies of the *Massachusetts Spy*, the inflammatory anti-British newspaper printed in Worcester between 1700 and 1776, which boldly supported the push for independence.

### General Information
For information, contact the **Worcester County Convention and Visitors Bureau** ( (508) 753-2920, 33 Waldo Street, Worcester, MA 01608.

## Where to Stay

There are many hotels in the Worcester area, particularly in the moderate to expensive range. Try the **Ramada Inn Worcester** ( (508) 832-3221 FAX (508) 832-8366, 625 Southbridge Street, 01501 (moderate).

## "FRUITLANDS"

The youth movement's "return to nature" in the 1960s could have been inspired by a curious 19th-century settlement in Harvard, Massachusetts, called **Fruitlands** ( (617) 456-3924, about 22 miles (35 km) north of Worcester on Route 110. Established in 1834 by transcendentalist Bronson Alcott (father of Louisa May Alcott, author of *Little Women*) and English activist Charles Lane, the little farm community attracted Utopians who gave up material goods, embraced vegetarianism and spent much time communing with their natural surroundings — the hilly beauty of the Nashua Valley. The community soon disbanded, but the old farmhouse at Fruitlands now houses a transcendentalist museum with displays of artifacts belonging to Alcott and other 19th-century transcendentalist writers and philosophers such as Thoreau and Emerson. Other museums on the grounds include a 1794 **Shaker House,** moved here after Harvard's Shakers (see also THE SHAKERS, page 147) left the village in the early 20th century. It is now filled with exhibits of handsome Shaker handiwork. Museum hours are Tuesday to Sunday as well as Monday holidays from 10 AM to 5 PM. Admission is $5 for adults, $4.50 for seniors and $1 for children aged seven to 16.

## THE NORTH SHORE

## SAUGUS

Many an 18th and 19th century New England sea captain harbored his merchant ship in ports along the North Shore. A trip north from Boston can be a journey through history. The **North of Boston Tourist Council** ( (508) 532-1449, P.O. Box 3031, Peabody, MA 01960, has prepared a wealth of literature on the area's museums and historic houses and public buildings.

Just north of Boston, off U.S. 1, is the **Saugus Iron Works**. A replica of an iron works built in 1650 by early Puritans, it demonstrates how settlers made and forged iron. Its workers toiled 12 hours a day, six days a week, in the white heat of the blast furnace, to the constant clanging of great hammers.

Today the iron works looks much as it did in the 17th century, complete with water wheel pits and slag piles. You can tour the furnace, forge, iron house and blacksmith shop; only the iron works house is original, dating to 1646.

## SALEM

### Background: The Witch Trials

"At first the girls would not answer, for fear of being discovered. They simply screamed and writhed or did blasphemous things, such as dashing a Bible against the wall. But gradually they began to give names."

Thus begins an inquisitor's account of Puritan Salem's 1692 Witch Trials, an American inquisition and reign of terror and hysteria. By the time it was over, 19 people had been hanged on Gallows Hill in one of the most notorious episodes in American history.

### What to See

This town, settled in 1626, leans heavily on its "bewitching" legacy. (Even its tourism slogan chips in with, "Stop by for a Spell.") If witches grab your fancy, head to the **Salem Witch Museum** ( (508) 744-1692, Washington Square (admission $4 with reductions for children and senior citizens, open daily 10 AM to 5 PM), where 13 life-sized stage settings present an historically accurate drama examining the hysteria.

The 1642 **Witch House**, Essex Street (admission $5; open daily 10 AM to 4:30 PM) is the restored home of Jonathan Corwin, one of the judges at the witch trials; preliminary examinations of more than 200 people accused of witchcraft were held here. The **Burying Point**, Charter Street, dating from 1637, is interesting for its 17th-century gravestones; the graves include those of judges of the witchcraft trials and a *Mayflower* passenger. The **Rebecca Nurse House** (in Danvers) belonged to a woman who was hanged as a witch; it overlooks a field where she is buried in an unmarked grave. And Gallow Hill is still here.

From the early 18th century, Salem was an important port and shipbuilding town, home of many wealthy merchants. Its seafaring legacy is apparent in the **Peabody/Essex Museum** ( (508) 745-9500, begun in 1799 by 22 sea captains who founded the East India Marine Society. By 1821 they had collected 2,000 items from all over the world for the museum; today, the collection numbers more than 300,000 artifacts and works of art exhibited in seven buildings and 30 galler-

ies. Included are ships' figureheads and models, paintings, gold, silver and textiles.

Of Salem's seafarers, Nathaniel Hawthorne wrote, "They sailed where no others dared to go, anchored where no one else dreamed of making a trade." Native son Hawthorne was a leading celebrity in the mid-1800s during the flowering of American literature. He was fascinated by both Salem's witch and sea legacies: he harbored a brooding sense of guilt about one of his ancestor's involvement in the witch trials and had turned to the sea for an occupation when he served as officer of the Custom House.

ABOVE: Witches were taken seriously by early New Englanders, but in Salem today their legacy is a tourist attraction. OPPOSITE: Salem Witch Museum.

At one time, 40 wharves stood on Salem's harborfront; the longest was **Derby Wharf**, which still stands today. Across the street, the 1819 **Custom House** ( (508) 744-4323 (open 8:30 AM to 5:30 PM every day except Thanksgiving, Christmas and New Year) contains restored offices, including Hawthorne's. Both above-mentioned are managed by the National Park Service, which offers daily guided tours in July and August. **The House of the Seven Gables** ( (508) 744-0991, Turner Street (admission $7 adults, reduced admission for children, open daily 10 AM to 4:30 PM) is the major Hawthorne relic. Featured in his novel of the same name, the 1668 house contains original Hawthorne furnishings and its share of secret stairways and passages. Other houses on the grounds include the 1750 Hawthorne birthplace and the 1655 Retire Becket house. The **Essex Institute** ( (508) 744-3390, Essex Street, preserves six houses spanning three centuries (the earliest dating from 1627) and its museum includes original witchcraft trial records.

Salem's **Heritage Walking Trail** maps supply an itinerary that includes most of the town's historical attractions; the path is marked by a red line drawn on the sidewalk.

### General Information

The **Salem Chamber of Commerce** ( (508) 744-0004 TOLL-FREE (800) 777-6848, Old Town Hall in Derby Square, can provide you with maps and other information.

### Where to Stay and Eating Out

In downtown is the **Hawthorne Hotel on the Common** ( (508) 744-4080 TOLL-FREE (800) 745-9842 FAX (508) 745-9842, 18 Washington Square and nearby is the **Lyceum** ( (508) 745-7665, 43 Church Street, which serves Continental menus. It was here that Alexander Graham Bell first demonstrated his telephone. Both are moderate to expensive.

## CAPE ANN

Cape Ann's rocky promontory and wild seas lure weekending Bostonians to its coastal villages, harbors and artists' colonies. Named for the Queen of England in 1614 by Captain John Smith, the Cape has always looked to the sea for its livelihood.

## GLOUCESTER

The first settlement on the Cape and the oldest seaport in the nation (1623), Gloucester continues to be one of the busiest fishing ports in the world, with a fleet of nearly 300 boats. Huge fish-processing plants line its shores, packaging the catch for shipment across the country.

The statue of the Gloucester fisherman (Man at the Wheel), which appropriately faces the sea, is a New England landmark, The statue's inscription simply reads, "They that go down to the sea in ships."

More than 10,000 Gloucester men have been lost in three centuries of fishing and almost every year another Gloucester boat and crew is claimed by the sea. Each June, the Blessing of the Fleet ceremony takes place during St. Peter's Fiesta.

**Whale-watching cruises** board at the docks in downtown Gloucester. For details contact **Cape Ann Chamber of Commerce** ( (617) 283-1601 TOLL-FREE (800) 321-0133, 33 Commercial Street, Gloucester, MA 01930-5034.

For a completely different perspective of this fishing village, head to the **Rocky Neck Art Colony,** East Main Street, East Gloucester, the nation's oldest working art colony, with galleries and shops.

### Where to Stay

The best hotels are along the beach on Atlantic Road. The **Best Western Bass Rocks Ocean Inn** ( (508) 283-7600 FAX (508) 283-7600, 109 Atlantic Road, is expensive, but the view is rewarding. Try **Gray Manor** ( (508) 283-5409, 14 Atlantic Road, East Gloucester, MA 01930, moderate to inexpensive.

### Where to Eat

For good New England seafood, stop at the **Easterly Restaurant** ( (508) 283-0140, 87 Atlantic Avenue (inexpensive to moderate).

## ROCKPORT

Rockport is a fishing village, artists' colony and tourist attraction rolled into one.

Picturesque Rockport Harbor.

Summer crowds throng Rockport's narrow streets; finding parking can be difficult. The village's quaint atmosphere attracts families, seniors and the usual seasonal tour buses.

Rockport is well known for its shops. Galleries, crafts and restaurants are crowded into both old and new fishing shanties along the narrow winding lanes of **Bearskin Neck**, a favorite gathering place for artists.

The quality of natural light on Cape Ann attracts artists and photographers to this picturesque village. Late afternoon is an especially popular time, as the setting sun focuses its fiery colors on the landscape and casts fleeting shadows over the craggy outcroppings along the shoreline.

A Rockport landmark is **Motif No. 1**, a weathered red lobster shack, a favorite subject for countless painters. It is actually a recent replica of the original, which was destroyed in a storm a few years ago.

Continuing around the head of the Cape, the shoreline scenery from Pigeon Cove to Annisquam is dotted with picturesque hidden bays and tiny coves.

**Where to Stay**

The best place to stay is **Peg Leg Inn ℂ** (508) 546-3038, 18 Beach Street. It is almost as old as the town itself and has moderate and expensive rooms depending on the view.

**Eating out**

Rockport is a "dry" town: no alcohol is served or sold. You can, however, bring your own wine into any of the restaurants that line Bearskin Neck. Seafood is the standard fare and prices are inexpensive to moderate.

## IPSWICH

A colonial town about 21 miles (34 km) north of Rockport on Route 1A, Ipswich still has nearly 50 homes built before 1725, with several from the 1600s. One of the finest is the **John Whipple House** (on Main Street), which dates back to 1640.

The **Richard T. Crane Beach Reservation**, at the end of Argilla Road on Ipswich Bay, is popular with the area's artists and the sandy beach which stretches for five miles (eight kilometers) is among the East Coast's finest. Here the **Pine Hollow Trail** leads hik-

ers on an hour-long trek along the shore and through a red maple swamp. Follow up a walk with a feast of a regional favorite, delectable Ipswich clams, available at any restaurant in the village.

## NEWBURYPORT

At the mouth of the Merrimack River, less than six miles (10 km) from the New Hampshire state line, is Newburyport. During the eighteenth and nineteenth centuries, the town's large merchant vessel fleet made local sea captains wealthy. Their Federal-style mansions lining High Street are a testament to their success. Tours around one of the finest, **Cushing House**, built in 1808 for Caleb Cushing, first United States envoy to China, show some of the artifacts he brought back from his tour of duty in the Orient.

Note the "widow's walks" atop many of the historic homes. Historians are divided as to their origin. Some say they were built for sea captains' anxious wives, who could gaze over the harbor and out to sea from their lofty perch, searching for their husbands' returning ships. Others contend that they were simply an affectation of style — an ornamental ironwork favored by one wealthy sea salt and then copied by his contemporaries.

The riverside **Market Square District** is also newly restored, its cobblestoned streets lined with handsome historic brick buildings which now house shops and restaurants.

Less than three miles (five kilometers) east of Newburyport is **Plum Island**, a national wildlife refuge where more than 250 species of migratory birds stop to rest along the Atlantic Flyway each spring and fall. Vistas of the island's dunes, marshes and its six-mile- (10km)-long beach can be enjoyed from an observation tower. In the fall, wild beach plums and cranberries can be found along the shore.

## THE SOUTH SHORE

While some visitors might make a quick stop at **Hingham's Old Ship Church** (1681), **Scituate's Lawson Tower and Light** and the

**Hull Lifesaving Museum**, most travel the South Shore along Interstate 93 and U.S. 6 only as a route from metropolitan Boston to Cape Cod. However, there are at least three sightseeing detours that should not be missed.

## QUINCY

Just south of Boston across the Neponset River, this former shipbuilding center was home to both John Adams and John Quincy Adams, the only father–son tandem to become presidents of the United States (they were the second and sixth presidents, respectively).

The **John Adams National Historic Site** ( (508) 773-1177, Adams Street, is the home bought in 1787 by the president and his wife Abigail. The varied styles of its original furnishings are the result of occupancy by four generations of Adamses. The **John Quincy Adams Stone Library** ( (508) 773-1177, on Franklin Street (open daily from mid-April to mid-November) has more than 14,000 books in nine languages. Guided tours lead you through the birthplaces of the Adamses, modest 17th-century colonial saltboxes containing family artifacts, including some of the famous letters Abigail wrote to John when he was a member of the Continental Congress in Philadelphia and, later, a negotiator at the Paris Peace Talks. Finally, the resting place of two presidents — John and son John Quincy — is the **United First Parish Church** ( (508) 773-1290, Hancock and Washington Streets.

## PLYMOUTH

Next stop is Plymouth, about 30 miles (50 km) south. Every American schoolchild knows about **Plymouth Rock**, the boulder where the Mayflower Pilgrims first stepped onto American soil on December 21, 1620. What is traditionally regarded as "The Rock" is covered by an elaborate Greek Classical pavilion on the Water Street Harbor shore and marked with a plaque.

Across the street, you can climb the 37 steps to the top of **Cole's Hill** to the burial place of the Pilgrims who died during that first bitter winter in the New World and to

a great view of Plymouth Harbor. Also on the harbor front, at State Pier, is the *Mayflower II* (admission $5.75 adults, open daily, April to November, weekends after Thanksgiving), a full-scale replica of the vessel which brought the 103 settlers from England. Guides, dressed in period costumes and playing the roles of the passengers and crew who made the treacherous crossing, demonstrate 17th-century skills and answer questions about the first colony of Pilgrims.

Tablets on **Leyden Street** mark the sites of the Pilgrims' first houses; however, the

1666 **John Howland House** (on Sandwich Street) is the only remaining Plymouth home where original Mayflower Pilgrims actually lived. The **Richard Sparrow House** (on Summer Street) is Plymouth's oldest, dating from 1640. In nearby Kingston is the 1674 **Major John Bradford House**. Possessions of the first Pilgrims are on display at the **Pilgrim Hall Museum** ( (508) 746-1620, Court Street (admission $5 with reductions for children and senior citizens, open daily 9:30 AM to 4:30 PM).

About three miles (five kilometers) south on Route 3A is **Plimouth Plantation** ( (508)

At Plymouth Plantation, seventeenth-century lifestyles are reenacted.

746-1622 (admission $15 adults, $8 children 5 to 12, open daily, April to November, 9 AM to 5 PM), a living-history museum that recreates the 1627 settlement of the Pilgrims. Men and women portray the dress, speech and manner of actual residents of the historic community, bringing to life the routines and activities of 17th-century Plymouth. You will get a good overview of the village, with its many thatch-roofed cottages, from the **Fort Meetinghouse.**

## Plymouth County

Southern Massachusetts produces more than 50 percent of the nation's cranberry crop. **Cranberry World** ( (508) 747-2350, off Route 44 (admission free; open daily, April to November 9:30 AM to 5 PM and July to August 9:30 AM to 9 PM), traces the history of this tangy red berry from colonial times to the present; features include tours of working cranberry bogs and cooking demonstrations.

Another way to enjoy the cranberry region is to board the **Edaville steam train** ( (508) 866-4526, Rochester Street, in nearby **Carver**, one of the state's cranberry capitals with more than 3,000 acres (1,200 hectares) under cultivation. The train takes you through six miles (10 km) of a 1,800-acre (730-hectare) cranberry plantation. Admission is $12.50 with reductions for children and senior citizens. Open April to December. The ideal time for a trip is during the fall harvest.

If your time is limited but you can't miss Cape Cod, then step aboard the **Cape Cod Clipper from Plymouth to Provincetown**, TOLL-FREE (800) 242-2469. The ferry cuts your traveling time in half and makes a great daytrip, beginning with a narrated tour of historic Plymouth. Once in Provincetown, you can easily explore the town and Race Point Beach on foot or hire a bicycle to go further afield. The ferry runs on weekends from late May to late September, daily from mid-June through Labor Day Weekend (first weekend in September) and on Tuesday, Wednesday, Saturday and Sunday in September. It departs from Plymouth Harbor at 10 AM arriving in P-Town at 11:35; at 4:30 it departs P-Town and arrives back in Plymouth at 6 PM. Fares are $23 for adults,

$14 for children aged 12 and under, $18 for seniors and $2 for bicycles.

### General Information

The **Plymouth County Development Council** ( (508) 826-3136, P.O. Box 1620, Pembroke, MA 02359, provides tourist information free of charge.

### Where to Stay

The **Sheraton Inn Plymouth** ( (508) 747-4900 TOLL-FREE (800) 325-3535 FAX (508) 746-2609, 180 Water Street, is in the moderate to expen-

sive catagory and offers high-quality service and rooms with an ocean view.

For a change of pace and an intimate look at New England living, **Be Our Guest** (P.O. Box 1333, Plymouth, MA 02360; ( (508) 837-9867) will book you a room in a moderately priced guest house or bed and breakfast.

### Eating Out

With a charm all its own, the **Lobster Hut** ( (508) 746-2270, Town Wharf, fixes simple seafood meals from $7 to $16. On hot summer days you can eat outside on the picnic tables.

OPPOSITE: Full-scale replica of the Mayflower mored at Plymouth. ABOVE: New England's seafaring legacy on display in New Bedford's Whaling Museum.

## NEW BEDFORD

In the second chapter of his classic novel, *Moby Dick*, Herman Melville says that Nantucket may have been the romantic home of whaling, but that it was New Bedford which made whaling an industry.

Indeed, New Bedford, a deepwater port on Buzzard's Bay, was once the greatest whaling center in the world, providing work for more than 10,000 men. By the 1850s, it harbored more than 300 whaling ships, some of whose voyages lasted up to five years. In New Bedford's heyday, whaling fleets generated more than $10 million in annual revenue.

Whaling built New Bedford. As Melville wrote, "all these brave houses and flowery gardens came from the Atlantic, Pacific and Indian Oceans. One and all, they were harpooned and dragged up hither from the bottom of the sea."

A good example of the prosperity derived from whaling is the many elaborate mansions of sea captains and maritime merchants along **County Street**, at the crest of a hill overlooking the harbor. The **Gilbert Russell House**, built in 1800 and remodeled in elaborate Italianate style in 1868, is one of the most spectacular.

The discovery of oil in Pennsylvania in the late 1850s marked the beginning of the end for New Bedford. With its whaling fleet badly depleted by the Civil War and losses in Arctic waters, New Bedford's whaling slowly gave way to textile manufacturing.

But much of the whalers' presence remains in New Bedford. The town's fishing fleet continues to rank among the top ten in value of catch landed in the nation. More than 200 vessels moor at the downtown waterfront.

From the **Waterfront Visitor's Center**, on Old Pier Three, it is a short trip up Johnny Cake Hill to the world's largest whaling museum, the **New Bedford Whaling Museum** ( (508) 997-0046 (admission $5 with reductions for children and senior citizens; open year round, except major holidays, Monday to Saturday 9 AM to 5 PM, Sunday 1 PM to 5 PM, summer hours vary). For 175 years, New Bedford's whalers were

known throughout the world and their legacy is preserved here. Perhaps the most interesting exhibit is the bark, *Lagoda*, the largest ship model in the world, built in 1915. This half-scale replica of a vessel that made 12 whaling voyages is outfitted with whaleboats, harpoons and other equipment. In the Panorama Room gallery, there are two 50-ft (15-m) sections from a quarter-mile- (400-m)-long painting depicting one year aboard an 1847 whaler. The museum library contains more than 1,100 logbooks from whaling journeys and the theater shows a film of an actual whaling expedition, complete with a "Nantucket sleigh ride," or whale chase.

Across the street from the Whaling Museum is the **Seamen's Bethel**, the

whaleman's chapel of Melville's *Moby Dick*. Built in 1832, it contains a pulpit resembling the hull of a ship and memorial tablets dedicated to sailors lost at sea.

**General Information**
**New Bedford Tourist Bureau** ( (508) 979-1745 TOLL-FREE (800) 508-5353 FAX (508) 979-1763, Waterfront Visitor Center, North Second Street, New Bedford, Masschusetts.

**Where to Stay**
On the outskirts of New Bedford are many moderately priced motels, including the **Comfort Inn** (/FAX (508) 996-0800, 171 Faunce Corner Road; the **Hampton Inn** (/FAX (508) 990-8500, One Hampton Way, Fairhaven, MA 02719; and **Day's Inn** ( (508)

997-1231 TOLL-FREE (800) 325-2525 FAX (508) 984-7977, 500 Hathaway Road, New Bedford, MA 02750.

## CAPE COD

A long spit of sand that curls out into the Atlantic Ocean for about 70 miles (113 km), Cape Cod is one of New England's premier resort areas, with 300 miles (480 km) of sandy beaches, coastal villages and isolated islands.

The Cape extends about 30 miles (50 km) into the warm Gulf Stream before it turns up

Tidy villages and natural harbors contribute to Cape Cod's summer popularity.

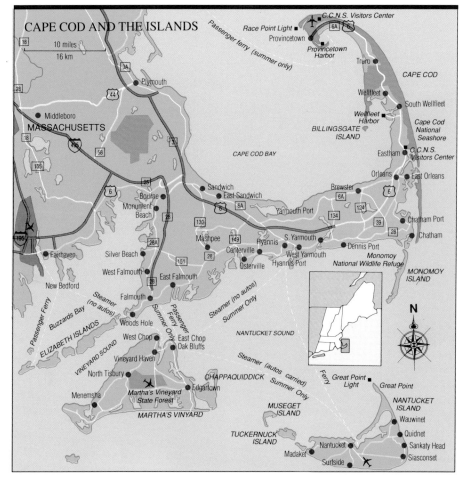

CAPE COD AND THE ISLANDS

at its "elbow." The weather is much milder here than on the mainland, with summers cooled by sea winds and winters warmed by Gulf Stream air.

The peninsula was a sleepy amalgam of small colonial fishing villages before the advent of the automobile. Then mobile visitors from nearby cities (Boston is only 70 miles or 113 km to the north and New York City is less than 250 miles or 400 km away) discovered its charm. Now swamped by visitors each summer, Cape Cod is a more intriguing destination in off-season months.

Cape Cod has preserved much of its beauty due largely to the **Cape Cod National Seashore**, 27,000 acres (10,930 hectares) of dunes and beaches, salt marshes, pine forests and cranberry bogs set aside to protect a remnant of the fragile ecosystems of the Lower Cape.

## GENERAL INFORMATION

In the summer, the **Cape Cod Chamber of Commerce** ( (508) 362-3225 TOLL-FREE (800) 739-7304, Routes 6 and 132, Hyannis, MA 02601, keeps its visitors center open daily from 9 AM to 7 PM. There you can pick up maps, guides and hotel information.

### Reservation Services

**Bed and Breakfast Cape Cod** ( (508) 775-2772 TOLL-FREE (800) 686-5252, P.O. Box 341, West Hyannisport, MA 02672, lists bed and breakfasts, inns and sea captains' houses throughout Cape Cod, Martha's Vineyard and Nantucket.

**Coastal Innkeepers Limited** ( (508) 430-3103 TOLL-FREE (800) 368-1180, 30 Earle Road, West Harwich, handles inns, bed and breakfasts, cottages, motels and condominiums in Yarmouth, Dennis, Harwich, Chatham and Orleans. The customers pays no fee. (Closed January and February.)

**Destinnations** ( (508) 420-3430, TOLL-FREE (800) 333-4667, P.O. Box 1173, Osterville, has properties on Cape Cod, the islands and offers a full-color catalogue listing historic village homes and inns.

**In Town Reservations** ( (508) 487-1883, TOLL-FREE (800) 67-PTOWN, 4 Standish Street, Provincetown, handles house rentals by the week, month or season, in Provincetown and North Truro. The firm also books reservations at inns, bed and breakfasts, guesthouses, motels and condominiums. There is no reservation fee.

**Orleans Bed & Breakfast Associates** ( (508) 255-3824, TOLL-FREE (800) 541-6226, P.O. Box 1312, Orleans, books traditional inns for a $10 reservation fee.

**Provincetown Reservations System** ( (508) 487-2400 TOLL-FREE (800) 648-0364, 293 Commercial Street, Provincetown, is a travel agency which handles rooms in more than 85 percent of the properties and more than 100 condominiums in Provincetown and the Beach Point section of North Truro. They lso make restaurant and show reservations. No reservation fee is charged.

---

## A DISAPPEARING LAND

A succession of glacial deposits and wind and wave erosion formed Cape Cod's present hook shape. This geologic history and ongoing ocean and climatic changes, spell a doubtful future for the Cape, one all too well known to its 175,000 residents. Studies seem to indicate that the roaring sea and northwest winds of the Atlantic are eroding the Cape a little more each year and that the land itself may be sinking into the sea.

Over the last century, the entire communities have been lost to the ocean. One report tells of Billingsgate Island, a fishing village off Jeremy's Point that once held a lighthouse, school and 35 family homes. By 1935, it had been completely washed into the sea. "Now all that is left of this island, which was first explored in 1620 by the Pilgrims, is a sand bar that surfaces at low tide — a grim

reminder of Cape Cod's tenuous future," the report read.

Scientists say that generations from now, the Cape will be only a memory, worn away to a few sandy shoals and that there is nothing modern-day technology can do to stop it. There are more alarming statistics: "Parts of the Cape are losing five acres (two hectares) a year to marine erosion," wrote Greg O'Brien, an expert on Cape Cod and the islands. "Chatham, on the Mid Cape's south coast, lost 10 ft (three meters) of shoreline a day to marine erosion during a recent winter."

A greater threat to the Cape is the rise in sea level brought about by the "greenhouse effect" — automobile, power plant and other human pollution melting polar ice caps. Scientists predict that within the next 40 years, shorelines from Provincetown to Bourne will retreat an average of 100 ft (30 m) and according to O'Brien, by the year 2100 more than 1,200 ft (366 m) of shoreline could be underwater. "Adding to this problem is the fact that while sea levels are rising, some coastal areas of the Cape, formed from silt sediments, are actually sinking — slowly compressing under their own weight."

---

Fences decrease the erosion of Cape Cod's dunes.

Provincetown, at the Cape's tip, finds itself in a most precarious position; the United States Geological Survey in Woods Hole predicts that the town "is headed for real trouble" which can be measured "in tens of years, not hundreds."

This is happening all over the Cape. The cliffs at Falmouth Heights are washing into Vineyard Sound; West Barnstable lost 15 ft (four and a half meters) of Sandy Neck beach in a severe winter storm; even the Wellfleet location where Marconi transmitted the first transatlantic cable 85 years ago, is now more

pact, the governing constitution of the Massachusetts Bay Colony.

By the 1630s, settlements had sprung up along the Cape, with fishing the mainstay industry. A whaling industry evolved and the Cape's fishermen commanded a fleet of vessels that sailed out of the ports of Truro, Wellfleet and Nantucket Island.

## OVER THE BRIDGE

On summer weekends, traffic to the Cape may be backed up more than an hour at the

than 200 ft (61 m) out at sea. Geologists give Nantucket Island only 700 years before it disappears under the ocean.

## PILGRIM BEGINNINGS

Cape Cod was inhabited by the Wampanoag Indians when explorer Bartholomew Gosnold landed in 1602. He named the peninsula for the great schools of cod found in the surrounding waters.

In 1620, the Mayflower Pilgrims landed at today's Provincetown before moving on to Plymouth, just across Cape Cod Bay. The Pilgrims stayed in plymouth for more than a month, exploring the area and working on what was to become the Mayflower Com-

bridges spanning the **Cape Cod Canal** and cars line up bumper-to-bumper along U.S. 6 and 6A, which together stretch the length of the Cape.

The Cape Cod Canal, which eliminates the need for ships to circumnavigate the peninsula, took 11 years to build and was finished in 1919 at a cost of $16 million. Because of it, there are only two road accesses to the Cape.

If you select the Bourne Bridge at the southern end of the canal, Route 28 will lead you first into the "Upper Cape," that part of the peninsula closest to the mainland, past West Falmouth and Falmouth and Marstons Mill before reaching Hyannis. If you cross at the Sagamore Bridge, at the canal's northern end, you can either continue on U.S. 6, a four-lane highway across the "Mid Cape" to Orleans, or Route 6A, a two-lane scenic road through several Mid-Cape towns. Highways 6 and 6A meet near Orleans and continue up the "Lower Cape" to Provincetown as rural Route 6.

## THE UPPER CAPE

The southwestern end of Cape Cod, on Buzzard's Bay, has spectacular coastline,

cy. Also on the village green is the birthplace of Katherine Lee Bates, who wrote the lyrics to *America the Beautiful*.

## Around Falmouth

From Falmouth you can bicycle along the old railbed from Falmouth to **Woods Hole**, a principal port on the Cape and a former whaling town from where ferries depart daily for the islands. It is also home to the **Woods Hole Oceanographic Institute** (WHOI), the **Marine Biological Laboratories** and the **National Marine**

historic houses and the Nobska Lighthouse overlooking Vineyard Sound. It was originally settled by Quakers in the 17th century; its first house was built in 1685.

## Falmouth

The main town on the southwestern elbow of the cape, Falmouth expanded around its village green, where many sea captains built fine houses at the height of the whaling industry's prosperity. The **Falmouth Historical Society Museum** ( (508) 548-4857, 55–65 Palmer Avenue (admission $2 adults, $0.5 children; open mid-June to mid-September, Monday through Friday 2 to 5 PM), which occupies two 18th-century houses on the Green records the town's whaling lega-

**Fisheries Service** — some of the world's most prestigious marine research institutions. The successful search for the *Titanic* was planned and launched by WHOI from Woods Hole in 1986. Only the Marine Fisheries Service is open to the public, allowing visitors to view its aquarium during the summer.

From the **bluff** where Nobska Lighthouse stands, you can see the boats traveling between Woods Hole and the islands, as well as those en route to New York and Boston.

North Falmouth's **Old Silver Beach** on Buzzard's Bay and Falmouth's **Surf Drive**

ABOVE: Beach huts stand like sentinels along the Cape Cod coast. OPPOSITE: Parking attendant looks out for business at a Barnstable beach.

**Beach** on Vineyard Sound, are two of the best beaches on the Upper Cape.

**General Information**

The **Falmouth Chamber of Commerce** ( TOLL FREE (800) 526-8532, P.O. Box 582, has a visitors center in downtown Falmouth in the Lawrence Academy building.

**Where to Stay**

EXPENSIVE

**New Seabury** ( (508) 477-9111 TOLL-FREE (800) 999-9033 FAX (508) 477-9790, Rock Landing

2000 TOLL FREE (800) 854-1507 FAX (508) 548-2712 at 291 Jones Road.

MODERATE

The **Capewind** ( (508) 548-3400 FAX (508) 495-0316, 34 Maravista Avenue Extension, offers quality rooms on a small scale. Also offering quality rooms and a pool, is the **Red Horse Inn** ( (508) 548-0053 TOLL-FREE (800) 628-3811, 28 Falmouth Heights Road.

INEXPENSIVE

Overlooking Vineyard Sound and within

Road, a resort complex with one- and two-bedroom luxury villas, private beaches, tennis courts and golf course. On the outskirts of town, overlooking a lake, is **Coonamessett Inn** ( (508) 548-2300 FAX (508) 540-9831, Jones Road, a former New England farm. More modern and less homey, are **Falmouth Inn** ( (508) 540-2500 TOLL-FREE (800) 225-4157 FAX (508) 548-9256, 824 Main Street; **Sea Crest Resort and Conference Center** ( (508) 548-3850 TOLL-FREE (800) 225-3110 FAX (508) 548-0556, Old Silver Beach, 350 Quaker Road; and **Quality Inn** ( (508) 540-

minutes of the beach the **Gas Light Inn** ( (508) 457-1647, 9 Fairmont Avenue, has one studio apartment and four guest rooms with private baths. Off-season rates are available making this an exceptionally good value.

**Eating Out**

Even if you are not staying at the **Coonamessett Inn** ( (508) 548-2300, consider having a traditional New England seafood meal there. Prices run from moderate to expensive. Another choice is the **Regatta** ( (508) 548-5400, 217 Clinton Avenue, overlooking the harbor. It specializes in seafood preparations. When you are looking for a hearty inexpensive stick-to-your-ribs meal,

ABOVE: Would-be dummies in Nantucket.
OPPOSITE: Memento artist in Cape Cod.

try **Cape Cod Chicken** ( (508) 457-1302, 235 Main Street, with delicious rotisserie chicken as well as roast pork, turkey or chicken pot pies and dozens of side dishes. Eat-in, carry out, or if you're staying within two miles of the restaurant, they'll deliver your order, free of charge. It's open for lunch and dinner and there is another location in Centerville.

## Sandwich

Sandwich, on the northwestern corner of the Cape just a few miles past the Sagamore Bridge, is the oldest town on the peninsula, dating from 1637. It is renowned for its Sandwich glass, produced between 1825 and 1888 in the workshops of the Boston and Sandwich Glass Company. The exquisite, lacy patterns are collectors items and quite valuable; see also the glass displays at the **Sandwich Glass Museum** ( (508) 888-0251, Town Hall Square, across from the village green (admission $3 with reductions for children and senior citizens; open April 1 to October 31, daily 9:30 AM to 4:30 PM ).

The **Hoxie House** and **Dexter Grist Mill** (on Water Street) are two of the village's restored 17th-century buildings; the mill still stone-grinds cornmeal. The **Heritage Plantation** ( (508) 888-3300, Grove and Pine Streets, offers more antiquities, including the 1931 Duesenberg used by actor Gary Cooper and a large selection of Currier and Ives paintings.

## Mashpee

At Mashpee, on the southern shore, live the few surviving descendants of the Massipee Indians, who lived on the Cape before the first European explorers arrived. The **Old Indian Meetinghouse and Burial Ground** dates back to 1684, making it the oldest in the state.

---

## MID CAPE

### Barnstable

Barnstable is just over 12 miles (20 km) along the Cape's north shore from Sandwich and faces Cape Cod Bay. It has a fine beach on **Sandy Neck**, a seven-mile (11-km) spit of sand that protects the harbor. Cabin cruisers, schooners and other boats are often docked here.

The old **Custom House** (now called the **Donald G. Trayser Memorial Museum**), located on Main Street at Cobb's Hill, has interesting displays of the town's maritime history.

As a county seat, Barnstable is the political hub of the Cape. The two cannons in front of its courthouse were brought by oxen from Boston during the war of 1812. The **Sturgis Library**, built in 1644, is the oldest library in the country; among its

collections are genealogical records of the Cape's families.

### Yarmouth Port and Dennis

**Yarmouth Port** has a row of sea captains' homes on Main Street; botanic trails past Miller's Pond can be found off Route 6A.

**Dennis** is less than five miles (eight kilometers) to the east. From its **Scargo Hill Tower**, in clear weather, one can have fine views of both the bay and ocean extending from Plymouth to Provincetown at the tip of Cape Cod. Dennis is also where Henry Hall developed commercial cranberry growing in the early 18th century; now cranberry bogs are common on the Cape landscape.

## Hyannis

Flights to Cape Cod arrive at Hyannis Airport. Hyannis is the Cape's main vacation and shopping center and a good base for visits up and down the strand. Ferry services leave from here (summer season) to Nantucket Island and to Martha's Vineyard. National attention focused on the Cape in the early 1960s when native son John F. Kennedy became President. "I always go to Hyannis Port to be revived, to know again the power of the sea and the Master who rules over it all and all of us," said the President, whose family still owns a large estate in this exclusive waterside village. The estate is protected by a tall fence and is not open to the public, but the **John F. Kennedy Memorial** is located on Ocean Street.

The **Cape Cod & Hyannis Railroad** ( (508) 771-1145, provides daily excursions of varying time lengths around the Upper and Mid Cape's spectacular coastline, salt marshes and cranberry bogs (Main Street, Hyannis).

## Centerville

Just west of Hyannis, Centerville is adjacent to **Craigville Beach**, one of the most popular swimming spot on Nantucket Sound.

### Where to Stay

The **Cape Codder Hotel** ( (508) 771-3000 TOLL-FREE (800) 843-8272, Route 132 and Bearse's Way (expensive), is a 260-room affair with all sorts of extras like a recreation program for the kids and "mixers" or outdoor barbecues for the grown-ups, free shuttle service around Hyannis, and a wide range of sports facilities. There's also a restaurant and tavern with live entertainment. The hotel has double and loft suites, some with two bathrooms.

The five-room (moderate) **Inn at Sea Street** ( (508) 775-8030, 358 Sea Street, was the first bed and breakfast in Hyannis. A full breakfast with homemade bread is served in the dining room where tables are set with silver, crystal and fresh flowers.

Its a short walk to the beach and downtown Hyannis. In the off-season you'll find the (moderate) **Ramada Inn Regency** ( (508) 775-1153 TOLL-FREE (800) 762-9563, in the inexpensive range. In any season, guests here

enjoy the glass-walled pool area, the green lawn with lounge chairs, and the dining room that hosts dinner theater and other live entertainment. Some rooms have kitchenettes. A health club with weight lifting equipment, sauna and steam room, and a game room for the children round out the amenities here.

The **Cascade Motor Lodge** ( (508) 775-9717, 201 Main Street, is conveniently located, just steps away from the island ferries, train and bus stations, restaurants and shops. Rent a bike at the motel and ferry over to the Vineyard or Nantucket for a two-wheel tour (inexpensive).

### Eating Out

On the **Cape Cod Dinner Train** ( (508) 771-3788, Main Street (expensive) diners are seated at four-person tables for a three-hour ride from appetizer to dessert, passing by Cape Cod cranberry bogs and salt marshes. This is a semi-formal affair with linen and silver; jacket or tie required for men, and only children over the age of 14 are invited. The menu features such items as broiled salmon, swordfish, and tenderloin of beef with port wine. The train operates on weekends in March through May; Wednesday through Sunday in June; Tuesday through Sunday in July and August; Wednesday through Sunday from September through October and weekends only in November and December. It is closed in January and February.

Another special eatery — though very much on the other end of the scale from the dinner train — is **The Egg and I** ( (508) 771-1596, 521 Main Street (inexpensive). This is where hungry partiers go in the wee hours of the morning for that all important breakfast. Huge portions and a mammoth menu, fresh ingredients and friendly staff make this unassuming restaurant memorable. It's open for breakfast daily all year round from 11 PM (that's right, PM!) until 1 PM.

---

## LOWER CAPE

### Chatham

Located on the southeastern tip of the Cape, Chatham is protected from fierce ocean storms by Morris Island, part of the nationally-protected seashore. **Fish Pier**, off Shore Road, is home to the large fishing fleets that unload their catches in the late afternoon.

The **Chatham Lighthouse** Beach offers panoramic views of the bay and **Nauset Beach**, the Cape's first true ocean beach and among the most popular. Just off the coast is **Monomoy Island**, a 10-mile- (16-km)-long sand spit protected as a wildlife refuge, with more than 250 species of birds.

### Cape Cod National Seashore

Established in 1961, this 27,000-acre (11-hectare) refuge of wind-sculpted dunes, deserted ocean beaches, spectacular cliffs and salt pond marshes dominates the seashore from Orleans to Provincetown.

The **Salt Pond Visitor Center** in Eastham and the **Province Lands Visitor Center** ( (508) 349-3785, provide literature on the Seashore, schedules for guided nature walks and pamphlets on biking and hiking trails; the Cape Cod National Seashore's headquarters is located in South Wellfleet.

Seashore highlights include nine scenic hiking trails, including **Nauset Marsh Trail**, a beautiful 30-minute walk among salt ponds and marshes; **Atlantic White Cedar Swamp Trail**, a 35-minute trek through a white cedar swamp, beginning near Marconi Station; **Beech Forest Trail** near Provincetown, a 40minute walk through sand dunes and beech forests; and **Cranberry Bog Trail**, east of Truro, which leads through natural wild cranberry habitat.

### Where to Stay

There are 17 major campgrounds on Cape Cod, but the oldest and largest is **Nickerson State Park** ( (508) 896-3491 or (reservations) (508) 896-4615, 3488 Main Street (Route 6), Brewster. Roland Nickerson was a multimillionaire who founded the First National Bank of Chicago. His estate once sat upon 1,900 hemlock, spruce, and pine forests. Nickerson's wife, Addie, donated the land to the state in 1934 in honor of their son, a victim of the 1918 flu epidemic. This park, one of Massachusetts largest, isn't typical of cape topography, though—no salt marshes, no dunes. Instead, you'll find eight *kettel ponds*, reminders of the Ice Age and formed by the glaciers that once dominated the landscape. You can spot many rare species of plants and wildflowers growing on the edges of the kettel ponds; it's against the law to trample or pick them. The choice of activities here are for practically endless: motorboating or swimming in the beach-edge Cliff Pond, birding, biking, and fishing. Nickerson is open year-round and winter visitors can ice skate, ice fish, or cross-country ski through the woods. There are 420 campsites at within the state park at $6 per night, but they do not offer recreational vehicle hookups. Early reservations are essential.

### Wellfleet

Historic towns also edge the seashore. One of the most picturesque is **Wellfleet**, once a great whaling port. It is still home port for a large fishing fleet. In true seafaring spirit, the downtown church tolls "ship's bells."

---

## PROVINCETOWN

At the tip of the peninsula, Provincetown is a lively amalgam of tacky tourist shops, chic boutiques, fishing fleets manned by burly Portuguese sailors, whale-watching cruises, wide beaches, wind-swept dunes, an artists colony and more recently, a meeting place for gays.

P-Town, as locals call it, looks out on some of the Cape's most spectacular scenery. The **Pilgrim Monument**, at Town Hill off Bradford Street, is a 252-ft- (77-m)-high Italianate bell tower commemorating the Pilgrims' "landing" at Provincetown in 1620 (they were blown off course); the view from the tower's observation deck takes in all of the Cape. Nearby hiking trails take visitors past marshes, ponds and pine forests. **Herring Cove** and **Race Point** beaches provide a spectacular setting for swimming and sun bathing.

A tour of Provincetown begins on **Commercial Street**, the main village thoroughfare, lined with galleries, shops, restaurants and bars. The population swells from less than 4,000 to nearly 80,000 at the height of the summer season and it seems that everyone is walking along this street at the same time; sometimes it is simply impassable — a tangle of people, cars and bicycles.

Once it was the third-largest whaling port in the world. Today, its fishing village legacy continues, with boats arriving during late afternoon at **MacMillan Wharf** to unload their catches.

Early this century, artists and writers were drawn to this isolated outpost on the Atlantic Ocean by Charles Hawthorne's Cape Cod School of Art. In 1916, the Provincetown Players launched the careers of playwrights Eugene O'Neill, Tennessee Williams and Sinclair Lewis.

## Where to Stay

The keyword at the **Ramada Western Tides Beachfront** ( (508) 487-1045 fax (508) 487-3557 toll-free (800) 528-1234 (expensive), is the eponymous "beachfront". With 64 rooms, all well above the standard motel stock and many of them smack on the water's edge, you can go to sleep with the sound of the surf and wake up for an early morning stroll on the sand. There's a pool, badminton courts, free parking and a restaurant that serves breakfast and lunch.

Here's something unique: park yourself on an old fishing wharf. **Captain Jack's Wharf** ( (508) 487-1450, 73A Commerical Street (moderate) has 13 rustic apartments each with individual character and quirks, but all comfortable and charming. During the high-season, apartments rent by the week; off-season by the week or day. Pets are welcome.

There's not an hotel or motel to be found in P-Town in the inexpensive range (unless you are visiting in the off-season), but the **Outermost Hostel** ( (508) 487-4378, 28 Winslow Street (*very* inexpensive), offers shoestring budget travelers the chance of a lifetime — to stay in P-Town at the unbeatable price of $14 per night, per person. This is a privately owned hostel with 30 beds in five white-washed cabins. There is a common living room and kitchen in one cabin and the big yard has barbecue grills and picnic tables. The Outermost has no curfew and is open mid-May to mid-October.

## Eating Out

The tiny **Café Heaven** ( (508) 487-3314, 338 Commercial Street (expensive; no credit cards), serves breakfast, including fresh-squeezed orange juice and delicious omelets; and is open daily until 3 PM. They also serve lunch and dinner when you can order brie cheese and garlic burgers. Heaven is open from mid-May to late October.

For take-out, **Clem and Joe's** ( (508) 487-8303 (inexpensive), 338 Commercial Street, offers good home cooking such as rotisserie chicken with corn bread, gravy and side dishes, meat loaf, glazed baked ham or chili. Specialty sandwiches, pies, cakes and cookies are also on offer. During the season, you may find a seat at the outdoor tables. Clem and Joe's will also deliver locally. They're open daily mid-April through October.

Informal and inexpensive, the **Governor Bradford** ( (508) 487-9618, 312 Commercial Street, is one of the hippest spots in town. You can eat indoors or on the patio and choose from a variety of burgers and seafood. There's also a children's menu. It's open for lunch and dinner daily all year.

**The Moors** ( (508) 487-0840, 5 Bradford Street Extension (moderate), serves the best Portuguese food in town. Try the *porco em pau* (marinated pork cubes). It's closed mid-October through mid-April. Lunch is served in July and August only.

**Napi's** ( (508) 487-1145, 7 Freeman Street (moderate) has the honor of being known as "Provincetown's most unusual restaurant" — lofty distinction in a town that often strives for the outlandish. The decor is industrial-antique; the menu reads like a novel. The fare travels the globe with entrées like Brazilian shrimp, Szechwan stir-fry, or Russian oysters. During the season, Napi's serves dinner nightly. In the off-season, Napi's serves lunch and dinner, and on off-season holidays and weekends, they serve brunch.

## Shopping

Provincetown streets are lined with shops selling everything from snow globe souvenirs, to top-of-the-line sporting equipment, to fine art. Browsing is the order of the day. But, be sure to take a peek in **Marine Specialties** ( (508) 487-1730, 235 Commercial Street. Housed in a former stable, this huge store is crammed floor to ceiling with interesting stuff. The front of the shop is where you'll find great inexpensive souvenirs — the usual geegaws packed in among some intriguing oddities. My favorite, the last time I was there, were the wooden hands once used in shop windows as glove mannequins. Delve deeper and you'll find a large stock of military surplus from around the world — including quite a lot of fascinating USSR military cast-offs. Finally, in the way-back, there's a well-organized camping and fishing supply area. The store is open daily in season and weekends only from Christmas through mid-March.

**Whale Watching**
Whether sailing off Cape Ann, north of Boston, or near Cape Cod to the south, **whale-watching cruises** have been cited as a great way to "witness the miraculous." One little girl on a cruise marveled that a whale once came so close "he sprayed us when he blew." A chance to see these marvelous mammals at close range is a thrilling adventure indeed.

You will also quite likely see schools of porpoises and dolphins, sea turtles, sharks, seals and sea birds playing very close to the ships.

However, all whale-watching operations are not alike. Some boats are no more than floating fast food and souvenir stands that happen to ply the waters the whales frequent. Others offer marine biologist-led narrated tours of prime whaling areas, video replays of the day's sightings and good food. A few more enterprising cruise operators "guarantee" whale sightings, claiming a 95 percent success rate; if you fail to spot any whales, you are offered a free trip to try again.

If time permits, choose a whale-watching cruise off Cape Cod. Daily morning and afternoon cruises, offered April to October, last anywhere from three to four hours. While many cruise operators vie for your dollar, the **Whale Watch Dolphin Fleet** ( (508) 255-3857, of Provincetown on the tip of the Cape, likes to claim that they are the cream of the crop.

The Dolphin Fleet originated whale-watching on the East Coast and it is also the largest and most successful of all the operations, having made more than 6,000 trips

since 1975. Their boats, built especially for whale-watching, are exceptionally stable. (The boats' seating capacity is 270 passengers, but only 145 people are permitted on each cruise to ensure a satisfying trip.) Cruises are led by scientists from the Center for Coastal Studies, one of the world's leading whale research and conservation organizations and acknowledged authorities on the humpback whales that live in local waters. A portion of each ticket sale is donated to help "save the whales."

Dolphin Fleet ships head offshore about six miles (10 km) to the Stellwagen Bank, the main whale feeding ground in Massachusetts Bay. Through years of research, Coastal Studies scientists have identified several hundred individual humpbacks and will offer you their individual histories, as well as stories of the finback and right whales found here. There are morning, afternoon and sunset cruises lasting four hours; reservations are recommended.

For additional information about Cape Cod whale-watching cruises, contact the **Massachusetts Department of Commerce and Development** ( (617) 727-3201, Division of Tourism, 100 Cambridge Street, Boston, MA 02202.

**GETTING THERE**

**Buses** ply the route to Cape Cod with service from Boston and New York through Greyhound TOLL-FREE (800) 231-2222, to Bourne with connecting service to Woods Hole (where you can hop the ferry to Nantucket or Martha's Vineyard) and Hyannis. Bonanza TOLL-FREE (800) 556-3815 runs six daily trips from Boston to Bourne, Falmouth and Woods Hole.

The only **rail service** is through Amtrak TOLL-FREE (800) 872-7245. The train runs every Friday, from mid-June through Labor Day weekend only. The Cape Codder runs to Hyannis from Washington, DC, Baltimore, Philadelphia, New York, Stamford and New Haven, Connecticut, and Providence, Rhode Island.

**By car** from Boston, take Interstate 93 south to Route 3; continue south to U.S. 6 to Provincetown at the Cape's tip. (See also, PLYMOUTH — CAPE COD CLIPPER, page113).

To reach the Whale Watch Dolphin Fleet office, turn left on Conwell Street, right on Bradford, then left on Standish.

It is only 114 miles (184 km) from Boston to Provincetown, but allow at least three hours to get through the sometimes maddening traffic on the Cape.

**Cape Air** ( (508) 771-6944 TOLL-FREE (800) 352-0714 connects Boston, Hyannis with New Bedford and Martha's Vineyard year round.

## THE ISLANDS

### MARTHA'S VINEYARD

"Island in Troubled Water" screamed the headline in the *Vinyard Gazette*, the 151-year-old newspaper that serves Martha's Vineyard, the bucolic island seven miles (11 km) off the Cape Cod coast. The piece was in response to a decision of the state legislature that would allow private developers to run wild over the island's South Beach.

Developers as bogeymen have always been a rallying point for the island's 12,000 full-time residents, who include celebrities such as newsmen Walter Cronkite and Mike Wallace, singers James Taylor and Carly Simon and cartoonist Jules Feiffer. The family of former first lady Jacqueline Kennedy Onassis still maintains her estate on the island, as well. As a result of the concern expressed by such influential residents, the decision was reversed and the island's spectacular beauty and miles of beaches and woodlands remain comparatively unspoiled.

The triangular-shaped island was named by the explorer Gosnold in 1602, when he found wild grapes growing everywhere. The grapes are gone, but what remains is a fascinating landscape dotted with little fishing villages and summer resorts.

**Vineyard Haven**, the main port of entry for visitors, is an old whaling town, much of which was destroyed in the Great Fire of 1883. Some pre-1883 houses can still be

found on Williams Avenue and the **Seamen's Bethel** is another original harborfront building. Along **Main Street**, you'll find shops and cafés, along with a Daughters of the American Revolution museum.

Two of the Haven's most familiar landmarks are the **West and East Chop Lighthouses** on the cliffs at the entrance to the harbor.

However, many visitors head straight for **Edgartown**, the oldest town (1642) on Martha's Vineyard. This whaling port of the early 19th century is charming, with elegant sea captains' houses (complete with widows' walks) and weathered saltboxes houses lining North and South Water Streets, overlooking the harbor.

Other architectural delights include the 1840 **Fisher House** on Main Street, called by many the most elegant residence in town; the 1843 **Methodist Church**, with its massive pillars and tower; and the **Cooke House**, a 1765 shipbuilder's house that is now home to the Dukes County Historical Society.

Board the *On Time* ferry (an island joke — it has no regular schedule and can transport only three cars at a time) at Edgartown to reach **Chappaquiddick Island**, 200 yds (180 m) across the harbor. The island is a paradise of thick woodlands, wildlife refuges and unspoiled beaches.

**Oak Bluffs**, located between Vineyard Haven and Edgartown, has a unique history. In the 1830s, Edgartown Methodists came to Trinity Park each summer to meet and pray at extended revival meetings. By 1850, the revival, held in an oak grove at the town's north end, was drawing 12,000 people. Soon tents were replaced with small cottages — the so-called **Cottage City**. Today, these colorful cottages with their gingerbread turnings, fish scales and lacy fretwork remain one of the most charming symbols of Vineyard living.

Up-island towns are few and far between. **Chilmark** offers excellent views of Vineyard Sound; and **Menemsha** is largely a working fishing village renowned for its picturesque moors.

**Martha's Vineyard State Forest**, in the center of the island, has hiking paths through dense stands of pines.

---

OPPOSITE TOP: Many of the Cape's vacationing visitors take advantage of its relatively undeveloped shorelines and relaxed atmosphere. BOTTOM: A short distance off the coast of Cape Cod, the island of Martha's Vineyard is a world unto itself.

However, the westernmost tip of the island is the most spectacular. The brilliantly colored **Gay Head cliffs** rise 150 ft (45 m) above the stormy Atlantic. Ripples of blue, red, white and orange run through the clay, whose strata contain fossils of camels, whales and other animals millions of years old. Because of erosion problems, you can no longer walk down the face of the cliffs to the beach below, but a winding path eventually gets you there.

The small towns around Gay Head are peopled by Wampanoag Indians, descendants of the island's original inhabitants.

## WHERE TO STAY

### Expensive

**Thorncroft Inn** ( (508) 693-3333, 460 Main Street, Vineyard Haven, is one of the island's premier inns offering 14 guest rooms in two antique-filled houses on several acres. Rooms have private baths and central air conditioning. Several of the rooms have wood-burning fireplaces, three have two-person Jacuzzis, and two have 300-gallon (1,350-liter) hot tubs. In a word: nice. A full breakfast and afternoon tea are served; and the inn is open year round.

Like many of Edgartown's inns, the **Charlotte Inn** ( (508) 627-4751, 27 South Summer Street, Edgartown, began life as a sea captain's house. Built in 1860, it is today one of the best inns in Edgartown and on the island. Each of the inn's 25 rooms was individually decorated by the innkeepers. L'Etoile Restaurant, inside the inn, features excellent French cuisine. The inn welcomes children older than the age of 14 and is open throughout the year.

**Duck Inn** ( (508) 645-9018, State Road, Gay Head, lies at lands end with incredible views of the Gay Head Cliffs and Lighthouse. To get to this cozy five-room, 200-year-old farmhouse you must take a dirt road. One room has a private bath, as well as a fireplace, all others share bathrooms. Miles and miles of the island's most secluded beaches lie just outside the door. Duck Inn is open all year long and children are welcome. Pets are welcome during the summer.

### Moderate

**The Hanover House** ( (508) 693-1066 TOLL-FREE (800) 339-1066, 28 Edgartown Road, Vineyard Haven, is a cozy, quiet bed and breakfast inn located near the harbor. Each of the inns' 12 rooms has private bath, two double or one queen-sized bed, air conditioning and cable TV. Complimentary breakfast includes homemade breads and muffins and fresh-ground coffee. The innkeepers ask that you inquire before bring along infants or children. The inn is open year round.

**Dockside Inn** ( (508) 693-2966, (800) 245-5979, Circuit Avenue Extension, Oak Bluffs, is — for starters — a lovely building, painted a combination of ivory, pink and pastel blue, with matching chairs lining its generous front porch. The Dockside has 20 rooms with air conditioning, private baths and cable TV; most rooms have queen-sized beds. Three kitchen suites are also available. The Dockside, convenient to all the Oak Bluffs attractions, is open from April to November.

At the **Governor Bradford Inn** ( (508) 627-9510 TOLL-FREE (800) 696-2723, 128 Main Street, Edgartown, start the day with a breakfast of freshly baked muffins and scones in the sunny tea room. In the afternoon, enjoy a cup of tea and sample some pastries or relax in the parlor or on the porch sipping complimentary sherry. The inn's 16 rooms have private baths, ceiling fans and king-sized four-poster beds. This is a delightful and elegant Victorian inn with a convenient location along historic Main Street — just a short walk to the shops along Edgartown's waterfront. The inn is open year round.

**Up Island Lambert's Cove Country Inn** ( (508) 693-2298, Lambert's Cove Road, West Tisbury, is where you get away from it all. Off Lambert's Cove Road you take an unpaved path through wooded wilderness to this place hidden amid tall pines, 150-year-old vine-covered stone walls, rambling gardens and and an apple orchard. The inn has 16 rooms, eight in the original 1790 main building and the remainder in the restored carriage house and converted barn. All rooms have private baths, air conditioning and some have private sun decks. A full breakfast is provided and the inn is also home to one of the island's finest dining rooms. Though Lambert's Cove is in a country setting away from the shoreline, guests are entitled to passes to the two private West Tisbury beaches.

### Inexpensive

For $12 (AYH members) to $15 (non-AYH members) a night you can stay at **Manter Memorial AYH Hostel** ( (508) 693-2665, Edgartown-West Tisbury Road, West Tisbury, a quaint country inn on the edge of Manuel E. Correllus Forest. The hostel has a fireplace in the common room, a volleyball court, a sheltered bike rack and a kitchen. Five dormitory rooms contain 80 bunkbeds; lockout is from 9:30 AM to 5:30 PM. The hostel fills up quickly; make reservations (especially during the high-season) at least two weeks in advance. It's open from mid-March to mid-November.

The **Martha's Vineyard Family Campground** ( (508) 693-3772, Edgartown-Vineyard Haven Road, Vineyard Haven, is located about a mile from Vineyard Haven center. Each campsite is allowed one motor vehicle and either one large tent or two small tents. Trailer sites are also available. Both types of sites include electric and water hookups; the trailer sites also include sewer. Rates at the time of writing were $26 per night for a campsite and $29 for a trailer site. These rates are for two adults and any children younger than 18. Additional adults are charged $9 per night. Also, there are one- and two-room cabins and tent trailers available for hire. Facilities include: table tennis, billiards, biking, baseball, a store and a playground. Cable television is also available. There are 180 sites; and the grounds are open mid-May through mid-October.

---

### EATING OUT

Note: Only restaurants in Edgartown and Oak Bluffs are allowed to serve alcoholic beverages. The other island towns are "dry," but most allow you to bring your own bottle.

### Expensive

The **Black Dog Tavern** ( (508) 693-9223, Beach Street Extension, Vineyard Haven, resting just steps away from the waters of Vineyard Haven Harbor, is a rustic wooden building decorated with nautical items. The windows provide spectacular views of the harbor; but you'll have to arrive early to get window table (no reservations are accepted). This landmark restaurant serves good seafood and pasta. Also on the grounds are The Black Dog General Store and the Black Dog Bakery.

At **David Ryan's Restaurant Café** ( (508) 627-4100, 11 North Water Street, Edgartown, dine on Menemsha swordfish, blackened or grilled with citrus herb butter or Vineyard crab cakes with Jonah crab served with remoulade. The café is closed during January.

**L'Etoile** ( (508) 627-5187, 27 South Summer Street, Edgartown, located at the Charlotte Inn (see WHERE TO STAY page 128), is an exquisite French restaurant featuring the artistry of chef/owner Michael Brisson. Entrées includes sautéed fresh Dover sole fillets with fried green tomatoes and saffron-poached potato batons, roasted spice-rubbed Australian lamb with artichoke, goat cheese, sunflower seed, couscous mélange. Dinner is served nightly from June through September; Wednesday through Sunday for the remainder of the year. L'Etoile is closed in January. Reservations are required.

The restaurant at **Up Island Lambert's Cove Country Inn** ( (508) 693-2298, Lambert's Cove Road, West Tisbury (see WHERE TO STAY page 128), is housed in a 1790 building in a romantic country setting at the end of an unpaved woodland path. The restaurant has an elegant dining room, and an outside deck where diners can look out over the apple orchard. It's open year round; seven days a week during the summer months. During off-season you should call ahead for days and hours of operation. Reservations are suggested but not required.

The **Feast of Chilmark** ( (508) 645-3553, State Road, Chilmark is aptly named — serving up plenty of seafood, and other specialties such as roast rack of lamb with spinach and cognac glaze. The Feast is open from mid-May until the end of October; during the months of May, June, September and October, the restaurant is closed on Monday. Reservations are suggested.

Since 1931, the **Homeport Restaurant** ( (508) 645-2679, 512 North Road, Menemsha, has been offering spectacular views along with great seafood. It's located on the Menemsha fishing port with its weathered shanties lining the harbor (Quint's home port for you *Jaws* fans). The Homeport is open from mid-April to mid-October.

## Moderate

On summer weekend evenings patrons line up to get into **Giordano's** ( (508) 693-0184, 107 Circuit Avenue, Oak Bluffs (no credit cards). It is worth the wait — the food here is hearty and wholesome; with heaping plates of cutlets and *cacciatore*, pizza, pasta, fried clams and seafood. There is a noisy ambiance about the place, but it's all part of the charm of this family dining experience. Children's meals are offered at substantially lower prices. Lunch and dinner are served daily from mid-May through mid-September. Reservations are not accepted.

Views from **The Aquinnah's** ( (508) 645-9654, Gay Head Cliffs, Gay Head, open porch are breathtaking. A Gay Head landmark since 1949, the Aquinnah features plenty of great seafood and plenty of crowds. Patrons are offered both indoor and alfresco dining, with take-out windows catering to those sitting out of doors to enjoy the awesome views. You can also buy clams and scallops by the pint and quart. Breakfast and lunch are served spring, summer and fall; dinner during the summer months only.

## Inexpensive

If you love a good breakfast then tuck in at **Linda Jean's** ( (508) 693-4093, 124 Circuit Avenue, Oak Bluffs (no credit cards). This is a year-round family-owned restaurant, and a favorite spot for locals and visitors alike. Linda Jean's also serves lunch and dinner; try the seafood platter with a full plate of clams, scallops, shrimp, haddock, fries and cole slaw.

**Mad Martha's** ( (508) 693-9151, 117 Circuit Avenue, Oak Bluffs, dishes up more than two dozen flavors of delicious ice cream. Established in 1971, Mad Martha can be found at several other locations throughout the island: Dockside Market Place in Oak Bluffs, Lake Avenue in Oak Bluffs,

Union Street in Tisbury and North Water Street in Edgartown. Besides serving ice cream, Mad Martha's also offers burgers and "grinders" (submarine sandwiches) from early June to Columbus Day.

After an evening out on the town, stop into Edgartown's **Espresso Love** ( (508) 627-9211, Two South Water Street, Edgartown, for a cup of coffee or a late-night sweet. Breakfast and lunch are also served at Espresso Love which is open 10 months of the year; closed January and February.

The **Main Street Diner** ( (508) 627-9337, 65 Main Street, Edgartown, is bit hard to find, but the journey is worth it. You approach it from Main Street by following a long, well-lit, flower wallpapered hallway. Along the way you'll pass all sorts of American memorabilia — on the wall at the end is an American flag with 36 states. Take a left and then a quick right, open the door and you're there. The food is good old-fashioned American "eats" and entrees are about $5. Main Street Diner serves breakfast, lunch and dinner year round.

**Shindigs** ( (508) 645-3443, Gay Head Cliffs, Gay Head, open from May to the end of October, offers fried seafood for hungry tourists who have come to see the cliffs. Though small and unassuming, the view from the restaurant's window seats is terrific.

## GETTING THERE

Access to Martha's Vineyard is provided by the **Steamship Authority Ferry** ( (508) 540-2022, which has daily services between Woods Hole and the harbor at Vineyard Haven; the trip takes about 45 minutes. (Car ferries fill up quickly, so you should call well in advance to reserve space on the boat.) Or you can fly with **Cape Air** ( (508) 771-6944 TOLL-FREE (800) 352-0714, which connects the Vineyard with Boston, Hyannis, New Bedford and Nantucket year round.

## NANTUCKET ISLAND

Some 30 miles (50 km) south of Cape Cod is Nantucket Island, for almost 100 years — until the 1830s — the world's greatest whaling port. Today it is one of the most charming and picturesque destinations on the East Coast, its streets lined with well-preserved houses and its landscape graced with long stretches of lovely beaches and open green moors.

Visitors arriving by ferry from Woods Hole (a three-hour ride) are often confronted with a mysterious, fog-shrouded island seascape that obscures the main port, **Nantucket Town**. But once ashore the beauty is astounding. As one writer put it, "This is not just an island; it is an experience."

Early Nantucket settlers were taught by the Indians how to harpoon whales from the shore and soon the settlers were setting out to sea to do their whaling.

By the early 1800s, Nantucket Town had more than 10,000 residents. Its cobblestone streets, elegant houses and tall elm trees were testament to the successes of its sea captains, ship owners and merchants.

When the new, larger ships could no longer dock in shallow Nantucket Harbor, the island lost many of its whalers to the deep port in New Bedford. After the Pennsylvania oil boom hit in the 1840s, Nantucket's fortunes declined even further, along with the whaling industry's. Today, its year-round population numbers around 3,500.

Fine 17th- and 18th-century houses can be seen on Main Street. The local **Historical Association** ( (508) 228-1894, provides pamphlets outlining a self-guided walking tour of the town.

One of the best preserved is the **Hadwen House** (Main and Pleasant Streets), a Greek Revival mansion built in 1845 for a whale oil merchant; it contains original furnishings of the whaling era.

The oldest existing house in the village was built in 1686 by **Jethro Coffin** on Sunset Hill. This **saltbox** is a fine example of 17th-century colonial architecture. The horseshoe-design in the chimney brick was meant to ward off witches and other evil spirits. The **Old Mill**, on Mill Hill, built in 1746 by wood salvaged from wrecked ships, is still used to grind corn.

Nantucket's **Whaling Museum** ( (508) 228-1736, on Broad Street, was closed at the time of publication; call for an update.

At **Straight Wharf**, at the beginning of Main Street, is the *Lighthouse Nantucket*, a double-masted lightship formerly moored offshore to guide ocean vessels around the island's dangerous shoals. The wharf's fishing sheds have now been transformed into shops and restaurants.

**Around the Island**

Just outside the town, the **Nantucket Moors** are windswept hills of bayberry, wild rose, heather and brambles that burst into vibrant color in summer and fall. Nestled among these hills are the villages of Wauwinet, Quidnet and Siasconset.

**Wauwinet** is the gateway to the **Coatue**, a 10mile (16km) sand spit that protects Nantucket Harbor from the more turbulent Nantucket Sound. You can walk along the spit to its northern tip, where the 1818 **Great Point Lighthouse** marks the site of treacherous sandbars in the Sound.

**Siasconset** sits on the easternmost edge of the island. By the end of the 19th century, this village, which became a popular destination for both artists and tourists, was linked to Nantucket Town by a railroad.

Nantucket beaches offer something for everyone — **Jetties Beach**, located near the channel leading into Nantucket Harbor, has warm Sound swimming and gentle surf; **Children's Beach**, with broad shallow flats, is a protected swimming area for bathers.

The beaches of the island's south shore are often washed by powerful breakers. **Surfside** and **Cisco Beaches** are popular with surfers; **Madaket Beach**, at the island's western end, is good for surf casting.

WHERE TO STAY

The Victorian-style **Centerboard Guest House** ( (508) 228-9696, 8 Chester Street (expensive), has six rooms with private bath, phone, refrigerator and TV and a continental breakfast is served. If a large resort appeals, **Harbor House** ( (508) 228-1500 TOLL-FREE (800) ISLANDS (expensive) has more than 100 rooms and cottages, a dining room, tennis courts (with resident pro), nightly entertainment, and a pool. It's open April through December. Cottages are another option on the island; **Wade Cottages** ( (508) 257-6308, Siasconset (expensive) are

on the grounds of a former estate and offer the solitude of a private beach. The rooms have private or shared baths and the apartments have one to four bedrooms. The facility is open May to October. During the season, you are not likely to find accommodation in the moderate price range. However, for cyclers and backpackers, the **Star of the Sea Youth Hostel** ( (508) 228-0433, Surfside (inexpensive), with 72 beds and cooking facilities is a lifesaver — having been, literally, at one time a lifesaving station; the front door still indicates where the lifeboats are located. The cost is $10 a night for members and $15 for non-members; and it's open April through October. (See also, CAPE COD, RESERVATION SERVICES, page 116).

EATING OUT

**Arno's Restaurant** ( (508) 228-7001, 41 Main Street, Nantucket Town (moderate), serves a big breakfast (until 2 PM), lunch and dinner. This is a good place to people-watch while you enjoy your meal. There's a children's menu available and Arno's is open all year round.

At **The Boarding House** ( (508) 228-9622, 12 Federal Street, Nantucket Town (expensive), the cuisine has Mediterranean and Asian influences. You can choose from a bistro menu or more formal fare. Seating is in a romantic dining room with low-beamed ceilings, or in the comfortable bar area or, in summer, outside on the patio. Lunch and dinner are served year round.

A cozy atmosphere is one of the recommendations of **The Brotherhood of Thieves** (no phone; no credit cards), 23 Broad Street, Nantucket Town, where low, oak-beamed ceilings, wood paneling and lots of candlelight create warmth. The corkscrew fries are recommended. This is a casual pub and is open daily year round for lunch and dinner, with evening entertainment. No reservations, so you may have to wait for a table outside.

According to the *Wine Spectator,* **The Chanticleer** ( (508) 257-6231, 9 New Street, Siasconset (expensive), has the best wine list on Nantucket, and the French cuisine is an island classic. It opens for the season on Mother's Day and closes in October.

On a beach vacation, you can't miss with an eatery called **Provisions** ( (508) 228-3258, Straight Wharf, Nantucket Town. This year-round gourmet deli is has soups, salads and very good sandwiches, as well as pâtés, cheeses and French bread. In good weather you can enjoy your lunch on the benches outside. Provisions is open for breakfast, too, and they will pack picnic lunches for you to take away.

## GETTING THERE

Regular ferry service throughout the year leaves Cape Cod from Woods Hole and Hyannis. **Hy-line Cruises** ( (508) 778-2600, Ocean Street Dock, Hyannis, and ( (508) 228-3949, Straight Wharf, Nantucket, offers seasonal passenger-only ferry service from May to October. The trip takes two hours and reservations are not required. The one-way fare is $11 for adults and $5.50 for children ages three to 12. First-class tickets are $21 one-way. Hy-line also offers seasonal service between Martha's Vineyard and Nantucket. **The Steamship Authority** ( (508) 477-8600, South Dock Street, Hyannis, provides year-round ferry service for passengers, bicycles, automobiles and pets. Reservations are required for cars, but not for passengers. The trip takes a little over two hours and the cost one-way is $10 for adults and $5 for children ages five to 12. Bicycle fare is an additional $5 each way. It's expensive to bring your car over, and permits are required for driving on beaches and in conservation areas. Ferry reservations for automobiles cost $90 one-way from May 15 to October 15; the fare drops to $70 from mid-October to May. Reservations must be made several months in advance. Flights to Nantucket Memorial Airport are available through a number of carriers, including: Ocean Wings Air Charter ( (508) 228-3277 TOLL-FREE (800) 253-5309, Colgan Air ( (508) 325-5100 TOLL-FREE (800) 272-5488, Continental Express TOLL-FREE ( (800) 345-3400, and US Airways TOLL-FREE ( (800) 428-4322.

OPPOSITE: On July 4th, many Bostonians dress in period costume to commemorate their Colonial heritage.

# Central Massa- chusetts and the Berkshires

## CENTRAL MASSACHUSETTS

Leaving historic Boston, the coastal region and Cape Cod, central Massachusetts offers a quite different ambiance. An area of lakes, trails, colleges and cornfields, it stretches north to New Hampshire and west to the foothills of the Berkshires.

### SPRINGFIELD

Springfield is a sprawling industrial city,

Arts (European and American primitive paintings) and the Smith Art Museum (Oriental and American art and furnishings).

Also worthy of attention is Springfield's massive **Eastern States Exhibition**, or "Big E" as it is called, which is held each September to display the year's agricultural and industrial achievements.

In 1891, Dr. James Naismith of Springfield College invented a game whose object was to toss a ball into a peach basket. He called it basketball and after he realized that removing the basket bottoms would add

home to more than 200 factories and manufacturing plants. The city is located in the geographical center of the state at the crossroads of two interstate highways (Interstate 90 and Interstate 91).

Springfield is best known as the home of America's largest weapons arsenal, **Springfield Armory**. The Armory manufactured the first American musket in 1795, supplied Union weapons during the Civil War and produced the famous Springfield rifle. It now houses the **Benton Small Arms Museum**, with displays of weapons dating from the 15th century.

The Armory, on the Quadrangle (Chestnut and State Streets), is part of a cultural complex that includes the **Museum of Fine**

momentum to the game, it became wildly popular.

Now basketball is part of the American way of life and its heroes and their hours of glory are the pride of the nation's shrine to hoops, the **Basketball Hall of Fame** ( (413) 781-6500, Springfield Center, off Interstate 91. Admission is $8 for adults with reductions for children and senior citizens and it is open year round.

The inventor is honored with a large memorial and a replica of the original YMCA gymnasium where the first game was played. It differs from other major sports'

ABOVE: Flower market in the Pioneer Valley.
OPPOSITE: Picnicking near the Mohawk Trail.

halls of fame in that it honors great players from amateur and college as well as the professional ranks. Besides old balls, jerseys, trophies and videos, the hall offers a "shooting gallery" with basketballs delivered on a conveyor belt to visitors who stand behind a rail and "shoot some hoops."

## General Information

For information, contact the **Springfield Convention and Visitors Bureau (** (413) 787-1548 TOLL-FREE (800) 723-1548 FAX (413) 781-4607, 56 Dwight Street, Springfield, MA 01101.

## Where to Stay

The **Ramada Sovereign Hotel and Conference Center (** (413) 781-8750 FAX (413) 733-8652, 1080 Riverdale Street, West Springfield (expensive), has comfortable lodgings and children stay free.

You can also count on **Plantation Inn (** (413) 592-8200 TOLL-FREE (800) 248-8495 FAX (413) 592-9671, 296 Burnett Road, Chicopee (moderate to expensive); or the **Quality Inn (** (413) 739-7261 TOLL-FREE (800) 228-5151 FAX (413) 737-8410, 1150 Riverdale Street, West Springfield (moderate).

---

The living-history museum of Old Sturbridge Village in central Massachusetts recreates nineteenth-century New England life.

## AROUND SPRINGFIELD

### Old Sturbridge Village

Just 30 miles (48 km) east of Springfield is **Old Sturbridge Village (** (508) 347-3362 (admission $15 adults, $6 children; open daily 9 AM to 5 PM, closed holidays and Mondays from November to April), a living-history museum that recreates life in an 1830s rural New England town. More than 200 acres (81 hectares) of rolling landscape, woodlands, country pathways, a working historical farm and more than 40 historic buildings form part of the village, which opened in 1946. Guides in historical dress demonstrate 19th-century skills and share the customs, work and celebrations of early Massachusetts with visitors.

**Center Village** is the heart of Old Sturbridge. Its Common is lined with historic homes such as the rustic 1704 Fenno House, the 1740 Richardson House Parsonage of a saltbox design and the Center Meeting House, which dominates the head of the Common with its Greek Revival columns and tall white-clapboard spire.

Take one of the footpaths leading off the Common to the **Pliny Freeman Farm**, which demonstrates typical 1830s community life in New England. It is one of the liveliest spots in the entire village, with costumed men and women performing daily farmstead tasks. The seasonal rhythms are also very evident — with the birth of baby lambs and calves and the plowing and planting of fields each spring; crop harvesting in the fall; and preparations for the long New England winter.

In addition to their daily tasks, village residents recreate special events such as the festive Fourth of July celebrations which include a parade, music and a reading of the Declaration of Independence. The village also conducts regular programs, seminars and workshops in field archaeology, spinning and blacksmithing.

### Where to Stay

Hotels here are more reasonably priced and smaller, than in Springfield: **Old Sturbridge Village Lodge (** (508) 347-3327 TOLL-FREE (800) 733-1830 FAX (508) 347-3018, U.S. 20;

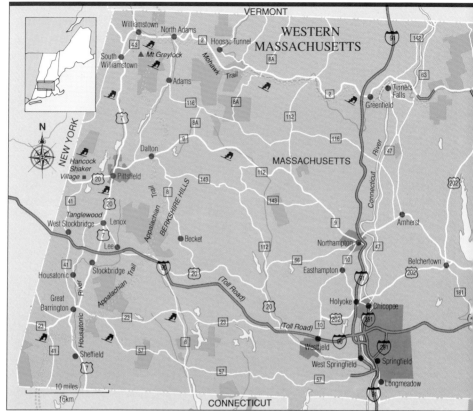

and **Quality Inn Colonial** ( (508) 347-3306 TOLL-FREE (800) 228-5151 FAX (508) 347-3514, U.S. 20, are both in the moderate price range.

## QUABBIN RESERVOIR

The Quabbin Reservoir covers 128 sq miles (332 sq km) and supplies drinking water to the Boston area. To build the reservoir, engineers dammed the Swift River, flooding four river valley towns and in the process, created a recreational wonderland offering fishing, hiking and scenic shore drives along U.S. 202, Routes 9 and Alt. 32. From an observation tower off **Windsor Dam** (Route 9, two miles or just over three kilometers from Belchertown) one can view nearly 50 reservoir islands, created by valley hills that rise above the water line.

## THE PIONEER VALLEY

Several well-known college campuses can be visited in the Pioneer Valley.

In **Amherst**, the Amherst College campus is a tree-shaded green; the high-rise University of Massachusetts towers above the surrounding corn fields. The town itself was home to three celebrated American poets — Robert Frost, Emily Dickinson and Eugene Field. One University of Massachusetts French professor is reputed to have the state's most extensive private library.

In nearby **Northampton**, Smith College, founded in 1875 to produce "intelligent gentlewomen," is now co-educational. Just north of town are many restored homes, including the 1658 Parsons House and 1796 Shepherd House. With Hampshire and Mount Holyoke colleges as well, the Pioneer Valley is blessed with cultural attractions and college-style nightlife.

## THE MOHAWK TRAIL

The Mohawk Trail follows the trace of an ancient Indian footpath from New York's

Finger Lakes to central Massachusetts. One of the first historical references to the trail notes that the Pocumtuck Indians, under pressure from the expanding colonists, retreated from their villages on the banks of the Connecticut River near what is now Greenfield, Massachusetts, in 1663 to invade the lands of the Mohawks, in the area of what is now Troy, New York. In the ensuing war, the Mohawks annihilated the Pocumtucks, virtually wiping out their legacy in North America. Later, pioneers traveled along the Mohawk Trail from the Massachusetts Bay Colony to the Berkshires, then on to Dutch settlements in the Mohawk and Hudson valleys.

The Mohawk Trail became a major path for moving colonial forces to New York to defend British outposts during the French and Indian wars. These troops included a young Paul Revere, then making his first trip away from his Boston home.

Soon after Independence, the Mohawk Trail was used by covered wagon trains

moving west, as it provided the easiest way over the mountains. In 1786, it became America's first toll-free interstate road.

The 19th century brought stagecoaches to the trail, as more and more settlers moved westward. But it was not until 1914 that the Mohawk Trail was opened to automobile travel.

Today, the Mohawk Trail extends 63 miles (100 km) along Massachusetts Routes 2 and 2A, from Millers Falls on the Connecticut River to Williamstown, near the Massachusetts–New York state line. It is one of the nation's prettiest highways, ascending from the Connecticut River valley past farms and orchards into the rugged forested slopes of the Berkshires and ending, at Williamstown, in one of New England's most renowned villages.

## ALONG THE TRAIL

### Millers Falls
Spanning the Connecticut River just west of Millers Falls is the **French King Bridge**, 750 ft (228 m) long and 140 ft (43 m) above the water. The northern side of the bridge provides an excellent view of the river and of **French King Rock**, supposedly the site of the first planting of the French flag in this region by French explorers.

### Greenfield
Farther west, Greenfield is known for its involvement in the Indian wars and for its fine colonial architecture. Here in Greenfield, a **covered bridge** spans over the Green River. The **"Poet's Seat Tower"** on Greenfield Mountain (east on Main Street toward High Street, then follow the signs) affords a panoramic view of the lush Greenfield Valley.

### Deerfield
South of U.S. 5 and settled in the mid-1600s this famous colonial town has Indian and Revolutionary War monuments and pre-Revolutionary War houses lining its Main Street, with many open to visitors. Deerfield was the site of two attacks in the French and Indian wars, the Massacre of Bloody Brook in 1675 and the Deerfield Massacre in 1704.

The restoration of Deerfield's historic structures was the first project of its kind in the United States. Period artifacts can be viewed at **Old Deerfield Village and Memorial Hall Museum**. The Museum also offers guided tours of a street lined with 12 colonial-era houses.

Back on the Mohawk Trail, you can stop in **Shelburne Falls** to see the "**Bridge of Flowers**," an arched trolley bridge that has been maintained as a "hanging garden" by the Shelburne Women's Club since 1929. Flowers cover the bridge from spring to fall.

featuring classical American and European chamber music (May to October) in the historic, yet acoustically perfect, **Charlemont Confederated Church**.

Charlemont's landmark is the 900-lb (409-kg) bronze cast statue (at Indian Bridge spanning the Deerfield River), "Hail to the Sunrise," depicting an Indian with arms outstretched to the "Great Spirit," a 1932 memorial to the Mohawks. Unfortunately, commemoration of America's original inhabitants occurred only long after they had been annihilated.

The 400-ft (122-m), five-arch concrete bridge was built in 1908 across the Deerfield River to carry trolley tracks between Shelburne and Buckland, but was abandoned in the late 1920s as transportation patterns changed.

Also worth seeing are the impressive glacial potholes visible at **Salmon Falls** (follow the signs from the bridge), reputed to be some of the largest in the world.

## Charlemont

The trail's half-way point, this town, settled in 1749, offers "Mohawk Trail concerts"

**Bissell Bridge**, a recreated covered bridge built in 1951 across Mill Brook, is just off Route 2 on Heath Road.

## Charlemont to North Adams

West of Charlemont, the Mohawk Trail climbs into rugged **Hoosac Range**, a wall of granite (once nicknamed the "Berkshire Barrier") that isolated the northern Berkshires from the rest of Massachusetts until 1875, when the Hoosac Tunnel was blasted through the rock. Soon after, one enters the superb mountain scenery of the **Mohawk Trail State Forest**. The forest has excellent hiking trails, including an easy slope to the peak of Forbidden Mountain, good picnic areas and campgrounds.

ABOVE: Fall colors on the Mohawk Trail.
OPPOSITE: Massachusetts' tourist industry attempts to capitalize on its Native American heritage.

**Whitcomb Summit**, just north of the town of Florida, offers the Trail's highest viewpoint (2,200 ft or 670 m) with a panorama of the Deerfield River and the Hoosac Tunnel.

Built to reduce the grade for trains traveling between Boston and Troy, New York, the **Hoosac Tunnel** is four miles (six kilometers) long. It took 25 years to complete, finally opening in 1873 after claiming the lives of nearly 200 men and costing more than $15 million. It had to be blasted through solid granite and involved the first working use of nitroglycerin; constant accidents earned the Tunnel the nickname of the "Bloody Pit." It is now considered by many local residents to be haunted by the ghosts of the men who died building it.

To reach the tunnel's eastern entrance, take Whitcomb Hill Road south to the Deerfield River, then turn left on River Road until you reach the railroad tracks.

Just west of Florida is the **Western Summit**, with fantastic views of North Adams, Williamstown, the Hoosac Valley and the Green Mountains, along with Mt. Greylock, the highest mountain in the Berkshires. Hang gliders launched from the summit often reach altitudes of more than 3,500 ft (1,067 m).

As the Trail descends toward North Adams, be careful to slow for the **Hairpin Turn**, a 180-degree curve memorable for its configuration and its spectacular views of the surrounding countryside. Off-road parking provides access to an observation platform. Here the **Golden Eagle Restaurant** has a second-story, outdoor verandah with panoramic views of three states: Massachusetts, Vermont and New York. The Trail continues down to the factory town of North Adams.

## North Adams

Once a busy 19th-century mill town, North Adams has seen its commercial prominence vanish with the textile industry. It is now a year-round recreation center, with **ski areas** minutes away and abundant summer activities. It also puts on a **Fall Foliage Festival**, when the surrounding hills are a palette of scarlet, gold and crimson.

Its 150-year-old **Cider Mill**, one of the largest restored mills in New England, makes tasty golden apple cider. The **Natural Bridge**, located on Route 8 North, is another North Adams attraction. A rock formation about 550 million years old, it is a marble chasm 475 ft (145 m) long and 60 ft (18 m) deep. This unique geological feature is the only natural, water-eroded bridge in North America and can be traversed from May through October for a small admission charge. North Adams has also recently created the $72 million **Massachusetts Museum of Contemporary Art**, located in a 28-building industrial complex.

High over the town looms the magnificent granite bulk of **Mt. Greylock**. At 3,491 ft (1,064 m), it is the highest point in

Massachusetts. From its rocky barren summit the hiker is rewarded with a fine vista of the Berkshires and western Massachusetts, the Green Mountains of Vermont and the Hudson River Valley of New York. The surrounding peaks and forests have many well-marked hiking trails, including part of the Appalachian Trail, which crosses Mt. Greylock.

## WILLIAMSTOWN

Williamstown is only five miles (eight kilometers) west of North Adams on Route 2, but it is a universe apart. Hawthorne once remarked that Williamstown is "a white village and a steeple set like a daydream

among the high mountain waves." In the late 19th century, it was a spa and summer resort. Set in a hollow of the surrounding Berkshires and in the shadow of Mt. Greylock, Williamstown remains one of New England's loveliest villages. The 1793 **Williams College**, long rated the country's best liberal arts college, is situated in this town. Known for its stringent intellectual requirements and brilliant, demanding professors, Williams College is well worth a visit by those whose children might someday seek the best American education has to offer.

Deerfield's historic church has long been one of the town's most prominent attractions.

Williamstown's **Sterling and Francine Clark Art Institute** (South Street, just west of the town center) houses one of the world's largest private collections of Renoirs, as well as works of other Impressionists and is one of the finest small art museums in the country.

At the information booth, Main and South Streets, you may obtain a self-guided touring map to explore Williamstown's rich past. On Main Street, many of the large and lovely homes date from the 1750s. One of the most interesting college buildings is Lawrence Hall, part of the **Williams College Museum of Art**, an octagonal Grecian rotunda inspired by Thomas Jefferson's *Monticello*.

The **Williamstown Summer Theater Festival**, founded in 1955, is an annual event featuring some of the country's most celebrated actors. The main venue is at the nation's finest summer theater, Williamstown Theater on Main Stage. The festival has featured actors Christopher Reeve and Richard Thomas, director Joanne Woodward and playwright like John Guare. Other choices include: Adams Memorial Theater's "Cabaret," which presents an early revue and a late cabaret that often includes stars from the Main Stage; Thespis Productions, now over 15 years old, at the Clark Institute; the Calliope Theater Company; a women's theater group; and the Spring Street Ensemble Theater, which showcases experimental productions.

Just a half-hour drive away are the Oldcastle Theater Company in Bennington, Vermont; the Theater Barn in New Lebanon, New York; the Berkshire Public Theater in Pittsfield, Massachusetts; Shakespeare & Company in Lenox, Massachusetts; and the Berkshire Theater Festival in Stockbridge, Massachusetts — to name a few. You can watch a different theater production in Williamstown or one of its neighboring towns every night of the week, at less than half the cost of a ticket to one of New York's Broadway shows.

**Where to Stay and Eating Out**

For a college town, Williamstown has many hotels and restaurants. Recommended hotels are **The William's Inn** ( (413) 458-9371 TOLL-FREE (800) 828-0133 FAX (413) 458-2767, on the Green (expensive); **The Orchards** ( (413) 458-9611 FAX (413) 458-3273, 222 Adams Road (expensive), which is near the museums.

South of town is **Best Western — The Springs Motor Inn** ( (508) 347-9121, U.S. 7, New Ashford (moderate to expensive). See also listings for nearby towns in the next section.

The best restaurant is **Le Jardin Inn** ( (413) 458-8032, 777 Cold Spring Road, which specializes in lamb and duck dishes.

## THE BERKSHIRES

"There's no tonic like the Housatonic," said Oliver Wendell Holmes about the river that snakes through the Berkshire Hills and winds into Connecticut. It creates an idyllic setting for the well-preserved little towns that dot the Berkshires in the westernmost county of Massachusetts. Village greens are surrounded by stunning colonial architecture; white clapboard church steeples pierce the blue skies; and tall shade trees line quiet residential streets. A plethora of cultural

Hancock Shaker Village is a study in simplicity.

activities include nationally-renowned theater and music festivals.

Its extraordinary variety of landscapes — open meadows and rolling farmlands, valleys dotted with shimmering lakes, wooded hills and green mountains, rushing rivers and plummeting waterfalls — is a major ingredient of the Berkshires' magic; this area is also the heart of Massachusetts' ski country.

Stretching from the Vermont border in the north, down the old "York State" line to the south, the Berkshire Hills remained a

From Williamstown you can continue north to Burlington, Vermont, or turn south on Route 7 toward the lower Berkshires.

Along the way you will pass the popular **Jimmy Peak** and **Brodie Mountain** ski areas near the town of Hancock.

## THE SHAKERS

A detour off U.S. 7 onto U.S. 20 at Pittsfield brings you to **Hancock Shaker Village**, an authentic community of the Shaker religious sect that thrived from 1790 to 1960. It is

wilderness until 1725, when pioneer Matthew Noble erected a log cabin in what is now the town of Sheffield. Soon dense forests were cleared for farmland and towns appeared along the Housatonic River. In the 19th century, the Berkshires were mined for iron used on the railroads. Marble was also quarried here and transported to construct such edifices as the Capitol dome in Washington, D.C.

The Berkshires attracted urban dwellers wishing to "escape" into the country, including some of America's wealthiest families (such as the Carnegies and the Vanderbilts), who built elegant mansions (quaintly called summer "cottages") and used them for less than three months of the year.

today a living, working museum of Shaker rural life, with 20 restored buildings on 1,000 acres (405 hectares).

The Shaker movement started in England in 1747 as an offshoot of Quakers. Manchester's Ann Lee first led eight followers to the American colony of New York and founded a settlement near Albany. For a time, they were known as "shaking Quakers" because "dances" during religious services made their bodies shake and tremble. Eventually, the Shakers' pronouncements and beliefs in four principle doctrines (separation from the outside world, common property, confession of sins and celibacy, with separation but equality of the sexes) took hold. By the mid-19th century, the Shaker movement reached its zenith, with 19 communities in the United States.

Strolling through the village on a guided tour, you will notice that the buildings are austere but elegant and the craftsmanship outstanding. Shaker ways of coping with the material world are sometimes ingenious, while their keen grasp of the concepts of purity and functionalism have raised the design of their buildings, furniture and common utensils to an art form.

The village's finest example of Shaker architecture and ingenuity is the magnificently restored **Round Stone Barn**. Built in 1826, the barn's upper level could be accessed by horses and wagons, which unloaded their harvest into a central haymow and then proceeded around a track to another exit. This eliminated the problem of backing hitched teams out of the barn, an often difficult task. Cows were stabled on the ground floor.

It is also interesting to note how separation of the sexes was carried to an extreme. **The Brick Dwelling** (community dining room, sleeping rooms and kitchen) which housed 100 brothers and sisters, is divided exactly in half; it is also very light and airy, with more than 3,000 windowpanes.

Hancock tours also include 19th-century **craft demonstrations** and a walk through the site's farm and herb garden (the seed industry was a Shaker specialty).

## PITTSFIELD

Returning toward U.S. 7, you will arrive at Pittsfield, whose **concert hall** has been the scene of distinguished music since 1918 and is now home to the South Mountain Concerts series. Artists who have appeared here include Leonard Bernstein, Leontyne Price, Rudolf Serkin and the Tokyo Quartet. Concerts are held during late summer and fall. The Berkshire Ballet offers a six-week series of classical, modern and contemporary dance at the **Koussevotzky Arts Center** on the Berkshire Community College campus.

Pittsfield is also home to the **Berkshire Museum**, a fine collection of 19th- and 20th-century American paintings and

Hawthorne memorabilia. The **Berkshire Athenaeum's Melville Room** has a unique selection of books, letters and pictures of the author. Melville's home, "Arrowhead," in Pittsfield, is filled with personal artifacts from his occupancy (1850–1863). Melville wrote part of *Moby Dick* here, where he could gaze out over the Berkshire Hills, which he said reminded him of rolling waves and gray humpback whales.

### Where to Stay
The **Hilton Inn Berkshire** ( (413) 499-2000 TOLL-FREE (800) 445-8667 FAX (413) 442-0449 is on Berkshire Common (expensive).

## LENOX AND TANGLEWOOD

**Lenox** became popular as a summer resort when the Boston Symphony Orchestra chose it in 1939 as the site of its annual **Berkshire Festival of Music**. The festival is held at **Tanglewood**, one-and-a-half miles (just under three kilometers) southwest on Route 183. The 210-acre (85-hectare) estate is where Hawthorne once lived and wrote *The House of the Seven Gables*. The site takes its name from *Tanglewood Tales*, which he also wrote here.

The Boston Symphony and guest artists perform here every July and August. The main "Music Shed," designed by Eero Saarinen, seats only 6,000, but an expansive lawn allows thousands more to enjoy the evening's music.

During Boston Symphony concert nights, Tanglewood is a mass of traffic and humanity. It is best to arrive early to find a spot in the parking lot and maybe bring along a picnic meal; it is not unusual for people to arrive more than three hours before a scheduled performance. Special bus excursions to Tanglewood concerts are offered by a number of local tour agencies.

You can enjoy, as well, one of the many non-Boston Symphony concerts, recitals and full orchestra presentations; nearly 50 of these performances are held throughout the summer. The **Popular Artists' Series** consists of rock, pop and folk concerts, while

OPPOSITE: The Chapel of Williams College, one of the nation's highest-ranked liberal arts colleges.

the **Stockbridge Chamber Concerts** at Seven Hills offers a year-round program of music in the great estates, halls and historic churches of the Berkshires.

On Lenox's Main Street is the 1805 "Church on the Hill." Several other streets offer glimpses of mansions once owned by business and industrial magnates (Harrimans, Biddles, Stuyvesants) who had summer "cottages" in Lenox. Most of these houses are not open to the public, although one — Wheatleigh — now operates as an elegant country inn and restaurant.

## BECKET

**Jacob's Pillow Dance Festival**, which takes place in Becket over 10 weeks each summer, offers some of the country's best dance and music. Since its inception more than 50 years ago, the program has commissioned new dance works from many innovative and renowned choreographers. Performers have included Martha Graham, Merce Cunningham and the Alvin Ailey Repertory Ensemble. Besides main theater performances, the

### Where to Stay

**Wheatleigh** ( (413) 637-0610 TOLL-FREE (800) 321-0610 FAX (413) 637-4507, West Hawthorn Road (expensive); **Village Inn** ( (413) 637-0200 TOLL-FREE (800) 253-0917 FAX (413) 637-9756, 16 Church Street (moderate to expensive) and **Quality Inn** ( (413) 637-4244 TOLL-FREE (800) 228-5151 FAX (413) 637-1969, 390 Pittsfield Lenox Road (moderate to expensive), are recommended in the area.

### Around Lenox

Nearby the **Pleasant Valley Wildlife Sanctuary** is a Massachusetts Audubon preserve of native plants and landscapes, including beaver ponds, open meadows and more than seven miles (11 km) of walking trails.

Pillow's "Inside/Out Series" presents a free, hour-long show on an outdoor stage that includes works in progress, discussions with dancers and choreographers and audience questions.

## STOCKBRIDGE

Stockbridge is a stately New England town with fine houses, quaint shops, historical attraction and a lively arts community. Established as an Indian mission by preacher and theologian John Sargeant (whose 1739 home, the **Old Mission House**, is open for tours), the town has evolved into a grand summer resort. The **Norman Rockwell Museum** ( (413) 298-4100, a restored 18th-century mansion in the Old Corner House, on Main Street (admission $9 for adults and $2 for children; open year-round except January 15 to 31), exhibits a large permanent collection of his paintings.

Other attractions worth visiting include **Chesterwood**, off Route 183 in Glendale, the summer estate of Daniel Chester French, sculptor of the Lincoln Memorial in Washington, DC and the *Minuteman* in Concord, Mass. His mansion, studio, barn gallery and period garden are open for guided tours, along with nature trails that offer views of Monument Mountain.

The **Berkshire Theater Festival**, one of the nation's top summer theaters, has performed here for more than 60 years. Classical works with name actors are staged June through August in the large Playhouse; new plays and children's theater from around the world are set in the barn, as part of the Unicorn Theater Company.

### Where to Stay

The antique-filled rooms, flower-laden courtyard and front porch lined with comfortable rocking chairs of the **Red Lion Inn** ( (413) 298-5545 FAX (413) 298-5130, Main Street (moderate to expensive), have made it a regional favorite for years. Smaller, with 12 rooms, and of equal quality is **The Inn at Stockbridge** ( (413) 298-3337 FAX (413) 298-3406, 30 East Street, U.S. 7 (expensive).

### Around Stockbridge

Just west off Interstate 90, is **West Stockbridge**, its Main Street lined with 1800s-style storefronts housing galleries, specialty stores, antiques and other tourist shops. A number of fairs and festivals are held here during the year. The **Williamsville Inn** ( (413) 274-6118 FAX (413) 274-3539, Route 41 (expensive), has an excellent dining room.

**Berkshire Scenic Railway** is a "rolling museum" that operates over a portion of the historic New Haven Housatonic Valley Line with vintage railroad equipment and comfortable 1920-vintage coaches. It rambles at a leisurely 10mph (16kph) pace for 15 miles (24 km) between **Lee** and **Great Barrington**. With an open or round trip ticket you can stop anywhere you wish along the line and board a later train to complete your journey. The train follows the path of the Housatonic River, past mills, waterfalls, meadows and mountains. Although the train is stationed at Lee, you can also board in Stockbridge, Housatonic and Great Barrington.

**Tyringham**, about five miles (eight kilometers) south of Lee along Tyringham Road, is noted for its **Gingerbread House** and **Tyringham Art Galleries**. The thatched cottage with rock pillars and grottoes, built in the 1930s by sculptor Sir Henry Hudson Kitson, now houses several art galleries, beautiful sculpture gardens and woodland walking trails.

## GREAT BARRINGTON

A short scenic drive south on U.S. 7 leads to Great Barrington, the largest town in the southern Berkshires resort area. The Mohican Indians built their "Great Wigwam" at a ford here in the Housatonic River. The village gained prominence in 1774 when its residents seized the courthouse from the British, committing the first act of open rebellion in the colonies against the Crown. And William Stanley (founder of General Electric) helped to light up the town with electricity as early as 1886. A booth on Main Street in the center of town provides visitor information.

Great Barrington was a station on the Underground Railroad transporting fugitive slaves to freedom. W.E.B. du Bois, the author and editor, lived here, as did James Weldon Johnson, co-founder of the National Association for the Advancement of Colored People (NAACP).

This part of the southern Berkshires is an antique hunter's delight. Scores of antique shops can be found in Great Barrington, South Egremont, Sheffield, New Marlboro and along the winding back roads of the Berkshire farm country nestled cozily in gentle hills. As with all antique shops, beware of fakes and inflated prices.

### Where to Stay

The best of Great Barrington's hotels are **Windflower Inn** ( TOLL-FREE (800) 992-1993 FAX (413) 528-5147, Route 23 (moderate to expensive); **Monument Mountain** ( (413) 528-3272 FAX (413) 528-3132, 249 Stockbridge Road (moderate to expensive); and **Briarcliff Motor Lodge** ( (413) 528-3000 FAX (413) 528-3000 (U.S. 7 (moderate to expensive).

### Around Great Barrington
**Sheffield**, founded in 1733 and the oldest village in the Berkshires, is the only Massachusetts town with two **covered bridges**.

Farther south, off Route 7A, is **Ashley Falls**, location of Berkshire County's oldest

**Monument Mountain.** Two trails lead to the summit. An easy two- to three-hour round trip offers spectacular views of Squaw Peak. Monument Mountain is also known as the site of an 1850 meeting between Melville and Hawthorne, which began their friendship.

### ANTIQUE HUNTING IN THE BERKSHIRES

The Berkshire Mountains offer some of the best antique-hunting grounds in the region. Many shops are located in New England's

home, the 1735 **Ashley House** (open for tours May to mid-October) and **Bartholomew's Cobble**, a national natural landmark renowned for its native ferns and wildflowers. Six miles (10 km) of hiking trails skirt the banks of the Housatonic River.

About 12 miles (19 km) past South Egremont (off Route 41, then follow the signs almost to the New York state line) is **Bash Bish Falls**, a 275-ft (84-m) waterfall plunging down a steep gorge. Legend has it that an Indian girl jumped to her death here; her spirit is said to haunt the pool beneath the falls.

Less than five miles (eight kilometers) north of Great Barrington off Route 7, is

beautiful towns, so whether you're seriously looking for antiques, just browsing, or simply wandering the region's back roads, you should have a pleasant and interesting journey. (See page 46 and 272.)

---

Antiques and objets d'art can be found in New England's many antique shops.

# Maine

BY FAR the largest New England state, Maine is also in many ways the purest remnant of the old New England spirit of hard work, honesty, thrift and personal ethics — in a word, the "soul" of New England. Looking down on its neighbor states as too soft, too modern, too flamboyant and too money-oriented, Maine has been hardened by its long, cold winters and constant battle with the sea.

Although the state's stunning beauty, lovely architecture and largely undeveloped backcountry continue to draw more and more visitors (and new residents) each year, native Mainers still retain a certain sense of privacy which seems to exclude newcomers — a newcomer being anyone whose family has not lived in the state for at least several generations. And although in recent years there has been a rise in "anti-outsider" sentiment, the traveler is still welcomed for himself more than for the money he might spend.

## "DOWN EAST"

A fabulous landscape of 10,000 lakes and 10,000 offshore islands, Maine is as far east as the traveler can go without leaving the United States. For a Maine resident, to travel northeast toward Canada is to go "down east" a term that has come to be identified with the state itself. Maine's coastline juts north and east into the cold, stormy Atlantic; to the north Maine is bounded by the endless spruce and fir forests of the Canadian provinces of Quebec and New Brunswick. Only on its western border does Maine touch the United States, along the state line with New Hampshire.

In his famous journal of exploration, *The Maine Woods*, Henry David Thoreau termed the state the last remaining wilderness east of the Mississippi. Even then, however, most of the towering white pines that gave the state its nickname had been cut down for ships' masts. Today, nearly 90 percent of Maine remains uninhabited spruce, fir and pine forests, which are, however, heavily overlogged by the paper industry, furnishing, as one Maine conservationist complained, "half of America's toilet paper."

## THE MAINE ETHIC

Maine's wild coastline is the longest and most varied in New England, stretching for 3,500 miles (5,600 km).

A jagged panoply of inlets, islands, peaks, peninsulas, bays, reefs and stony headlands washed by the cobalt sea and hammered by white surf and crashing winter storms, the Maine coast has given rise to countless legends and tragedies of the north Atlantic and has prepared many thousands

of young fishermen and sailors for a life at sea.

Similarly so, the backwoods of Maine, which gave rise to generations of lumberjacks, woodsmen, trappers and guides, remain a marvelous experience for the more adventurous and hardy visitor — the largest undeveloped forest area in the United States east of Montana. For those willing to take the time and trouble, Maine's extensive northern river system offers perhaps the best long-distance canoeing in the lower 48 states, where the traveler can lie at night under the undimmed stars and hear the

OPPOSITE: At anchor in Rockport, one of many excellent harbors along the Maine coast.
ABOVE: Local color at the Fryeburg Fair.

lonely, half-mad laughter of the loons across vast and silent lakes.

Less well known is Maine's major, though lessening, agricultural role. Before the United States took over the Indian lands west of the Mississippi, Maine provided sheep and cattle for much of the northeast. And until federally-subsidized irrigation projects made it possible to grow potatoes cheaply on arid western farmlands, Maine potatoes were known as the nation's finest — which indeed they still are.

As with most unique places, Maine suffers from numerous clichés: rough-and-tumble lumberjacks and log cabins, salty

The Fryeburg Fair is the "Maine" event in late September or early the October of every year.

lobster fishermen and tight-lipped natives whittling wood on the porch of a century-old general store while they talk about the "comin' nor'easter," of wandering moose, howling wolves and L.L. Bean.

But the lumberjacks have been largely replaced by huge belching combines that grind their way through the north woods, uprooting trees and snipping off their tips and roots. Like most of their fellow Americans, unfortunately, the natives are more likely to be watching television than whittling wood and the general store is probably filled with trinkets for the tourist trade. The moose still wander, except in hunting season when they try to keep their heads down, but no wolves have howled in Maine for nearly a hundred years — although their

again there is fishing, hiking, wandering and enjoying the outburst of blossoms and flowers that foretells the coming summer.

For warm-season vacationers, late June through August is best, when the temperatures generally hover between 70°F and 80°F (21°C and 27°C) during the day and slightly lower at night. For skiers, Maine's cold winter weather is a blessing, for it brings heavy falls of snow. Western Maine's ski retreats, mountains surrounded by lush forests, provide a magnificent wilderness setting in which to enjoy the slopes and trails.

**General Information**
To help plan your trip, the **Maine Publicity Bureau**, 325B Water Street, Hallowell, ME 03437, will provide free maps and brochures. For travel information, call (out-of-state) TOLL-FREE (800) 533-9595 or (in-state) ℂ (207) 623-0363 FAX (207) 623-0388.

## BACKGROUND

### THE DAWN PEOPLE

Maine's first known inhabitants were the tribes of Paleo and Algonquin Indians who, 10,000 to 25,000 years ago, wandered down from what is now Canada and the western United States, probably along the St. Lawrence River, until they reached the sea. Called "the dawn people" because they had traveled so far east, toward the dawn, they were roughly divided, in Maine, into Algonquins in the south, Penobscots in the middle and Micmacs and other coastal tribes in the north.

ecological niche is being taken over by coyotes, wilier and less afraid of humans.

## YEAR-ROUND VACATIONS

For vacationers, Maine (33,215 sq mile or 86,050 sq km) offers unique experiences on a year-round basis. In summer you can swim in its crystalline, unpolluted lakes, swim and sail on the coast, fish the lakes, streams and ocean, visit its lovely colonial towns, canoe its rivers, or hike its mountains. In the fall Maine's wonderland of autumn colors provides a dramatic backdrop for hikers, hunters and fishermen. In winter the visitor can cross-country or downhill ski, skate, or ice fish. And in spring

They tended to winter along the coast and travel inland in the late spring, summer and fall for hunting and gathering. The Penobscots, whose name means "the rocky place," describing a bouldered series of rapids on the river of the same name, spent their winters along Penobscot Bay, where they lived off the shellfish, fish and shore animals. In warmer months they traveled in small clans and hunting groups far up into the vastness of the Allagash and upper Penobscot watersheds, even into what is now Canada, returning with moose, caribou and deer. Although they apparently lived in relative peace among themselves, the Maine tribes were threatened by raiding parties of fierce Mohawk warriors from upper New York state and later by the colonists.

## EUROPEAN EXPLORERS

Tenth-century Norsemen were probably the first European explorers to land on Maine's shores. But the region was largely ignored until John Cabot passed in 1497. In the 1600s, colonists began to move north from what is now Massachusetts and the French started to travel south from Acadia into Maine; there were soon frequent skirmishes between British and French troops, which continued until an eventual British victory in 1763.

The colony of Massachusetts bought what is now Maine for $6,000 in 1677; and this area remained part of Massachusetts until 1820, when it entered the Union as a free state under the Missouri Compromise. The young state quickly distinguished itself in its opposition to slavery, its commercial power and the contribution which its brave regiments made in several major Civil War battles. It had some moral surprises in store for its sister states as well: in 1851, Maine became the first state to enact a law prohibiting the manufacture of alcoholic beverages; the law remained in force until 1934. More recently, in 1949, Maine voters sent their Congresswoman Margaret Chase Smith to the Senate, making her the first woman to serve in both houses of Congress.

## THE SOUTH COAST

Maine's south coast draws many of the state's visitors to its wide beaches and sparkling surf. There are many lovely beaches along the coast, with the water gradually getting colder as one moves northeast. Well-known is the 11mile (18km) **Old Orchard Beach**, a traditional haven for families from Quebec; it is the smoothest, hardest sand beach in Maine.

## KITTERY

Most travelers enter Maine at its southern-most point, from Portsmouth, New Hampshire. The first town on the Maine side of the border is Kittery, once the home of pioneers and Revolutionary War heroes. This sea village — Maine's oldest community, established in 1623 — was once the backbone of the young nation's shipbuilding industry. Its legacy can be traced to Kittery's Portsmouth Navy Yard, which built John Paul Jones' ship, *Ranger*, in 1775. The *Ranger* was the first ship to fly the Stars and Stripes and took to France the news of General Burgoyne's surrender, thus receiving the first salute ever given an American ship by a foreign power.

Today, the shipyard builds primarily submarines and no visitors are allowed. But at the private boat yards on the Piscataqua River, the visitor can watch pleasure craft being built. The **Kittery Historical and Naval Museum ℂ** (207) 439-3080, Rogers Road, off U.S. 1 (admission $2 with reductions for children, families and senior citizens, open Monday to Saturday, 10 AM to 4 PM, closed October 15 to Memorial Day except Saturdays, 1 PM to 4 PM), has an interesting collection of artifacts from Kittery's past.

Another Kittery landmark is **Fort McClary** (1809) on Kittery Point, which defended the townspeople against Indian attacks. A restored hexagonal blockhouse and the original granite sea walls remain standing.

The **Isles of Shoals** can be seen just off shore. They once harbored pirates who plundered ships after luring them to their doom along the rocks by placing false lights near the shallows.

### Around Kittery

Historic sites north of Kittery include the **Sarah Orne Jewett House**, birthplace and home of the noted 19th-century novelist and the **Hamilton House**, a fine 1787 Georgian mansion overlooking Salmon Falls River, both in Berwick. But perhaps the most notable historical complex is **York Village ℂ** (207) 363-4974, 207 York Street, in the village. A self-guided tour includes several

Kittery, just north of the New Hampshire border, is Maine's oldest community.

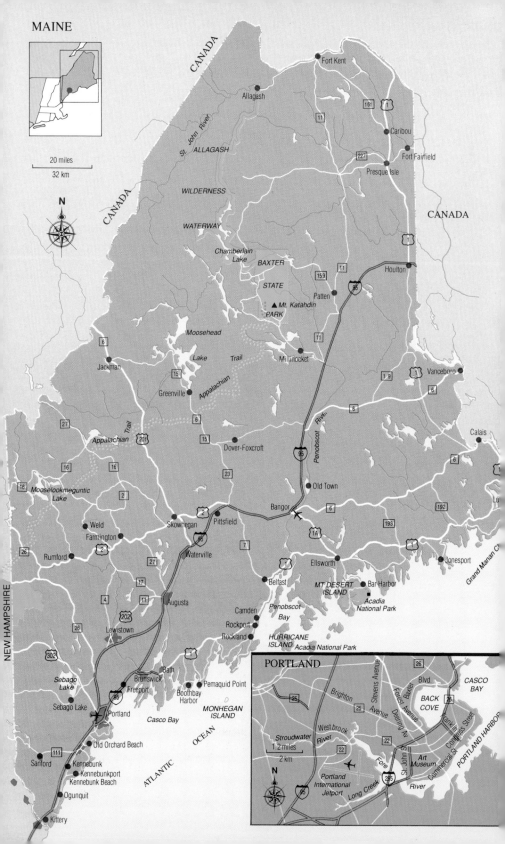

historic buildings and a colonial-period cemetery.

Well worth a visit is the **Old Gaol**, a stone jail built in the 1600s on a knoll overlooking York, complete with dungeons, cramped cells, jailers' quarters and a most gruesome pit—an oozing, wet hole in the ground used for unruly prisoners. It continued to be used as a jail until the 1860s.

Other local attractions include the one-mile (1.6-km) **York Beach**, **Wild Kingdom Amusement Park** and a never-ending string of fast-food fish restaurants.

On leaving York, you have the choice of touring Maine via Interstate 95, making quick loops at various exits to harbor towns and other attractions, or taking U.S. 1, a two- to three-lane highway that bisects the commercial districts of most coastal communities.

### Where to Stay

To ensure lodging during the busy summer season, reserve several days in advance: **Coachman Motor Inn** ( (207) 439-4434 TOLL-FREE (800) 824-6183 FAX (207) 439-6757, Route 1, Kittery (moderate); **Days Inn** ( (207) 439-5555 FAX (207) 439-5555, 2 Gorges Road, Route 1, Kittery (moderate).

### Eating Out

Fresh seafood is the standard fare at Kittery's restaurants. Here you can find good restaurants in every price category: **Warren's Lobster House** ( (207) 439-1630, Route 1, Kittery (expensive); **Bill Foster's Down East Lobster and Clambake** ( (207) 363-3255, Route 1A, York Harbor (moderate); and **Weathervane** ( (207) 439-0330, Route 1, Kittery (inexpensive).

---

### OGUNQUIT

Going north on U.S. 1 along the coast, the next major community is Ogunquit, whose Indian name means "beautiful place by the sea." The name is well-suited, as the beach here is a three-mile (five-kilometer) stretch of white, inviting sand. The town itself is also lovely, with shady streets and fine colonial architecture.

From the center of town, **Marginal Way**, a one-mile- (1.6-km)-long path winds

along the ledges high above the Atlantic, providing walkers with superb vistas of the ocean and shoreline tidal pools. Follow the path as it crests the 100-ft (30-m) peak of Bald Head Cliff and then meanders into the fishing port of **Perkins Cove**, a welcome hodge-podge of lobster shacks and craft-shops.

With its cliffs, sandy beaches and peaceful backdrop of rolling dunes, it is no surprise that Ogunquit and Perkins Cove became a destination for artists at the turn of the century. A number of small art galleries

(along with a jumble of shops) can be found in the village.

The **Ogunquit Summer Playhouse** ( (207) 646-5511, the oldest in Maine, stages a different play each week during the tourist season. Started half a century ago in a local garage, it has become one of the premier summer stock theaters on the East Coast, with its drama school attracting students from around the country.

### Where to Stay

**The Cliff House** ( (207) 361-1000 FAX (207) 361-2122, Bald Head Cliff, 94 rooms (mod-

---

The Kittery Point Lighthouse marks the entrance of the Piscataqua River to the harbor.

erate to expensive) sits atop a bluff and most rooms have sea views. The **Sparhawk** ( (207) 646-5562, Shore Road (expensive) also has excellent views and good service.

### Eating Out

It is not unusual for diners to travel from nearby New Hampshire and Massachusetts to eat at **Hurricane** ( (207) 646-6348, Perkins Cove (expensive); or **Gypsy Sweetheart** ( (207) 646-7021, 10 Shore Road (expensive).

For less expensive Maine seafood dinners, there are **Clay Hill Farm** ( (207) 646-2272, Agamenticus Road (moderate to expensive), which also serves prime rib and **Old Village Inn** ( (207) 646-7088, 30 Main Street (moderate). In **Perkin's Cove**, **Barnacle Billy's** ( (207) 646-5575, serves fresh seafood; lobster is a specialty.

---

## THE KENNEBUNKS

The next set of villages along this picturesque coastline — Kennebunk, West Kennebunk, Kennebunk Beach and Kennebunkport, collectively called The Kennebunks — is a vastly popular vacation spot made more so during George Bush's presidency.

**Kennebunk**, settled in 1650, was once the shipbuilding capital of York County. But as the boatwright trade declined, the town became a fishing and tourism center. What remains of those affluent days when shipbuilders were king are some imposing homes, stately trees and typical New England churches, including the 1772 **First Parish Church** (on Main Street) which has a bell cast by Paul Revere & Sons.

Perhaps the town's most beautiful and unusual building is the **Wedding Cake House**. It was apparently built by a sea captain who, about to marry, was suddenly called on duty. With little time to spare, the wedding took place but without a wedding cake. The captain promised his bride that when he returned he would build her a house frosted like the cake she had wanted. The ornate gingerbread trim on the spectacular two-story, 1826 house does indeed make it look like a lacy wedding cake. It is not open to public tours, but is one of the most photographed buildings in Maine.

For an inside look at Kennebunk's historic houses, some dating back to 1724, contact the **Brick Store Museum** ( (207) 985-4802, 117 Main Street, for details of its 90-minute architectural walking tour which is available during summer only.

**Kennebunkport**, another picturesque town at the mouth of the Kennebunk River, is the summer hometown of former President George Bush. In summer, Kennebunkport is transformed into a vacation boom town. It has the standard quota of quaint shops, old inns and fancy private estates. Historical attractions include the **Seashore Trolley Museum** ( (207) 967-2800, on U.S. 1, just north of town (admission $6 for adults with reductions for children, families and senior citizens; open daily 10 AM to 5:30 PM, May to mid-October, limited hours in spring and fall). It displays 150 antique streetcars from the United States and abroad. You can have a good **swim** at the beaches of Arundel, Cleaves Cove or Goose Rocks.

### Where to Stay

Reservations can be hard to come by. If you are keen to stay here, the following are recommended:

**The Captain Lord Mansion** ( (207) 967-3141 TOLL-FREE (800) 522-3141 FAX (207) 967-3172, Pleasant and Green Streets (expensive); **Inn at Goose Rocks** ( (207) 967-5425 FAX (207) 967-0204, Dyke Road (expensive, near saltwater marshes and woods); **Old Fort Inn** ( (207) 967-5353 FAX (207) 967-4547, Old Fort Avenue (expensive); and **Village Cove Inn** ( (207) 967-3993 FAX (207) 967-3164, South Maine Street (expensive), which overlooks a private cove.

### Eating Out

Dinner reservations are usually easier to obtain than hotel accommodations during peak seasons and weekends. Recommended restaurants are:

**The Kennebunk Inn** ( (207) 985-3351, 45 Main Street (moderate to expensive), is a classic seacoast inn, providing accommodation as well as fine continental dining.

**Olde Grist Mill** ( (207) 967-4781, on Mill Lane (moderate to expensive), serves traditional Maine seafood in its converted mill.

**White Barn Inn** ( (207) 967-2321, Beach Street (moderate to expensive), is popular for its sirloin steak *au poivre*.

## OLD ORCHARD BEACH

Ten miles further north on U.S. 1, just east of Saco, is Old Orchard Beach, Maine's equivalent to Coney Island. Its seven-mile (11km) strand of flat, sloping sand was once the departure strip for early attempts to fly across the Atlantic and was long known for its stylish promenade and boisterous dance halls. Today its traditional boardwalk is lined with arcades and carnival rides. Perhaps because it is the first large saltwater beach south of Montreal, Old Orchard attracts large numbers of French Canadians. Many of the hotels and restaurants here employ bilingual staff to make these visitors feel at home.

### General Information

During the summer season, Old Orchard has many open air concerts and special events. The **Old Orchard Beach Chamber of Commerce** ( (207) 934-2500, P.O. Box 600, Old Orchard Beach, ME 04064, has a complete schedule of events, maps and other useful travel information.

### Where to Stay

Old Orchard Beach's popularity has spawned a wide array of lodging choices. Some good ones are: **Brunswick Inn** ( (207) 934-2171, West Grand Avenue (expensive); **Edgewater** ( (207) 934-2221, 57 West Grand Avenue (moderate to expensive) and **Royal Anchor Motor Lodge** ( (207) 934-4521, East Grand Avenue (moderate to expensive).

### Eating Out

For seafood and steaks, **Joseph's-by-the-Sea** ( (207) 934-5044, 55 West. Grand Avenue (moderate to expensive), is a local favorite.

## PORTLAND

Often called the San Francisco of the East, Portland dominates a long peninsula jutting into magnificent Casco Bay, with a panorama of the Bay's hundreds of islands. At both ends of the city, the land rises gently,

forming excellent viewpoints, the Eastern and Western Promenades, from which to view the islands to the east and the hills and mountains to the west.

### Background

First settled in 1631, Portland has been burned to the ground three times — by raiding Indians in 1676, by invading British troops in 1775 and by accident in 1866. Longfellow commented that the smoldering ruins of 1866 resembled the rubble of Pompeii.

Each time, Portland has rebuilt itself on its ashes, stronger than before. Today it is Maine's largest and most populous city (62,000 people), providing a center of culture and urbanity in a state best known for its backcountry and natural beauty.

From its very beginnings, the city was an important commercial and shipping center, its natural deep-water harbor being 100 miles (160 km) closer to Europe than any other port in the United States. From Portland's docks sailed many of the finest

Portland's famous Observatory, one of the nation's first.

sailing vessels and clipper ships built in the United States; in the eighteenth and nineteenth centuries the city was a major center for lumber export, fisheries and the West Indies sugar and molasses trade. Until the completion of the Saint Lawrence Seaway, much of Canada's wheat sold overseas was shipped from Portland; the city's large oil depots supply a regional network of pipelines. The Bath Iron Works has established a ship repair facility in Portland which has a constant stream of United States Navy vessels in its drydocks.

keeping in daily contact with clients elsewhere.

Portland remains a lovely city with its historic waterfront district, a magnificent skyline and architecture and many other fascinations for the travelers.

**General Information**

The city's **Chamber of Commerce (** (207) 772-2811 and **Visitors Bureau (** (207) 772-4994, both at 142 Free Street, supply brochures outlining a self-guiding **"Portland History Trail"** walking tour of nearly 40 historic buildings.

Overfishing of Atlantic fisheries and lobster beds, however, has cut into Portland's trade and many of the docks along the port have been turned to non-fishery uses. But the city continues to grow and diversify as many professionals from lower New England, New York and the Atlantic states arrive each year in search of a more peaceful, crime-free and pollution-free life. A not insignificant number still commute by plane to offices in New York and Boston; others find the telecommunications revolution has made it possible to live in Portland while

**The History Trail**

Parts of the waterfront district, now called the **Old Port Exchange** (Exchange and Pearl Streets), have been saved and resuscitated into a thriving commercial and tourist center of historic buildings and brick sidewalks, with cafés, good restaurants, bookstores, clothing stores and boutiques of all shapes and sizes amid lawyers' offices, ship chandlers and seamen's bars.

Portland also contains some of the most exquisite historic homes of New England, including the 1785 boyhood **home** of the poet **Henry Wadsworth Longfellow**, which was also the first brick building in the city (admission $4 with reductions for children;

OPPOSITE: Portland's docks harbor fishing boats, tankers and cruiseships alike. ABOVE LEFT: State Street in Portland. ABOVE RIGHT: Relaxing in the shade of Portland's tree-lined streets.

open Tuesday to Saturday, 10 AM to 4 PM, from June 1 to mid-October). The **Maine Historical Society**, a repository of information on four centuries of the city's life, is next door.

Also extraordinary is the **Victoria Mansion** ( (207) 772-4841, 109 Danforth Street (admission $4 with reductions for children; open Tuesday to Saturday, 10 AM to 4 PM, Sunday 1 to 4 PM, from June 1 to Labor Day, with shorter hours in September).

Both the **Eastern** and **Western Promenades** offer views of large and impressive

5 PM, Sunday, 1:30 to 5 PM, from June 15 to September 15).

### Museums and Entertainment

The art scene is also well represented in Portland. At the **Portland Museum of Art** ( (207) 775-6148, 7 Congress Square, a wing designed by I.M. Pei displays a fine selection of paintings by Maine artists Winslow Homer, Edward Hopper and Andrew Wyeth. Another fine museum is Westbrook College's **Payson Gallery**, with its collection of impressionist and New England art.

mansions. Nearly any downtown street has its share of colonial or Victorian masterpieces.

The city is a major educational center as well, with both the **University of Maine**'s southern campus and **Westbrook College** — the nation's first coeducational college, dating from 1831. The latter, located on Stevens Avenue, is a lovely tree-shaded campus of brick buildings.

Outside Portland, near the airport, the **Tate House**, built in 1755, offers a detailed view of life in the 18th century. It is located at 1270 Westbrook Street, off outer Congress Street at the airport turnoff (admission $4 with reductions for children; open Tuesday to Saturday, 11 AM to

The **Portland Civic Center** offers a variety of prominent sports events, conventions and concerts staged by the **Portland Concert Society**. The Visitors Bureau has schedules and ticket information.

### Where to Stay

EXPENSIVE

**Portland Regency** ( (207) 774-4200 TOLL-FREE (800) 727-3436 FAX (207) 775-2150, 20 Milk Street, is superbly situated in the Old Port with lovely rooms in a restored 19th-century armory. Outside the old town are the **Holiday Inn-Portland West** ( (207) 774-5601 TOLL-FREE (800) 465-4329 FAX (207) 774-2103, 81 Riverside Street; and the **Ramada Inn** ( (207) 774-5611 TOLL-

FREE (800) 272-6232 FAX (207) 761-1560, 1230 Congress Street. Near the Maine Mall is the **Sheraton Tara Hotel** ( (207) 775-6161 TOLL-FREE (800)325-3535 FAX (207) 775-0196, 363 Maine Mall Road.

MODERATE

**Susse Chalet** ( (207) 871-0611 FAX (207) 871-8234, 340 Park Avenue near the Maine Medical Center; and **Susse Chalet** ( (207) 774-6101 FAX (207) 772-8697, off the Maine Turnpike at Exit 8, Brighton Avenue, both can be reached TOLL-FREE (800) 524-2538.

**Eating Out**

**DiMillo's** ( (207) 772-2216, 121 Commercial Street (moderate), serves excellent food, including fresh lobster and other seafare, amid pleasant decor and interesting views aboard a large docked cruise ship. It is one of the very best restaurants in Portland; however, it does not accept reservations.

**Boone's** ( (207) 774-5725, 6 Custom House Wharf (moderate to expensive); and **Seamen's Club** ( (207) 772-7311, 375 Fore Street (moderate), also serve fresh seafood meals.

**The Village** ( (207) 772-5320, 112 Newbury Street (moderate) has fine seafood, New England and continental cuisine, with emphasis on the Italian.

**The Good Egg** ( (207) 773-0801, 705 Congress Street near Longfellow Square (inexpensive) has excellent downeast cooking, homemade hearty breakfasts including blueberry pancakes, real maple syrup and other delights.

**Amato's Sandwich Shops** pride themselves on their reputation as the originators in Portland of the Italian "submarine" sandwich with all the "fixin's". They can be found at 74 India Street, ( (207) 773-1682 and 1379 Washington Avenue, ( (207) 767-5916.

Another Portland tradition is **Three Dollar Dewey's** ( (207) 772-3310, 446 Fore Street (inexpensive), a fine drinking emporium with many excellent Maine-brewed and other beers on tap and famous chili, with lunch and dinner specialties.

Sebago Lake and Sebago Lake State Park provide natural opportunities for fishing, swimming and boating.

## AROUND PORTLAND

### CASCO BAY AND ISLANDS

A marvelous way to see Portland and its many beautiful neighboring islands is to take a cruise with **Casco Bay Lines** ( (207) 774-7871, on the corner of Commercial and Franklin Streets. Options include a six-hour trip to **Bailey's Island**, a circumnavigation of the bay stopping at all major islands including **Peaks, Great and Little Diamond** and **Chebeague**, on the Mail Boat and sunset and musical cruises. The islands are excellent for bicycling, strolling and getting away from the metropolis.

Portland is also the gateway to the Canadian province of Nova Scotia via the *MF Scotia Prince*, departing nearly every day from May through October, an 11hour overnight voyage. High season (June to September) rates are $55, half price for children, with an additional $98 to carry your car. A cabin for two people varies from $40 to $160 one way. In Portland call **Prince of Fundy Cruises** ( (207) 775-5616 TOLL-FREE (800) 482-0955 (within Maine) TOLL-FREE (800) 341-7540 (from outside Maine).

Finally, just south of the city is the historic **Portland Headlight**. This lighthouse dates from 1791, the first authorized by the United States, upon an order from George Washington.

### SEBAGO LAKE

About 12 miles (19 km) north of Portland is lovely Sebago Lake. The 14mile (23km) lake, second largest in Maine, lies in rolling hills of birch, maple, oak and pine and offers swimming, boating, fine salmon and trout fishing.

**Sebago Lake State Park**, at the north end of the lake, is a prime summer swimming area with wide sandy beaches, although it tends to be very crowded on weekends and holidays.

**Where to Stay**

**Migis Lodge** ( (207) 655-4524 FAX (207) 655-2054, off Route 302 (moderate to expensive), is on the lake shore in South Casco.

There are many motels and lakeside cabins for rent in the area.

## FREEPORT AND L.L. BEAN

North of Portland on U.S. 1 is **Freeport**, once a sleepy village, promoted to notoriety by L.L. Bean. For 365 days a year, 24 hours a day, L.L. Bean parking lots are crammed with the cars of shoppers who are confronted inside the building with an overwhelming array of fashions, camping gear,

hunting and fishing goods, wilderness and outdoor clothing and accessories.

It all started in 1912, when founder Leon L. Bean promoted a better boot for Maine hunters. His money-back guarantee earned him a lot of goodwill and soon the store began to grow, reaching almost legendary status by the 1980s. Now, the outlet's "wilderness clothes" are much sought-after by the yuppie generation. With success comes imitators. L.L. Bean has drawn a rabble of fashionable designer outlets and retailers to Freeport, transforming what was once a

lovely colonial town into a shopper's wasteland.

### General Information

The **Freeport Merchants Association** ( (207) 865-1212, has prepared a free brochure that list outlet stores, restaurants, bed and breakfasts, country inns and campgrounds. It is available in all the stores in Freeport. For a copy, call the Association or write to P.O. Box 452 DL, Freeport, ME 04032.

## AUGUSTA

Inland, just off Interstate 95, about 30 miles (48 km) north of Brunswick, is Augusta, the state capital. A small city of less than 25,000, Augusta is situated on the banks of the Kennebec River in the heart of the Kennebec Valley. Primarily a residential community with little industry or manufacturing, Augusta is largely dependent for its livelihood on the many offices of the state government.

Well worth a visit is the **Maine State House** designed by Charles Bullfinch, who was also the architect of the Boston State House. Located at State and Capitol Streets, the Maine State House was completed in 1832 and is topped by an impressive cupola. Across from it is the **State Museum** (admission free; open Monday to Saturday, 9 AM to 5 PM) which has dioramas that integrate live animals and plants and many interesting historical displays.

**Fort Weston**, on Bowman Street, is a restored 18th-century stockade. It is the site from which, in 1775, Benedict Arnold set out with his troops on the ill-fated march through the wilderness to attack Quebec.

From Augusta many scenic Kennebec Valley villages are an easy drive, including **Hallowell** and **Gardiner**. Further north is historic **Waterville**, home of prestigious Colby College.

---

### WHERE TO STAY AND EATING OUT

ABOVE: The placid bay of Freeport provides docking for many of the town's inhabitants.
OPPOSITE: Wild Mountain Man and his resume.

Lodging costs in the Augusta area are generally in the moderate to inexpensive category. One of the best is the **Best Western Senator Inn** ℓ/FAX (207) 622-5804, 284 Western Avenue (moderate). It is also recommended for fine cuisine and "Downeast" food. Also adequate is the **Days Inn** ℓ (207) 622-6371 FAX 621-0349, Western Avenue and Interstate 95 (moderate).

tend to find it too expensive and are apt to prefer baked beans, corn bread, fish and other traditional fare.

**General Information**

For more information, contact the **Down East Maine Association** ℓ (207) 667-3615, Box 662, Ellsworth, ME 04605.

## DOWNEAST MAINE

"Downeast" may be a confusing term to non-Mainers. It refers to the upper north-

### BRUNSWICK

Brunswick is an attractive town best known for its wide avenues, tall trees

ern portion of the Maine coastline. But confused or not, once you travel north to Brunswick, you are "down east." (The term was coined by sailors who were blown "down" the coast in their sailing ships by the prevailing winds of the region.)

For many travelers it is the lobster, taken from the frigid waters off downeast Maine's rocky coastline, that has become a drawing card.

Regional restaurants prepare this delicacy in every possible fashion, but perfectly steamed lobster dipped in melted butter is hard to beat.

Lobster, however, is far less consumed by Mainers than by tourists; natives of Maine

shading Federal mansions and the Bowdoin College campus.

**Maine Street** is the state's widest at 198 ft (60 m). Locals explain that the wide street was built to give marauding Indians fewer places in which to hide.

The **Federal Street** area contains some of Brunswick's most impressive and historic homes, including the 1806 **Stowe House**, where Harriet Beecher Stowe wrote *Uncle Tom's Cabin*. Nearby, the **Pejepscot Historical Society Museum**, housed in an 1858 sea captain's home, has a display of local seafaring artifacts.

The town's most important landmark, **Bowdoin College**, was established in 1794 and is considered one of the best private colleges in the United States. Acclaimed alumni include writer Hawthorne, poet Longfellow, President Franklin Pierce and polar explorer Admiral Robert Peary. The school's **Walker Museum of Art** has a fine collection of paintings, including a Gilbert Stuart portrait of Thomas Jefferson; and its **Peary-MacMillan Arctic Museum** houses artifacts from historic Arctic expeditions.

### Where to Stay and Eating Out

**Stowe House Motor Inn (** (207) 725-5543 FAX (207) 725-9813, at 63 Federal Street

(moderate to expensive), is an 1807 home converted into a comfortable inn.

For dining, **Bowdoin Steak House (** (207) 725-2314, 115 Maine Street (moderate) is excellent.

## BATH

In the last 200 years, more than 5,000 ships have been launched from Bath's historic shipyards at the mouth of the Kennebec River. Today, the **Bath Iron Works** continues the tradition. Since 1889, the company has made not only pleasure boats and freighters, but also destroyers, patrol boats and battleships; it remains one of the busiest boatyards in the nation for United States Navy ships. While national security interests keep the boatyard closed to visitors, boat launchings are still festive events in the town.

Bath's shipbuilding legacy comes alive at the **Maine Maritime Museum (** (207) 443-1316, Washington Street, just off U.S. 1. Several buildings exhibit models, gadgets and other seafaring artifacts; a working apprentice boatyard demonstrates various stages of boatbuilding.

## BOOTHBAY HARBOR

During the summer season, more than 60,000 visitors flock to Boothbay Harbor, a fishing town that lies at the end of a rugged peninsula between the Sheepscot and Damariscotta Rivers. Its streets are lined with small shops and seafood restaurants. At nearby wharves, fishermen unload catches of fish and lobster. In warm weather, dozens of ships and boats fill the harbor, creating an unmatched spectacle of masts, sails and colors. Special celebrations in the self-proclaimed "boating capital of New England" include **Windjammer Days** and **Friendship Sloop Days**, both held in July.

Charter boats such as the *Maranbo II* and *Balmy Days* offer **harbor cruises** that include stop-over island clambakes, seal watching, lobster hauling, scenic sunsets and more.

Back on dry land, the **Boothbay Railway Museum (** (207) 633-4727, on Route 27, a mile (just over a kilometer and a half) north of Boothbay Center, features a ride on a narrow gauge steam railway through a replica of an old New England village.

### Where to Stay

Some hotels in the Boothbay area are closed from late autumn to early spring. In the summer, demand is high so book early or call ahead.

The following provide good accommodations:

**Browns Wharf Inn (**/FAX (207) 633-5440, Atlantic Avenue (moderate to expensive); **Fisherman's Wharf Inn (** (207) 633-5090 FAX (207) 633-5092, 40 Commercial Street (moderate to expensive). **The Pines (** (207) 633-4555, Sunset Road, has a secluded setting a mile from town, ideal for families; and **Spruce Point Inn and Lodge (** (207) 633-4152, TOLL-FREE (800) 553-0289 FAX (207) 633-

Boothbay Harbor shops, crowded with trinkets, cater to summer's influx of tourists.

7138, Spruce Point on Route 27 (moderate to expensive), is a pleasant hotel.

**Eating Out**

For fresh lobster and local seafood, the **Brothers Wharf Restaurant** ( (207) 633-5440, Atlantic Avenue (moderate to expensive), is the best in town.

The **Lawnmeer Inn Dining Room** ( (207) 633-2544, Route 27, Southport (moderate), specializes in Downeast meals.

## PEMAQUID POINT

The **Pemaquid Point Light**, built in 1827, might be the most painted, photographed and sketched lighthouse in the country. It sits on a bluff at the tip of Pemaquid Point, a ledge jutting into the sea.

Photographers love to capture the lighthouse's reflection in the nearby shallow pools left by the retreating surf. A small fishermen's museum is located in the lightkeeper's house.

The Point, south of Damariscotta on Route 130, is also home to colonial **Pemaquid**. In 1965 amateur archaeologists uncovered here the foundations of 17th-century houses and other artifacts which included a human skeleton outfitted in armor, believed to be a Viking. These discoveries are displayed at the tiny archaeological museum.

## MONHEGAN ISLAND

Near **Port Clyde**, nine miles (15 km) off the coast, rise the dramatic cliffs of Monhegan Island, a ledge of rock and forest less than two miles (three kilometers) long and one mile (one and a half kilometers) wide. The ocean scenery and boulder-strewn coast are spectacular when viewed from atop **Lighthouse Hill**. Seventeen miles (27 km) of **hiking trails** traverse the 150-ft (46-m) cliffs. The open meadows are blanketed with wildflowers and **Cathedral Woods** display majestic pines and firs.

Leif Ericsson is said to have walked this island more than 1,000 years ago. English explorer John Cabot referred to it on his journeys. Its headlands were reputed to be hideaways for pirates, who plundered ships off the Maine coast.

The easiest way to get to Monhegan is aboard the **Laura B**, a converted trawler which ferries passengers from Port Clyde (at the bottom of Route 131). Along the way, the captain of the *Laura B* will stop to let his passengers watch dolphins and whales. From a distance, the island itself resembles a huge floating whale. No cars are permitted on the island.

## PENOBSCOT BAY

**Rockland**

Continuing north on U.S. 1, travelers pass through Rockland (north of Owls Head on the western edge of Penobscot Bay), a modern-day seaport that is the leading lobster distribution center in Maine. It is perhaps best noted for its **Maine Seafood Festival**, a three-day-long event held annually during the first weekend in August. Everything revolves around the catch — lobster boils, harvesting excursions and even displays of lobster trap building.

A windjammer fleet, offers week-long cruises along the coast and handsome schooners ply the waters on three- to six-day island cruises from May to October. The only original three-masted schooner in the famed Windjammer fleet, the *Victory Chimes* TOLL-FREE ( (800) 745-5651, sails out of Rockland Harbor. For other cruise options call **Maine Windjammer Association**, TOLL-FREE ( (800) 807-9463. **Owls Head Lighthouse**, four miles (six and a half kilometers) south of Rockland, sits atop a 100-ft (30-m) cliff and for lighthouse fans it is worth the short drive.

**Camden**

Camden, at the base of the Camden Hills with a long view of Penobscot Bay and its picturesque harbor, is a Maine classic. A yachting center and one of the loveliest towns in New England, it is also in its quiet, undemonstrative way an oasis of downeast wealth and glamour.

For a majestic panorama, head to **Camden Hills State Park** (two miles or just over three kilometers north of Camden on U.S. 1) where **Mt. Battie** at 800 ft (244 m) stands sentinel over the town; a stone viewing tower on top of the mount provides a spectacular view of the coast.

At the **William A. Farnsworth Library and Art Museum** ( (207) 596-6457, Elm Street, you can view works by master painters such as Jamie and N. C. Wyeth, Winslow Homer and Rockwell Kent. The collection is especially noted for its coastal landscape oils and watercolors by artists who lived and worked on the Maine Coast.

A publishing center and a renowned summer resort attracting Hollywood celebrities and lovers of the state's central coast, Camden is the publishing home of the quintessential Maine periodical, *Down East Magazine.*

**Sailing** is the primary attraction. In summer the harbor is filled with graceful yachts, sailboats with colorful canvases and every other kind of floating vessel imaginable.

Sightseeing cruises and sailing trips on old schooners depart from the **Town and Public landings** ( (207) 236-4404, offering tours of Penobscot Bay and views of Mounts Battie and Megunticook.

In winter, bitter winds laden with moisture sweep in from Penobscot Bay, which means plenty of snow for the **Camden Snow Bowl** ( (207) 236-3438, offering both downhill and cross-country runs. You can also ice skate on the vast **Lake Megunticook**. If you are in Camden during early spring, you can enter a local gambling pool, centered on the day that the ice will break on the lake.

At any time of year, you can browse through the expensive shops that cater to Camden's decidedly upscale clientele and to unwary tourists.

For those urban and suburban dwellers anxious to test themselves out-of-doors, there is the famous **Outward Bound School** on **Hurricane Island** ( (207) 594-5584 TOLL-FREE (800) 341-1744, P.O. Box 429, Rockland, ME 04841, in Penobscot Bay. This training school for wilderness survival skills claims that students should be prepared for the "most miserable, most wonderful days of your life." Two weeks of backpacking, rock climbing, or maneuvering tiny boats past bay islets is standard curriculum.

### Rockport

Located on U.S. 1 between Rockland and Camden, Rockport is a fishing town with carefully landscaped grounds along its waterfront.

### Where to Stay

The **Camden Harbor Inn** ( (207) 236-4200 FAX (207) 236-7036, 83 Bayview Street, Camden (expensive); and the old colonial **Whitehall Inn** ( (207) 236-3391, 61 High Street, Camden (expensive; open May to September), are the best accommodations in town.

**Samoset Resort** ( (207) 594-2511 TOLL-FREE (800) 341-1650, 220 Warrenton Street, Rockport (150 rooms and suites), a seaside haven built from the timbers of a Portland granary, overlooks Penobscot Bay.

### Eating Out

Dinners at the **Whitehall Inn** (expensive; see WHERE TO STAY, above) are unforgettably good; and **Belmont Restaurant** ( (207) 236-8053, 6 Belmont Avenue, in Belmont Inn, Camden (moderate to expensive), serves excellent French cuisine.

Dining at one of Bar Harbor's colonial mansions.

## MOUNT DESERT ISLAND

Even in Maine, a land of intense natural beauty, Mount Desert Island and its largest town, Bar Harbor, are unusual. The name "Mount Desert" is certainly a misnomer. Sixteenth-century French explorer Champlain noticed its treeless mountain peaks and gave the island its name. However, it is a place of dense forests, quiet bays and inlets and has the highest mountains on the Atlantic coast.

table that would descend from a retractable hole in a dining room ceiling — completely set for the meal, including food and drinks!)

In 1947, a great forest fire burning out of control for nearly a month destroyed much of the island, including most of the mansions. They were replaced by more modest motels and hotels and the island opened up to accommodate tourists of all means.

The few mansions that survived have been transformed into elegant inns, such as Cleftstone Manor in Bar Harbor, a 33-room house built in the late 19th century by the

### Bar Harbor

Bar Harbor is the gateway to the Acadia National Park and a good base for visiting the only national park in New England. It is a town which once rivaled Newport, Rhode Island, for its wealth and extravagance.

In the late 19th century the island attracted artists who came to paint its incredible beauty. They were soon followed by rich East Coast families, such as the Rockefellers and Vanderbilts, who built mansions and elegant summer "cottages," transforming Mount Desert and more specifically Bar Harbor, into their personal playground. (One mansion featured a massive banquet

Blairs of Washington, D.C. (the same family that built the Washington landmark house across the street from the White House where dignitaries stay when visiting the capital).

Today, almost three million people visit Mount Desert Island (pronounced "desSERT") annually. They come primarily to see Acadia National Park, for the yachting and for the sightseeing cruises that leave from Municipal Pier at West Street for the Bar's scenic bays and inlets.

### General Information

With year round outdoor recreation opportunities in the area, the **Bar Harbor Chamber of Commerce** ( (207) 288-5103, Bar

Harbor, ME 04609, has prepared several free brochures and maps for vacation planning.

## Where to Stay

There is no lack of good accommodations here, although they do tend to fill up during peak summer months: **Atlantic Eyrie Lodge** ( (207) 288-9786, Highbrook Road (expensive), open April to September; **Bar Harbor Inn** ( (207)288-3351 TOLL-FREE (800) 248-3351, Newport Drive, (expensive); **Bayview Inn** ( (207) 288-5861 FAX (208) 288-3173, 111 Eden Street (expensive); **Cleftstone Manor** ( (207) 288-4951 TOLL-FREE (800) 962-9762, 92 Eden Street (expensive); **The Ledgelawn Inn** (( (207) 288-4596 FAX (207) 288-9968, 66 Mount Desert Street (expensive); **Stratford House Inn** ( (207) 288-5189 TOLL-FREE (800) 550-5189, 45 Mount Desert Street (moderate to expensive); and **Wonder View Inn** ( (207) 288-3831 FAX (207) 288-2005, Eden Street (moderate to expensive).

## Eating Out

**Pier Restaurant** ( (207) 288-5033, West Street (expensive), is a seafood restaurant a cut above the others in town.

## ACADIA NATIONAL PARK

Acadia National Park (33,000 acres or over 13,350 hectares) occupies most of Mount Desert Island and is one of the nation's most distinctive national parks. Small by comparison with Yellowstone or Yosemite, it has nonetheless an equally grand diversity of landscapes, colors, geology, flora and fauna. It is the home of 250 different bird species and over 500 varieties of wildflowers. In ecological zones it varies from sandy and rock-strewn beaches to coastal coniferous forests to mountain rock and lichen. Miles of Park Service trails crisscross the island from beach to peak, through pine forest and meadows. Dominating Mount Desert Island above the bare granite of lesser peaks is majestic Cadillac Mountain, at 1,530 ft (466 m), the highest mountain on the East coast.

Much of the land comprising the park, established in 1916, was given by a wealthy Bostonian, George B. Dorr and by John D. Rockefeller, Jr., who also paid for construc-

tion of many of the park's roads. A good place to begin a tour of the park is at the **Visitor Center** ( (207) 288-3338 TOLL-FREE (800) 365-2267 (for camp reservations) FAX (207) 288-5507, Hull's Cove, Route 3. It is open June to November.

## Seeing the Park

Park rangers can help in planning tours, including **naturalist-led hiking treks** or self-guided 56mile (90km) auto tours, enhanced by prerecorded cassette tapes which describe points of interest, history and geography. **Guided bus tours** ( (207) 288-5218, depart from Main Street, Bar Harbor and motor through the park. You can also hop aboard a **sightseeing plane** of Air Acadia, Inc. (along Route 3). Another option is to

hike or bike the nearly 200 miles (322 km) of footpaths and trails. Unfortunately, Park Service budget cuts have closed many of the Park's trails, so check with Rangers for the latest details.

The 30-mile (48-km) **Loop Road** tour of the park offers memorable views. The Loop's Ocean Drive section is one-way for 11 miles (18 km) along the Park's eastern perimeter with the Champlain Mountain's pink cliffs ahead. A hike up the **Precipice Trail**, using ladders and handrails, is rewarded by a summit-top mountain vista. On the Loop's southeastern section, **Otter Cliffs** rise precipitously more than 100 ft (30 m) above the ocean.

The Park's most spectacular site is **Cadillac Mountain**, with its unparalleled views of breathtaking ocean views and rugged island interiors, including Mt. Katahdin, Maine's highest peak and the northern terminus of the Appalachian Trail. For those who prefer driving, there is an automobile road to the top.

## EASTERNMOST UNITED STATES

### LUBEC

Most visitors travel no further up the Maine coast than Bar Harbor. If you continue up U.S. 1, then Route 189 toward Lubec, you arrive at **Quoddy Head State Park** (just

Sunset at Acadia.

*Maine*

south of Lubec), the easternmost patch of land in the United States. It receives the warming rays of the sun earlier than any other point in the nation and likes to be called "Sunrise County." It also has the country's greatest variation in tides, with differences ranging to almost 30 ft (nine meters).

## CAMPOBELLO ISLAND

Lubec is also the gateway to Campobello Island, New Brunswick (Canada). Linked to the mainland by a bridge stretching over Lubec Narrows, Campobello is the location of President Franklin D. Roosevelt's family summer home, which still contains much of the original furniture. The **Roosevelt Cottage** is jointly maintained as an American-Canadian collaboration and is part of **Roosevelt Campobello International Park**, a 2,600-acre (1,050-hectare) nature preserve. At the **Visitor Center**, you can see films depicting Roosevelt's life, obtain maps for various walks and drives in the preserve and directions to the cottage. For further information contact **Campobello Island Chamber of Commerce (** (506) 752-2233.

## WAY UP NORTH

Most travelers never see the larger top half of the state of Maine, a vast wilderness of pines, balsam firs, spruce swamps and birch, pocketed with sandy-bottomed lakes and drained by countless trout-filled streams.

## BANGOR

En route to these northern wilds via the seacoast and Interstate 95, Bangor is the first stop and the last urban center south of Canada. This city on the west bank of the Penobscot River, once the "lumber capital of the world," was the brawling center of a young logging industry back in the days when Maine still had tall trees. In those boisterous times, lumbermen would come in after weeks in the woods, sailors would sail upriver after weeks or years at sea and a

wild and often bruising time was had in "Devil's Half-acre," the city's bar and brothel district.

Now, in more temperate times, the city maintains a giant statue of mythical lumberjack Paul Bunyan on Main Street opposite the Civic Center. Bangor still relies on the wood industries and pulp processing as the mainstay of its economy, although it is now diversifying rapidly. A Bangor Victorian mansion is the home of "horror" novelist Stephen King.

Above Bangor, the roads fan out northeast to **Moosehead Lake**, north to **Millinocket** and **Baxter State Park**, beyond to **Aroostook County** and west to Maine's major ski areas, **Sugarloaf** and **Saddleback Mountain** near Lake Mooselookmeguntic.

**Where to Stay**
**Holiday Inn (** (207) 947-8651 FAX (207) 942-2848, 500 Main Street (moderate to expensive); and **Ramada Inn Bangor (** (207) 947-6961 FAX (207) 945-9428, 357 Odlin Road (moderate to expensive).

## MOOSEHEAD LAKE

Moosehead, the largest lake in Maine, lies some 90 miles (145 km) beyond Bangor. It covers more than 120 sq miles (310 sq km), with a shoreline of 420 miles (677 km). Much of the shore is inaccessible except by canoe or float plane, both of which are available for hire or charter at **Greenville** at the south end of the lake. The region remains rich in wildlife, including, deer, bear and moose; the lake's waters abound with salmon and trout. For hunters and fishers, the region boasts an abundance of lodges and hunting camps.

The less adventurous can get a panoramic view of the north woods from the scenic chair lift at **Big Squaw Mountain Ski Area (** (207) 695-2272, about five miles (eight kilometers) northwest of town, off Route 15; the view in the fall is spectacular.

---

OPPOSITE: The craggy shores of Acadia National Park.

*Maine*                                                          *177*

## General Information

The **Moosehead Lake Region Chamber of Commerce** ( (207) 695-2702, P.O. Box 581D, Greenville ME 04441, claims no visitor will be disappointed with facilities in the area and provides free maps and brochures.

---

## ALLAGASH WILDERNESS WATERWAY

Not for the average traveler, this wonderland of lakes, rivers and forest is a remnant of the north woods as they used to be. Accessible by canoe, it is best known for the 98-mile (158-km) Allagash Wilderness Waterway, a superlative chain of lakes, some up to 20 miles long, linked by the thundering rapids and slick current of the Allagash River. Here the traveler goes at his or her own pace, paddling the long lakes and riding down the fast-moving river, camping at night with the song of loons and the Northern Lights for company. Hundreds of miles of rivers and lakes can be traveled this way, like the voyagers of old, portaging your canoe between watersheds. Many canoeists put in on the Penobscot River just east of Moosehead Lake, cross over into the Allagash drainage at Mud Pond and paddle all the way to the St. John River, or even down to Calais and the Atlantic.

Again, this is only for experienced canoeists and not to be done alone. Parts are difficult even for the most experienced; the fiercest stretches of Allagash Rapids and Falls are portaged even by the best canoeists.

An even longer voyage can be made down the **St. John River**. This tends to become shallow by late summer and is even wilder than the Allagash in early summer. Trips on the Penobscot and Kennebec Rivers can also begin here. Canoe tours are available for those not sufficiently experienced to try it on their own. For those who are, canoes can be rented at Greenville and then carried by car back to Greenville when you leave the River. Two cars are an advantage: one to leave at your destination and the other to bring back to Greenville or wherever you begin, or "put in," as Mainers say.

As with any trip to the North Woods, black flies are a major problem in May and June and mosquitoes in June through September.

For further information, contact the **Moosehead Lake Vacation and Sportsmen's Association** ( (207) 534-7300, Rockwood, ME 04478.

---

## BAXTER STATE PARK

Percival Proctor Baxter, Governor of the State of Maine, was an early environmentalist. Knowing that civilization would one day doom the wilderness, he dreamed to set aside great tracts of land in central Maine as a nature preserve in order that generations to come might enjoy the land as it once had been.

Unable during his two terms as governor to persuade the Legislature to support his intent, Baxter undertook nonetheless to make his dream a reality. A man of considerable wealth, he devoted his life to the purchase and consolidation of 200,000 acres (81,000 hectares) of wild land which he then deeded to Maine as a state park on condition that the land remain "forever wild."

The state park that bears this extraordinary man's name is located 18 miles (29 km) north of **Millinocket** and 75 miles (121 km) north of Bangor. It is an area of dense forests, pristine streams, lakes and mountains and shelters abundant wildlife. Apart from a few narrow unpaved roads, access to its interior is chiefly by the many hiking trails across it.

### Mt. Katahdin

Baxter State Park is dominated by Mt. Katahdin, at 5,267 ft (1,605 m) the highest peak in the state, second highest in New England and one of the highest points east of the Rockies. The Abenaki Indians' god Pamola lived on the summit, hurling thunderbolts and conjuring up fierce storms in times of anger. You can cross Pamola Peak by trekking the **Hunt Trail**, an 11-mile (18-km) path leading to the top of Katahdin. It is an all-day, very demanding hike; beware of high winds and treacherous weather.

Most of Baxter's wilderness attractions require hiking to reach them, but

the park's 162-mile (261-km) trail system
guarantees access. One of the park's loveliest sights, **Chimney Pond**, is accessible
by a three-hour moderate hike from the
Chimney Pond parking lot. A campground
at the pond (reservations usually necessary in summer) offers grand views of
Katahdin's sheer, massive granite walls
towering straight up from the far side of the
pond.

On **Sandy Stream Pond Trail**, moose
often linger at the pond; the **Cathedral
Trail** demands serious rock climbing tech-
niques to reach the Katahdin summit; and
the northern portion of the **Appalachian
Trail** leads to both **Big** and **Little Niagara
Falls**.

Baxter Peak is one of the four Katahdin
summits, the others being Hamlin, Pamola
and South. The last two are connected by
one of the park's most extraordinary geologic features: the **Knife Edge**, an extremely
narrow, serrated wall of granite 4,000 ft
(1,219 m) high.

**Park Information**
For more park information, contact the
Reservation Clerk, **Baxter State Park Head-
quarters** ( (207) 723-5140, 64 Balsam Drive,
Millinocket, ME 04462.

### AROOSTOOK COUNTY

Still farther northeast (from the Baxter Park
access road, hook up with Interstate 95,
go north to U.S. 1 and continue north) is
**Presque Isle**, the commercial center of
Aroostook County, Maine's prime potato-
growing country. Just south of town is the
**Aroostook Farm — Maine Agricultural
Station** ( (207) 768-8341, with 375 acres
(152 hectares) devoted to potato growing
research. By calling ahead, you can arrange
a free tour.

**Potato Blossom Festival**
**Fort Fairfield**, eight miles (13 km) north of
Presque Isle on U.S. 1, just a stone's throw
from New Brunswick, Canada, holds its
annual Potato Blossom Festival in July. This
is the height of the potato blossom season
and Aroostook is awash with pink, white
and lavender blooms.

### SKIING IN MAINE

Two of Maine's major ski areas, Sugarloaf
and Saddleback Mountains, lie 80 miles
(128 km) west of Bangor, near Lake
Mooselookmeguntic.

### SUGARLOAF MOUNTAIN

Sugarloaf is one of the highest peaks in the
east with a summit of 4,237 ft (1,291 m). With
an annual snowfall of 14 ft (just over four
meters), it seems, as skiers say, "to have been
created especially for skiing." A lattice-work
of 50 ski trails totaling more than 30 miles
(48 km), with a vertical drop of 2.637 ft
(804 m), offer something for every skier.

Novice runs drop off the hills into the
center of the ski village, which is filled with
shops, restaurants and watering holes.
Along the mountain's western edge, the intermediate Tote Road run stretches an incredible three miles (nearly five kilometers)
and the Narrow Gauge, a famous World
Cup run, offers the ultimate skiing experience for the expert.

**Sugarloaf USA** ( (207) 237-2000, is
Maine's premier ski resort and among the
most popular in New England. It is a blend
of old-time Yankee, deep-woods wilderness, refined hospitality and superb skiing
guaranteed to make any skier feel at home.

### SADDLEBACK MOUNTAIN

Saddleback Mountain ( (207) 864-5364, is
Maine's second-largest ski resort, about a
one-hour drive south from Sugarloaf. Its
summit rises to 4,116 ft (1,255 m), with a
vertical drop of 1,826 ft (557 m). There are
more than 40 runs, including Rustler's
Range and Bronco Buster — both steep,
mogul-filled slopes. Saddleback sponsors
an annual ski contest here in March —
anyone who can cruise Bronco from top to
bottom without falling or stopping earns
free ski passes.

# New Hampshire

IN HIS poem "New Hampshire," Robert Frost wrote:

*Just specimens is all New Hampshire has,*
*One each of everything as in a show case,*
*Which naturally she doesn't care to sell.*

Travelers to this state quickly discover what the poet meant. Despite its small size (180 miles or 290 km, from north to south and 100 miles or 160 km, at its widest point), New Hampshire has a variety of geographical and scenic features.

## SEVEN DISTINCTIVE AREAS

The **Hampshire seacoast** is less than an hour's drive from Boston and follows the Atlantic Ocean for 18 miles (29 km) between Maine on the north and Massachusetts to the south.

The **Merrimack River Valley** has a colorful history but is often now referred to as "The Golden Corridor" because of the many financial institutions and high-tech industrial firms which have located there.

The **Monadnock** region, on the other hand, is reminiscent of Currier and Ives prints: a rolling countryside of small villages, the land crisscrossed with hiking paths and ski trails.

Along the western border of the state, the **Hanover and Lake Sunapee** region is the home of venerable Dartmouth College and the locale, as well, of popular winter resorts that attract skiers from all over the East.

In the **Lakes region**, Lake Winnipesaukee draws many of the state's summer visitors. Its broad expanse, wooded shores and 274 islands offer a variety of summer pleasures for the vacationer.

The **White Mountains**, tallest in the East, tower over the Maine border and extend southwest through the center of the state. The scenery here is rugged and dramatic, with the mountains' granite faces staring down at the valley towns far below. It is a region of forests and whitewater streams that, with the changing colors of the autumn leaves, takes on a particular beauty.

The **Far North** area near the Canadian border is almost totally unspoiled and contains one of the most scenic waterways in the State.

These regions, each distinctive, can be found within the confines of a state that can be traversed from south to north in little more than three hours.

## GENERAL INFORMATION

The **New Hampshire Office of Travel and Tourism** ( (603) 271-2666 TOLL-FREE (800) 386-4664 FAX (603) 924-9441, 172 Pembroke Road, P.O. Box 1856, Concord, NH 03302-1856, has free maps and information which it will mail to you upon request.

## "LIVE FREE OR DIE"

Somewhat isolated geographically from the other New England states, New Hampshire was the only one of the thirteen colonies not invaded by British troops during the Revolution. The people of the state had then and still retain, a determined sense of independence and have embraced conservative democracy with a particular fervor. One of New Hampshire's major newspapers, *The Manchester Union-Leader*, has in its editorial policies and news coverage embraced one

ABOVE: A commemoration of emancipation from tyranny. OPPOSITE: A New Hampshire country hotel and its tranquil setting.

of the most ferocious right-wing stances in the nation. Although many New Hampshire residents would disagree, such attitudes seem to have filtered down into the daily attitudes of the population.

New Hampshire's strong-willed, independent attitudes manifest themselves in other substantive ways. New Hampshire has no state income tax or sales tax. State revenues are generated through so-called "sin" taxes on lottery tickets and liquor and cigarette sales. Most notably, the state's Bill of Rights recognizes "revolution" as a legiti-

mate means of carrying out the will of the people, hence the state motto: "Live Free or Die" found also on its license plates.

Political awareness and self-determination are also evident in New Hampshire's form of local government, the town meeting. Established early in New England's history, the town meeting was, in a sense, the genesis of American democracy, giving each member in the community an equal voice in local affairs. Town Meeting Day remains an important element of that process throughout New Hampshire. In the state government, more than 420 legislators constitute one of the largest legislative assemblies in the world.

## PRESIDENTIAL PRIMARIES

New Hampshire's presidential primary, the nation's first in a presidential election year, has become the forecast of success or failure

A New Hampshire license plate, the state's motto rooted in American Revolution history, and a friendly invitation.

for candidates for that office, a mega-media event that has somehow achieved "make or break" status on the political scene. Candidates who might otherwise have difficulty pointing out New Hampshire on a map of the United States descend quadrennially upon the state to offer political platitudes to this independent people.

But platitudes do not seem to work in New Hampshire. Its residents are straightforward, unpretentious Yankees who cut to the political quick of issues. They also have an uncanny record of reflecting the national mood. Around 75 percent of the time, New Hampshire Primary winners have become presidential candidates of both the Republican and Democratic parties.

## BACKGROUND

It is not surprising that New Hampshire residents relish their tough streak of independence. Ever since Englishman David Thomson and a small group of fishermen made the dangerous journey across the Atlantic, landing at Odiornes's Point (the town of Rye) in 1623 to establish a fledgling fishing industry, independence and self-reliance have been traits vital to survival.

Early settlers experienced severe hardships: the land had only a thin layer of topsoil, with a profusion of rocks and boulders (that's why you see so many old stone walls in the region); it was also heavily forested, requiring much hard labor to clear it before food crops could be planted; and winters were bitter, with sub-zero temperatures and mounds of snow.

Apart from subsistence farming, there were two basic means of support for the new settlement. Fishing fleets set sail from the state's only deep water port, now Portsmouth, to seek cod on the west Atlantic, while loggers cut down New Hampshire's 1,000-year-old pines for use as masts and shipbuilding timber.

By 1641, the struggling settlements had agreed to consolidate with the flourishing Massachusetts Bay Colony to the south. But the year-long King Philip's War (named for a Wampanoag Indian chief) caused much disruption when it began in 1675 and the

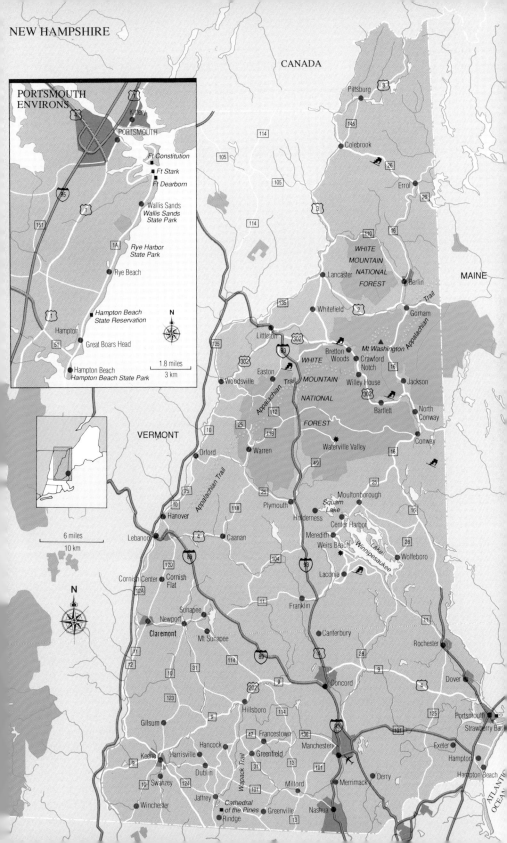

settlements did not recover until just before the American Revolution.

## THE NEW HAMPSHIRE SEACOAST

### INDEPENDENCE

New Hampshire received its "independence" from Massachusetts in 1679, when King Charles II declared it a royal province. John Wentworth, a successful merchant, was appointed to govern the colony in 1717; it prospered for a time, with Portsmouth taking on an English elegance that is still apparent today.

Later, the colony became caught up in the fervor for independence and Wentworth was forced to leave Portsmouth in 1775. One year later, on January 5, 1776, New Hampshire drew up its own constitution and declared its independence from England six months before the Declaration of Independence of July 4, 1776.

### ECONOMIC DIVERSIFICATION

In the 1800s, New Hampshire changed gradually from a logging, fishing and farming economy into a manufacturing center for cotton and wool.

Manufacturing continued to grow well into the 20th century, attracting thousands of French Canadians from poor farms across the border. Many factories, including the Amoskeag Manufacturing Company, then one of the largest mills in the country, drew immigrant workers from around the world who toiled long, grueling hours. The mills are said to have produced more than one mile (1.6 km) of cloth every working minute. However, the Great Depression, labor strikes and the changing economy combined to deal New Hampshire's economy a serious blow.

Today, a revitalized (and diversified) manufacturing industry combines with tourism, a relaxed lifestyle and a favorable tax climate to make New Hampshire an attractive place in which to live and work.

### PORTSMOUTH

New Hampshire's only seaport, Portsmouth was once the capital of the state and home port to a long-lived dynasty of merchant seamen. Great riches were amassed from their trade, which then were used to build handsome houses befitting their status, bringing to the settlement a veneer of refinement and culture.

The city has since experienced wildly changing fortunes and its "Golden Age" has long passed.

**General Information**

Travelers can still sample a bit of Portsmouth's colonial past by following the **Portsmouth Trail** which tours six of the city's finest 17th- and 18th-century homes. Tour guides (wearing period costumes) relate the history of the houses and tell anecdotes of their original owners. The city's **Historic Associates (** (603) 436-1118, offers combination tickets (sold at any of the houses) and tour maps. For more information contact the **Portsmouth Chamber of Commerce (** (603) 436-1118 FAX (603) 436-

ABOVE Portsmouth's historic churches and expansive mansions OPPOSITE were built when the town was a flourishing seaport during the eighteenth century.

5118, at 500 Market Street, Portsmouth, NH 03802, or the **Seacoast Council on Tourism** ( (603) 436-7678, TOLL-FREE (800) 221-5623, Box 4669, Portsmouth, NH 03801, which actively promotes tourism to the coast.

**Portsmouth Trail**

On Market Street is the **Moffatt-Ladd House**, built in 1763 by Captain John Moffatt as a wedding gift for his son, Samuel and noted for its elegant furnishings and 18th-century architectural style. Visitors are

Joseph Blackburn, including one of Polly Warner.

No less than George Washington called the **Governor John Langdon House**, on Pleasant Street, "the handsomest house in Portsmouth." Built in 1784 for a prominent Revolutionary War political leader who was twice governor of New Hampshire and first president *pro tempore* of the United States Senate, this elegant Georgian mansion remains one of the finest 18th-century homes in New England. The exterior proportions are enormous, while the gracious interiors

also welcome in the formal gardens, where peonies blossom in colorful splendor each June.

The **Warner House** (next to the Town Hall on Daniel Street), built in 1715 by another wealthy sea captain, was occupied by the old salt's descendants as late as 1930. It has been called "one of the finest urban brick residences of the first quarter of the 18th century" in America today. It is one of New England's most beautiful Georgian houses, with several historic murals hanging in their original positions along the staircase. Especially noteworthy is the lightning rod on the west wall, said to have been installed by Benjamin Franklin in 1762. There are also several portraits by

contain some of the finest hand carving in the city. The gardens have been restored to their original state, with rose and grape arbors, perennial garden beds and a handsome gazebo. Washington, Lafayette and other statesmen of the time were entertained here.

Other houses on the tour include the 1758 residence of famed American naval leader **John Paul Jones** (who, when beckoned by the British to surrender during one high-seas battle, uttered the renowned line, "We have not yet begun to fight"); the grand 1807 Federal mansion called the **Rundlet-May House**; and the **Wentworth Gardner House**, whose grand woodcarvings are said to have kept a master craftsman busy for more than a year.

**Strawberry Banke**

Named for the wild strawberries that grew here in abundance when early settlers arrived, Strawberry Banke ( (603) 433-1100, Hancock and Marcy streets (open daily May to October), is a 10-acre (four-hectare) outdoor museum preserving the historic waterfront neighborhood that was the site of the original Portsmouth settlement. About 35 **historic buildings**, dating from 1695 to 1940, are being restored. Ten are completed and open to the public (including the 1780 Captain John Wheelwright House) and are

furnished with period antiques. The restoration is so well done it appears as though people still live and work here — only momentarily absent. Also recently restored is the 1766 William Pitt Tavern, a former stagecoach stop and hotbed of Revolutionary politics. George Washington often came here when visiting local state officials.

Not only can you stroll among the historic structures (in many cases watching actual restoration taking place), but you can also participate in a number of interesting activities. Several of the historic homes have been transformed into workshops, where

Strawberry Banke ABOVE , an outdoor museum and restored neighborhood, preserves Portsmouth's past. OPPOSITE: Portsmouth's harbor.

programs geared to the family offer educational seminars on colonial crafts (including hands-on demonstrations), lectures and special events such as the December candlelight tour through the "village." Other houses contain craftshops of working artisans who display their handiwork. Even historic landscapes have been recreated, including 18th-century herb and vegetable gardens. Set your own pace; all tours are self-guided.

**Old Harbor**

The Portsmouth area has several other historical attractions, including **Fort Constitution**, the 1632 site of a British fort captured by the Sons of Liberty in 1774 (the gunpowder seized here was used in the battle of Bunker Hill); **Fort Stark State Historic Site**, the remains of a seacoast defense system dating from 1746; and the **Old Harbour Area**, located on the waterfront, now filled with crafts, antique shops and restaurants.

Both *Viking* and *Heritage* Portsmouth Harbor cruises offer narrated boat tours down the **Piscataqua River** — where 90 sawmills once cut the virgin pine trees used for masts in the Royal Navy — and out into the Atlantic, bound for the historic **Isles of Shoals**. Contact **Star Island Cruises** ( (603) 431-4620, P.O. Box 311, Portsmouth, NH 03810; and **Portsmouth Harbor Cruises** ( (603) 436-8084, 64 Ceres Street.

**Where to Stay**

EXPENSIVE

**Sise Inn** ( (603) 433-1200 TOLL-FREE (800) 267-0525, 40 Court Street, in the heart of the historic district, is a Queen Anne-style town house reminiscent of 19th-century Portsmouth. There are also several fine hotels located at nearby Hampton Beach (see page 189).

MODERATE

There is a wide variety in this category of accommodations. In the summer, they are frequently booked; reservations are advisable.

Some recommendations are: **Anchorage Inns** (/FAX (603) 431-8111, 417 Woodbury Avenue (Portsmouth Traffic Circle), Portsmouth; **Holiday Inn** ( (603) 431-8000

FAX (603) 431-2065, Interstate 95 and Woodbury Avenue; **Howard Johnson Hotel** (/FAX (603) 436-7600 (Interstate 95, exit 5, Portsmouth; **Port Motor Inn** (/FAX (603) 436-4378, 505 U.S. Highway 1 Bypass; and **Sheraton Hotel and Conference Center** ( (603) 431-2300 FAX (603) 433-5649, Interstate 95, exit 7, 256 Market Street.

## Eating Out

EXPENSIVE

**Porto Bello** ( (603) 431-2989, 67 Bow Street, Southern Italian cooking with a view of

## HAMPTON BEACH

Hampton Beach is located about eight miles (13 km) south of Portsmouth. This long, sandy beach provides excellent swimming, with arcades and rides for children and the **Hampton Beach Casino** which features top-name entertainment.

## Where to Stay

EXPENSIVE

The following inns with access to the ocean

the harbor makes this second-story dining room a fine choice.

The **Library at the Rockingham House** ( (603)431-5202, 401 State Street, a downtown landmark, serves continental cuisine in a literary setting.

On the waterfront in Portsmouth are two fine restaurants: **The Oar House** ( (603) 436-4025, 55 Ceres Street; and **Pier II** ( (603) 426-0669, next to Memorial Bridge.

MODERATE

Located in the Old Harbour area next to the tugboat docks in Portsmouth, **The Dolphin Striker** ( (603) 431-5222, 15 Bow Street, Portsmouth, has a pleasant ambiance and excellent food.

are recommended: **Hampton Beach Regal Inn** ( (603) 926-7758 TOLL-FREE (800) 445-6782, 162 Ashworth Avenue (closed late autumn to early spring); and **Kentville on the Ocean** ( (603) 926-3950 TOLL-FREE (800) 303-9933, 315 Ocean Boulevard (spring and autumn rates are moderate; closed late autumn to early spring).

MODERATE

Some recommendations are: **Ashworth by the Sea** ( (603) 926-6762 FAX (603) 926-2002, 295 Ocean Boulevard; **Best Western Seabrook Inn** ( (603) 474-3078, Route 107 and Stard Road; **Hampton House** ( (603) 926-1033 TOLL-FREE (800) 458-7058 FAX (603) 926-3473, 333 Ocean Boulevard; and

**Lamie's Inn and Tavern** ( (603) 926-0330 TOLL-FREE (800) 805-5050 FAX (603) 929-0017, 490 Lafayette Road.

**Eating Out**
**Lamie's Tavern** ( (603) 926-0330, specializes in New England dishes, while **Lincoln House** ( (603) 926-6069, 95 Ocean Boulevard, has spectacular ocean views and excellent value.

Seafood lovers should head for **Galley Hatch** ( (603) 926-6152, Route 1, the best in the area.

## THE MERRIMACK RIVER VALLEY

More than half of New Hampshire's population resides in the Merrimack Valley, which offers the traveler superb colonial architecture, clear streams and forests. It is also home to many of New Hampshire's high-tech industries.

### NASHUA

Just a short distance from either Portsmouth or Boston is Nashua, home of the University of New Hampshire. There are many hotels and restaurants in the area, including **Sheraton Tara Hotel** ( (603 888-9970 TOLL-FREE (800) 325-3535 FAX (603) 888-4112, Route 3, exit 1, 335 Tara Boulevard (expensive); **Comfort Inn** ( (603) 883-7700 TOLL-FREE (800) 228-5150 FAX (603) 595-2107, 10 St. Laurent Street, Route 3, exit 7E,

(moderate); and **Howard Johnson Lodge** (/FAX (603) 889-0173, 170 Main Dunstable Road, Everett Turnpike, exit 5E (moderate).

**Green Ridge Turkey Farm Restaurant** ( (603) 888-7020, Daniel Webster Highway, serves traditional Thanksgiving roast turkey dinners year-round for a moderate price.

**Mystery Hill**
Of interest in this area is Mystery Hill, which unashamedly compares itself to the massive stone structures found at England's Stonehenge. Located east of Nashua on Route 111, less than three miles (five kilometers) east of Interstate 93, it is proclaimed to be one of the oldest building sites in North America. Radiocarbon testing pinpoints the origin of these eerie stone buildings, walls, chambers and carvings at 4,000 years ago; numerous ancient hieroglyphics have been found, but few have been deciphered.

The question of who built these structures has sparked heated debate. Some argue for North American Indians and others for ancient seafarers such as the Phoenicians, or the Celts from the Iberian Peninsula. Whoever was responsible for constructing this awesome complex, they were masters of astronomy. Scientists have determined that the rings of carefully arranged stones pinpoint solstices, equinoxes and other astronomical phenomena. Trails to the astronomical stones, viewing ramp and self-guiding tour map (allow at least one hour) are available at the site headquarters, ( (603) 883-8300. Guided tours are offered in summer and on weekends during spring and fall.

### MANCHESTER

Manchester, 16 miles (26 km) north of Nashua on the Everett Turnpike, is worth the drive if only for the **Currier Gallery of Art** ( (603) 669-6144, 192 Orange Street (open daily except Mondays and holidays). It is a fine small art museum with a choice collection of American and European paintings.

The city — one of the state's textile centers — has attracted large numbers of

ABOVE: New Hampshire's Mystery Hill is one of the oldest building sites in North America. OPPOSITE: The Canterbury Shaker Village.

French Canadians, who crossed the border to work in the mills here. A large proportion of the city's population is bilingual.

Between Nashua and Manchester on the turnpike is the **Budweiser Brewery** in **Merrimack**, with its famous Clydesdale horses. Tours can be arranged by calling ( (603) 595-1202.

**Where to Stay**
With the exception of **Howard Johnson Hotel** ( (603) 668-2600 TOLL-FREE (800) 654-2000 FAX (603) 668-2600, Interstate 293, exit 4, Queen City Avenue (moderate), accommodations in this area are expensive: **Holiday Inn Center of New Hampshire** ( (603) 625-1000 TOLL-FREE (800) 465-4329 FAX (603) 625-4595, 700 Elm Street; and the **Four Points by Sheraton** ( (603) 668-6110 TOLL-FREE (800) 325-3535 FAX (603) 668-0408, Interstate 293, exit 1.

**Eating Out**
The most elegant restaurant in the city is the **Renaissance** ( (603) 669-8130, 1087 Elm Street (moderate to expensive), serving Greek and Italian specialties.

## CONCORD

Concord (40 miles or 65 km west of Portsmouth along U.S. 4), in the center of the valley region, is the state capital. It is a rather sleepy town, founded as a trading post in 1659, then later granted a royal charter in 1725, when its name was changed from the Plantation of Pennacook. Today, its most notable landmark is the golden dome of the **State Capitol** ( (603) 271-2154, on Main Street, with its hall of historic New Hampshire battle flags and statues of political favorite sons such as Daniel Webster and former president Franklin Pierce.

The **New Hampshire Historical Society** has an interesting collection of Concord Coaches dating from 1827. Many of the wagons that helped to open the American West were manufactured here.

South and west of Concord are the villages of **Hopkinton**, with its placid streets and **Henniker**, with its double-arched stone bridge — both are pleasant towns with handsome colonial homes.

**Where to Stay**
**Holiday Inn** ( (603) 224-9534 TOLL-FREE (800) 465-4329 FAX (603) 224-8266, 172 Main Street, Interstate 93, exit 14 (moderate to expensive); **Days Inn** ( (603) 224-2511 TOLL-FREE (800) 329-7466 FAX (603) 224-6032, 406 Main Street, Interstate 93, exit 12S (moderate); and **Comfort Inn** ( (603) 226-4100 TOLL-FREE (800) 228-5150 FAX (603) 228-2106, 71 Hall Street, Interstate 93, Exit 13 (moderate).

**Eating Out**
**Angelina's Restaurante** ( (603) 228-3313,

11 Depot Street (moderate), serves homemade breads and generous Italian entrées. **Hermanos Cocina Mexicana** ( (603) 224-5669, 11 Hills Avenue (moderate), serves appetizingly fresh Mexican fare. For those with a sweet tooth, there is **Thursday's Restaurant** ( (603) 224-2626, 6 Pleasant Street (moderate), where the meals are homestyle and the desserts excellent.

## CANTERBURY SHAKER VILLAGE

Located about 17 miles (27 km) north of Concord off Interstate 93, Canterbury Shaker Village ( (603) 783-9511 (open May to October, Tuesday through Saturday) was once home to 300 farmers and craftspeople who led a simple life governed by their belief in God, a communal lifestyle and a "Hands to Work and Hearts to God" philosophy.

The Shakers, a religious sect founded in 18th-century England, shunned contact with the outside world and demanded celibacy of their followers. As a result, they have all but disappeared from the modern American scene, but settlements such as Canterbury convey the eloquent simplicity of their world — a world that has become much-admired for ingenious solutions to complicated problems.

The Canterbury Shakers' two surviving members offer walking tours of the 22 historic Shaker buildings which date back to the 1780s. Tours last about 90 minutes. A museum displays Shaker crafts (famed for woodworking, basketmaking and sewing) and offers workshops. The Creamery Restaurant offers Shaker food specialties.

## THE VALLEY'S HISTORIC HOMES

**Daniel Webster's birthplace** is off Route 127, just south of Franklin. The small frame house where this noted political leader was born in 1782 is filled with family artifacts. Other historic Merrimack Valley homes open to tourists include **President Franklin Pierce's manse** in Concord, the **Pierce Homestead** in Hillsboro and poet **Robert Frost**'s 1880s white-clapboard **farmhouse** in Derry.

## THE MONADNOCK

This small region in southwest New Hampshire shares its border with Massachusetts to the south and the Connecticut River with Vermont to the west. Many of New Hampshire's 54 covered bridges can be found here and 18th-century villages are showcased against the backdrop of majestic Mount Monadnock. When it snows, these towns literally glow with the "Currier & Ives" imaginary romantic quality of colonial America.

### KEENE

The region's finest museum is located in Keene, which also has a 172-ft- (52-m)-wide,

oak tree-lined Main Street, believed to be the widest paved street in the world. **Colony House Museum** ( (603) 357-0889, 104 West Street, NH 03431, the 1819 home of Keene's first mayor, contains a fine collection of 19th-century Stoddard glass and Staffordshire pewter.

### Where to Stay

**The Coach & Four Motor Inn** (/FAX (603) 357-3705, Route 12 (moderate), is a well-run small motel, providing good service and clean rooms, as do the larger **Best Western**

**Sovereign** ( (603) 357-3038, TOLL-FREE (800) 528-1234 FAX (603) 357-4776, 401 Winchester Street (moderate to expensive); and the very comfortable four-room **Carriage Barn Guest House** ( (603) 357-3812, 358 Main Street, across from Keene State College (moderate).

### Eating Out

**Millside Café** ( (603) 357-4353, at Colony Mill Marketplace on West Street, Keene (moderate), is set in the warehouse of a restored woolen mill and serves continental cuisine.

ABOVE: Robert Frost's mailbox and his home. OPPOSITE: Dartmouth College, at Hanover.

For something more American, the **176 Main** ( TOLL-FREE (800) 865-3895, at the same address (moderate), serves gourmet cuisine with outdoor patio dining in good weather.

## AROUND KEENE

### Other Attractions

Other attractions in the region include **Francestown**, with its old colonial houses dating back to the town's 1772 beginnings; **Gilsum**, which has a stone arch bridge and offers maps of 56 local abandoned mines;

**Jaffrey Center's Old Town Burying Yard**, where novelist Willa Cather is buried; and **Hancock**, with its Revolutionary War graves in Pine Ridge Cemetery and a splendid covered bridge spanning the Contoocook River. In **Milford**, an 1802 Paul Revere bell in the town hall tower tolls every hour. **Dublin** is a resort colony that once attracted Mark Twain and other literary figures. It is the highest town in New England, at 1,439 ft (439 m) above sea level. **Swanzey** has four covered bridges and its theater continues to perform the 100-year-old play *Old Homestead* annually. Nearby **Winchester** has two covered bridges. And **Harrisville** has been called the "most paintable, photogenic mill town in the United States."

On Route 119 in **Rindge**, you will find the **Cathedral of the Pines**; thousands of visitors annually visit this pine forest memorial dedicated to a son lost in World War II.

### Hiking and Biking

The area provides some of New Hampshire's best hiking country, with trails through a variety of picturesque landscapes. The best is the **Wapack Trail**, which offers spectacular vistas along a 21-mile (34-km) marked path (look for yellow paint on the trees) following a high ridge from Mount Watatic in Massachusetts to the 2,280-ft (695-m) North Pack Monadnock near Greenfield.

Using Keene as a hub, the Monadnock has several scenic bicycle trails on roads with little or no traffic. One of the best follows the **Ashuelot River** and crosses many covered bridges. The **Keene Chamber of Commerce** ( (603) 352-1301, $^C/_o$ NEG, 8 Central Square, Keene, NH 03431, has regional biking trail maps.

*A warning to cyclists:* American drivers tend to be far less courteous to cyclers than European drivers, so be cautious, wear a helmet and avoid high-traffic areas.

### Monadnock State Park

Monadnock State Park (off Route 124, west of Jaffrey, then follow the signs) offers several trails leading to the summit of **Mount Monadnock**, one of the most-climbed mountains in the world. It is about a three- to four-hour round trip to the 3,165-ft (965-m) summit, but you will be rewarded by a commanding vista of the surrounding region. Among those who have climbed Monadnock are Emerson and Thoreau. The summit is quite barren, the trees and bush having been burned off in the 1820s by farmers. **New Hampshire Division of Parks and Recreation** ( (603) 271-3254, Box 856, Concord, NH 03301, has maps of the parks.

## HANOVER AND LAKE SUNAPEE

This is a region of lakes, picturesque villages and gentle mountains that line the Connecticut River.

## HANOVER

**Dartmouth College**, founded in 1769, dominates every phase of life in Hanover and is the cultural anchor for the entire region. Originally founded by Reverend Eleazar Wheelock "for the instruction of the Youth of Indian tribes," it now attracts well-heeled "youths" of every persuasion from all over the country.

Its handsome campus retains much colonial flavor, with stately Federal and Georgian buildings and an attractive village green. **Dartmouth Row**, located on the east side of the Green, has several white brick buildings dating from 1784 and the **Baker Memorial Library** displays frescoes by the famed Mexican artist Orozco. Guided campus tours are offered during summer only.

In town, the **Webster Cottage** on North Main Street was the residence of Daniel Webster during his final year at Dartmouth. **Lebanon Street** offers handiwork by the League of New Hampshire craftsmen. Hanover's streets are lined with bookstores, restaurants and shops.

### Where to Stay
The best accommodations in Hanover are at the 200-year-old **Hanover Inn** ( (603) 643-4300 TOLL-FREE (800) 443-7024 FAX (603) 646-3744, at the corner of Main and Wheelock Streets (expensive).

### Eating Out
There are many good restaurants in the Hanover area. Recommended are **Murphy's on the Green** ( (603) 643-4075, 11 South Main Street (moderate to expensive) and **Jesse's** ( (603) 643-4111, Route 120 (expensive).

### General Information
For maps of the area and information contact the **Hanover Chamber of Commerce** ( (603) 643-3115, P.O. Box 5105, Hanover, NH 03755.

## AROUND HANOVER

### Orford
The hamlet of Orford, about 17 miles (27 km) north of Hanover, has an interesting area called "The Ridge," with a half-dozen stately homes dating from the 1770s to the 1830s.

### Cornish
South of Hanover is the **Saint-Gaudens National Historic Site** ( (603) 675-2175, located on Route 12A north of the Cornish-Windsor covered bridge. Here are the summer home, gardens and studio of American classical sculptor Augustus Saint-Gaudens and many examples of his work.

The town of **Cornish** was home to the famed **Cornish Colony** for artists and

writers; set up in 1885, it "officially" lasted for 50 years. Reclusive J.D. Salinger, author of *The Catcher in the Rye*, still lives in this town. Cornish also has the longest remaining **covered bridge** in the United States. Built in 1866, it stretches 466 ft (142 m) over the Connecticut River to Vermont.

Still farther south is the **Fort at N° Four**; ( (603) 826-7751, a reconstruction of an original 1746 fortified settlement which defended the region during the French and Indian Wars. Its buildings appear much as they did in the 18th century. Colonial craft demonstrations (candlemaking, weaving, etc.) and reenactments of a soldier's life in the colonial militia are part of the "living history" show.

**Mount Sunapee State Park**, outside **Newbury** (on Route 103), offers gondola rides up to the mountain's 2,700ft (823m) summit, with panoramic views of Lake

OPPOSITE and ABOVE: New Hampshire's larger lakes are well-used by pleasure boaters and fishermen in summer.

Sunapee, known for its fine salmon and lake trout fishing, the Green Mountains in the distance to the west and the White Mountains to the northeast.

## THE LAKES REGION

It is the 600 lakes and ponds in east-central New Hampshire that gives the Lakes Region its name. With their romantic Indian names, deep fish-filled waters and good harbors, the lakes invite a leisurely, unhurried pace of life. **Lakes Region Association** ( (603) 569-1117, Box 300, Wolfeboro, NH 03894, has brochures about recreation in the area. For information, contact the **Greater Laconia/Weirs Beach Chamber of Commerce** ( (603) 524-5531 TOLL-FREE (800) 531-2347, 11 Veteran's Square, Laconia, NH 03246.

### WOLFEBORO

Wolfeboro, on Route 28 between Lake Winnipesaukee and Lake Wentworth, is the heart of the lake region, although the largest

town of the region is Laconia, on Route 3 to the southwest of Lake Winnipesaukee.

Wolfeboro claims to be the country's oldest summer resort. Governor John Wentworth built a summer mansion here on **Lake Wentworth** in 1771. The **Wolfeboro Railroad** offers 24mile (39km) two-hour round-trip tours, with antique steam engines, along Lake Winnipesaukee's southeastern shore. These trips are especially rewarding during the fall foliage season.

### LAKE WINNIPESAUKEE

*Winnipesaukee* is an Indian word meaning "smile of the great spirit." Lake Winnipesaukee covers 72 sq miles (186 sq km), with 283 miles (456 km) of shoreline and coves, 274 habitable islands and eight towns on its shores.

Perhaps the most active lakeside town is the tacky, overbuilt **Weirs Beach**, on the western shore, offering a taste of Atlantic City in New Hampshire. In addition to visual pollution, it also offers the jaded traveler an assortment of band concerts, fireworks, boat races, seaplane rides, water skiing shows, arcades, miniature golf links, slot cars, a surfcoaster water park and a 325-ft (99-m) water slide where

Faces of New Hampshire.

revelers plummet down flumes to the pool below.

This is, however, great boating country, whether you own, charter, rent or take public cruises. The largest boat on the lake is the 230-ft (70-m) *Mount Washington*, which offers narrated 50-mile (81-km) **cruises** departing from **Weirs Beach** and ending at nearby Wolfeboro. There are also breakfast, lunch, dinner and moonlight cruises and several so-called theme trips — Fabulous Fifties, Hawaiian Luau, Buccaneers Ball and Irish Fling. Another Weirs Beach option is a cruise on the *SS Mailboat* which makes two-hour mail trips to islands on the western side of the lake. For information and booking for the above cruises call **Mount Washington Cruises** ( (603) 366-5531.

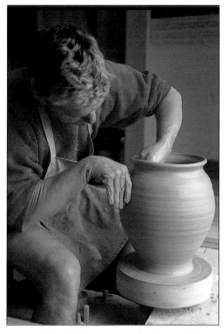

Excellent lake trout and salmon fishing can also be found here, but you will need a boat to escape the crowded and noisy docks.

Another way to get away from the crush of summer visitors is by biking around Lake Winnipesaukee along a series of back roads and uncrowded highways.

**Summer Music**
Professional musicians have gathered at Center Harbor on the northern end of Lake

Winnipesaukee for six weeks each summer since 1952 to perform orchestral concerts, chamber music and original commissioned pieces at the **New Hampshire Music Festival** ( (603) 253-4331, c/o NEG, P.O. Box 147, Center Harbor, NH 03226.

## SQUAM LAKE

Squam Lake, just northwest of Winnipesaukee — the filming location for the Henry and Jane Fonda drama *On Golden Pond* — is the second largest lake in the state. The Manor in **Holderness** northeast shore of Squam Lake ( (603) 968-3348 TOLL-FREE (800) 545-2141 FAX (603) 968-2116, offers two-hour cruises that take you to *On Golden Pond* film locations and provide commentary on the lake's loon population. Hiking trails in the area lead to the summit of the Squam Mountain.

## OTHER LAKES REGION ATTRACTIONS

**Moultonborough**
Just north of Center Harbor on Route 25 is Moultonborough, known for the **Castle in the Clouds**, a 6,000-acre (2,430-hectare) mountaintop country estate built in 1910 by eccentric millionaire Thomas Gustav

Plant at a cost oi $7 million. It provides a 75-mile (121-km) panorama of Lake Winnipesaukee.

**Plymouth**
North of Laconia just off Interstate 93 in Plymouth are the **Polar Caves**, glacial caverns that are said to have been a last refuge for the Pemigewasset Indians when they were attacked by settlers in colonial times.

Some moderately-priced places in Wolfeboro are: **Bayside Inn** ( (603) 875-5005 FAX (603) 875-0013, Route 11D, Winnipesaukee, where the price includes continental breakfast; **Lakeview Inn & Motor Lodge** ( (603) 569-1335 FAX (603) 569-9246, Route 109, Exit 17; and **Wolfeboro Inn** ( (603) 569-3016 TOLL-FREE (800) 451-2389 FAX (603) 569-5375, 90 North Main Street, 43 rooms.

In **Laconia**, the largest town in the area, there are several good establishments: **The Anchorage on Lake Winnisquam** ( (603) 524-3248 FAX (603) 528-1028, RFD#1, Laconia (moderate); **Christmas Island Resort Motel** ( (603) 366-4378 TOLL-FREE (800) 832-0631 FAX (603) 366-2457, 630 Wiers Boulevard, Route 3, Laconia (moderate); **The Margate on Winnipesaukee** ( (603) 524-5210 TOLL-FREE (800) 627-4283 FAX (603) 528-4485, Route 3, Laconia (expensive); and **Shalimar Resort Motel and Spa** (/FAX (603) 524-1984 TOLL-FREE (800) 742-5462, Route 3, Laconia (expensive).

**Wolfeboro Inn** ( (603) 569-3016, Route 109 (expensive) serves excellent New England dinners, as does **Blackstone's at the Margate** ( (603) 524-5210, 76 Lake Street (moderate to expensive) in nearby Laconia. **Hickory Stick Farm** ( (603) 524-3333, southeast of Laconia, is a three-star restaurant renowned for its roast duckling.

**WHITE MOUNTAINS**

No visitor to New Hampshire should miss its breathtaking White Mountains. Long a

wild, forbidding region almost inaccessible from the rest of the state, these grand mountains are now one of New England's prime natural vacation areas, with year-round attractions.

WHITE MOUNTAIN NATIONAL FOREST

The White Mountain National Forest, which covers much of the White Mountain region, extends over 760,000 acres (307,700 hectares). Access is facilitated by more than 100 miles (160 km) of roads, which cut across whitewater rivers (totaling 650 miles or 1,048 km of fishing streams), dense forests with mountain lakes, ponds and deep valleys. It is also a hiker's paradise, with nearly 1,200 miles (1,935 km) of foot trails.

The standard United States Forest Service policy of clearcutting huge patches out of the forest to prevent their being designated as Wilderness Areas seems less active here, with the logging generally in smaller areas and even European-style selective cutting being practiced.

Here the **Appalachian Trail** snakes across some of its most spectacular scenery, including several of the tallest peaks in the East. The **Appalachian Mountain Club** ( (603) 466-2727, Pinkham Notch, Gorham, NH 03581, provides information about hikes and lodging along the Trail; the **Mount Washington Valley Chamber of Commerce** ( (603) 356-3171 TOLL-FREE (800) 367-3364, Box 385S, North Conway, NH 03860, has more general information about the area.

An hour's drive north of Mount Washington, the stately **Balsam's Grand Resort Hotel** ( (603) 255-3400 TOLL-FREE (800) 255-0600 (out of state) (800) 255-4221 (in New Hampshire) FAX (603) 255-4221, Dixville Notch, NH 03576, is an oasis of gentility in the state's remote northernmost reaches.

MOUNT WASHINGTON

The tallest peak in the White Mountain chain, Mount Washington is 6,288 ft (1,916 m) high; seven other peaks rise to more than a mile (1,609 m) high and 22 others reach

Fall in the White Mountains.

more than 4,000 ft (1,219 m) but despite such imposing statistics, the White Mountains are not that difficult for the traveler to negotiate. Most highways are well-maintained, including the 90-minute round-trip road leading to the summit of Mount Washington (but some eight miles, or 13 km, of braking can be tough on some cars). Those who do make it to the top in their own trusty vehicle, can sport — like thousands of other New Englanders — the bumper sticker: "This car climbed Mount Washington". However, if you have any doubts, leave your car at the

foot of the mountain and take a shuttle (chauffeured van service) to the top.

While several hiking trails accommodate even the casual stroller, some leading to the Mount Washington summit may require more than a few hours of moderate to tough hiking. The climb to the summit is not a casual climb. Although the terrain is neither too rough nor too steep, the mountain peak is susceptible to sudden weather changes that bring in sudden blizzard conditions that have resulted in the death of unprepared hikers. Rewards include spectacular views of waterfalls, deep gorges, rushing streams and peaceful valleys.

Mountain weather can be treacherous. Even in the middle of summer, violent blizzards and freezing temperatures do occur; winds of 231 mph (372 kph), the highest ever measured in the world, have been recorded at the summit of Mount Washington. Unless you are an experienced, well-supplied hiker, it is advisable to keep to the short, heavily-used trails. The White Mountain National Forest, **Forest Supervisor's**

**Office (** (603) 528-8721 TOLL-FREE (800) 283-2267, 719 Main Street, P.O. Box 638, Laconia, NH 03247, will gladly advise hikers on trail conditions and assist in selecting the best routes for day outings or longer treks.

## Mount Washington Cog Railway

Another option for a visit to the White Mountains is a ride on the **Mount Washington Cog Railway (** (603) 846-5404 TOLL-FREE (800) 922-8825 (fare $39 adults, $35 for seniors and $26 for children, free for children under six; open April to mid-October). It and leaves from the Base Station, one mile (just over one and a half kilometers) north of Crawford Notch on U.S. 302. Since the mid-19th century, the train has hauled tourists to the summit of the White Mountains' tallest peak — the highest north of the Carolinas and east of the Rockies.

Hailed in 1869 as a marvel of "modern" technology, this was the world's first mountain climbing cog railway. The "cog" is a toothed or notched wheel that latches on to a center track, pulling and lowering the train up and down the mountain.

Today the train, powered by steam locomotives, climbs three miles (five-kilometers) to the summit on the second steepest railway track in the world. (Only a track in the Swiss Alps beats it.) One trestle, "Jacob's Ladder," registers an incredible 37 percent grade. Each locomotive consumes a ton of coal and 1,000 gallons (3,785 liters) of water while making the one-hour climb to the top.

On clear days the view from the summit's observation center spans four states. Often, however, the mountain is shrouded in gray clouds and thick mist and the train literally climbs through the fog.

## CRAWFORD NOTCH

The narrow, rugged mountain pass of Crawford Notch, off U.S. 302 north of **Bartlett**, offers some incomparable views of the Presidential Range, including the 4,052-ft (1,235-m) **Jackson Mountain**. The Saco River also runs through the Notch, creating some of the tallest and most spectacular waterfalls and cascades in New Hampshire. **Arethusa Falls**, the state's highest, is a 50-minute walk from the parking area; **Silver Cascade**, a 1,000-ft (305-m) cataract, is visible from the highway.

A plaque marks the site of **Willey House**, a stopover for bygone wagon teams traveling between northern New Hampshire and the seacoast. The Willey family was killed here in 1826 when they fled their home during a rock slide; ironically, the house was untouched.

Crawford Notch is also the site of the first attempt at a tourist industry in the White Mountains. It is named for Abel and Ethan Crawford, who in 1819, blazed the first foot-

touring options available. Go north from Manchester on Interstate 93, then east on one of several roads until you reach Route 16 and turn north to North Conway.

Perhaps the easiest way to get a quick overview of the region is by boarding the **Conway Scenic Railroad** ( (603) 356-5251 TOLL-FREE (800) 232-5251 (open May to October), at the Main Street depot, a canary yellow building built in the 1870s. Steam locomotives puffing billows of black smoke pull restored turn-of-the-century coach cars through the **Saco River Valley** on one-hour

path to the summit of Mount Washington, then advertised their services as tour guides and lodging arrangement for visitors .

## NORTH CONWAY

There are few interstate or major highways in New Hampshire, so travelers wishing to explore the heart of the White Mountains region must abandon the four-lane roads and continue their journey on country back roads. This is a bonus rather than an inconvenience, since "Sunday driving" is one of the most enjoyable ways to explore the state's natural wonders.

North Conway is the heart of the Mount Washington Valley region, with several

train rides. The 11-mile (18-km) round trip also offers first-class service on an 1898 Pullman observation car.

Another option is to take a short drive to **Mount Cranmore** and board the *skimobile* ( (603) 356-5543, Routes 16 and 302. In operation for more than 50 years, it is the oldest operating ski lift in the country. Its colorful cars glide smoothly up a trestle to the summit of Mount Cranmore, which also provides fine winter skiing.

Those with more time might consider a guided whitewater or a calmer canoe

ABOVE: Lake Sunapee, New Hampshire, a popular summer destinations, was once the home of Indian tribes. OPPOSITE: An engineer for the Mount Washington Cog Railroad.

tour on the **Saco River**, which winds through the splendid wilderness scenery of Mount Washington Valley. The **Saco Bound Northern Waters** ( (603) 447-2177, P.O. Box 113, Conway Center, NH 03813, two miles (three kilometers) east of Conway Center on U.S. 302, provides guide services.

Several stables in the region offer guided trail rides through the mountains. **The Riding Place** ( (603) 278-1836 in Bretton Woods, tours the 75 miles (121 km) of scenic bridle paths belonging to the venerable Mount Washington Hotel; and the **Nestle-**

**nook Inn and Equestrian Center** ( (603) 383-9443, in Jackson, offers all-day trail rides over Black Mountain and through local farmlands.

If mountain biking from country inn to country inn is more your style, consider one of the special weekend tours put together by **New Hampshire Bicycle Touring** ( (603) 428-3147, 10 Maple Street, Henniker, NH 03242. Yet another way to experience the region is from the air. Scenic flights aboard a jet helicopter operate out of North

Conway's **White Mountain Heliport** ( (603) 356-2930 or 356-2946, P.O. Box 679, North Conway, NH 03860.

**Autumn Foliage**

In addition to its other attractions, the region offers a dramatic display of fall foliage. While the weather can play havoc with the change of seasons, the most colorful time is traditionally the first two weeks in October. More than a half-million people jam New Hampshire's roads each year to have a glimpse of nature's annual color extravaganza, so it is advisable to take the back roads to avoid the crowds.

Before you leave North Conway itself, make certain to catch the view of Mount Washington from the middle of Main Street; it has been called "one of the great views in the East."

**Where to Stay**

EXPENSIVE

**Attitash Mountain Village** ( (603) 374-6500 TOLL-FREE (800) 862-1600 FAX (603) 374-6509, Route 302 near **Bartlett**, originally built for the ski season now stays open year-round. Of a similar style is **Best Western Red Jacket Mountain View** ( (603) 356-5411 TOLL-FREE (800) 752-2538 FAX (603) 356-3842, Route 16. Ask about package deals at both of these resorts.

**Isaac E. Merrill House Inn** ( (603) 356-9041 TOLL-FREE (800) 328-9041 FAX (603) 356-9055, Kearsarge Road; and **Snowvillage Inn** ( (603) 447-2818 TOLL-FREE (800) 447-4345 FAX (603) 447-5268, Stuart Road, are traditional New England country inns. A mile and a half (two kilometers) from the center of town is **Cranmore Mountain Lodge** ( (603) 356-2044 TOLL-FREE (800) 526-5502 FAX (603) 356-6052, Kearsarge Road. The 10 rooms in the old lodge have shared baths and are less expensive. The remaining seven are in the recently renovated loft of the barn.

MODERATE

**Eastern Slope Inn Resort** ( (603) 356-6321 TOLL-FREE (800) 258-4708 FAX (603) 356-8732, Main Street, Routes 16 and 302, is next door to the summer theater and has clay tennis courts. Children stay free here.

ABOVE: Steam engine on display at Clark Trading Post in Franconia. OPPOSITE LEFT: The Old Man of the Mountains. OPPOSITE RIGHT: The quiet, simple style of North Woodstock.

The Riverside ( (603) 356-9060, Route 16A, is a small country inn with only seven rooms (four have shared baths). Rates include breakfast.

In nearby **Gorham** is the **Tourist Village Motel** ( (603) 466-3312 TOLL-FREE (800) 437-3529 FAX (603) 466-5800, 130 Main Street.

INEXPENSIVE
With only ten rooms, it is more like staying at home than a hotel at the **Wildcat Inn** ( (603) 356-2642, Main Street, North Conway.

### Eating Out
The inns all have their own dining rooms which also serve non-residents, but there are other fine restaurants in the area.

As its name would indicate, the **Scottish Lion** ( (603) 356-6381, Route 16 (moderate) serves Scottish-American cuisine. **Horsefeather's** ( (603) 356-2687, on Main Street, downtown North Conway (moderate), is a popular eatery serving light fare in a casual atmosphere.

## FRANCONIA NOTCH STATE PARK

Franconia Notch State Park is another New England tourist shrine, but well worth a visit nonetheless. The Notch is a deep val-

ley cut between the towering peaks of the Franconia and Kinsman mountain ranges, with the granite-walled, 4,200-ft (1,280-m)-high **Cannon Mountain** on the east and the twin 5,000-ft (1,524-m) peaks of **Mounts Lafayette and Lincoln** to the west. It also contains some of the region's most familiar landmarks.

### Flume Gorge
The spectacular Flume Gorge extends for 800 ft (244 m) at the base of **Mount Liberty**, down which cascades the **Pemigewasset**

**River** flanked by 90-ft (27-m) granite walls. Close up views (accessible by stairs and walkways) yield glimpses of rare mountain flowers and luxuriant mosses that cling to the moist walls. Nearly a half-million travelers visit the gorge annually.

### Great Stone Face
**Old Man of the Mountain** (also known as the Great Stone Face) is a natural granite profile of a man's finely detailed face jutting from a sheer cliff 1,200 ft (366 m) above **Profile Lake**. Carved by nature over millions of years, it is formed by five separate ledges of granite and measures 40 ft (12 m) from jutting brow to bearded chin.

## Other Park Features

Panoramic views of the mountains and distant valleys are provided by the **Aerial Tramway**, which carries tram cars more than a mile (1.6 km) at an average height of 2,022 ft (616 m) to the summit of Cannon Mountain at 4,180 ft or 1,263 m.

South of the Notch are three other natural phenomena. **The Basin** has a deep glacial pothole 20 ft (six meters) in diameter at the foot of a waterfall. **Indian Head** is a 98-ft-(30-m)-high profile carved by the elements in granite; its scowling visage is likened to that of an Abenaki chief. **Lost River** and the **glacial caves**, both west of Lincoln, owe their existence to the passage of glaciers which gouged out depressions and then receded north, leaving unique boulder-strewn ravines and tunnel-like caves.

## American Indian Crafts

Today, in a kind of legacy from New Hampshire's native Algonquin Indians, who crafted birch bark canoes, split ash baskets and snowshoes, the White Mountain region offers works by some of the state's finest craftspeople. One can find fine displays of their handiwork at the **Franconia League of New Hampshire Craftsmen (** (603) 823-9521, Access Road, off U.S. 3.

## Where to Stay

EXPENSIVE

At the top of the line in **Franconia** are the **Franconia Inn (** (603) 823-5542 TOLL-FREE (800) 473-5299 FAX (603) 823-8078, Easton Road; and **Sugar Hill Inn (** (603) 823-5621 TOLL-FREE (800) 548-4748 FAX (603) 823-5639, 117 Sugar Hill, Route 117, (moderate in the off-season). Guest are required to take dinner at the inn.

MODERATE

In this category the traveler can find the following: **Gale River Motel (** TOLL-FREE (800) 255-7989, Route 18; **Ledgeland (** (603)

*Walkway gives visitors a chance to marvel at the rare mountain flowers and luxuriant mosses that cling to the moist walls of the spectacular Flume Gorge which extends for 800 ft (244 m) at the base of Mount Liberty.*

823-5341 FAX (603) 823-5227, Route 117;
**Lovett's by Lafayette Brook (** (603) 823-7761
TOLL-FREE (800) 356-3802, Routes 18 and 141;
**Stonybrook Motor Lodge (**/FAX (603) 823-
8192 TOLL-FREE (800) 722-3552, Route 18N;
and **Sunset Hill House (** (603) 823-5522 TOLL-
FREE (800) 786-4455, Route 117.

INEXPENSIVE
**Pinestead Farm Lodge (** (603) 823-8121,
Route 116, with nine rooms, is the best buy
in the area and is often fully booked for the
summer.

**Eating Out**
For a river view and good seafood meals, the
**Rivagale Inn (** (603) 823-7044, Main Street,
(moderate) is recommended.

The **Horse and Hound Inn (** (603) 823-
5501, off Route 18 (expensive), has an
excellent wine list to complement its
continental cuisine.

The **Franconia Inn (** (603) 823-5542
Route 116 (expensive) serves local veal and
excellent desserts and **Lovett's Inn (** (603)
823-7761, Routes 18 and 141 (expensive)
also has an excellent dining room.

The Mount Washington Hotel OPPOSITE, one of
New Hampshire's most stylish hotels. Fly-fishing
purists ABOVE enjoy luxurious accommodations as
well as the state's rivers and streams.

## SKI THE WHITE MOUNTAINS

The White Mountains provide the best
skiing, both alpine and nordic, in the state.
Ten full-service "Ski the White Mountains"
resorts offer a panorama of slopes and
cross-country ski trails against a backdrop
of snowcapped peaks and serene New England scenery. **Attitash**, in **Bartlett**, offers
some of the most consistently fine skiing in
the state and is one of six nationwide United
States Ski Team training centers. In **Bretton
Woods** (in the shadow of Mount Washington), snow squalls known as "Bretton Woods
flurries" blanket a landscape that offers
some of the best views in the east. **Waterville
Valley**, after a new $30 million expansion,
even has its own snowboarding park — the
newest rage in American winter sports.
Then there's **Tuckerman Ravine**, about
12 miles (19 km) north of **Jackson**, a huge,
precipitous, steep-walled bowl that is regarded as the only authentic Swiss-style alpine ski area in the east.

### General Information
Package plans include lift tickets and
lodging, with several midweek specials. For
more ski information, contact the **Mount
Washington Valley Chamber of Commerce (** (603) 356-3171 TOLL-FREE (800) 367-
3364, Main Street, P.O. Box 385, North
Conway, NH 03860.

### Where to Stay
In a class by itself is **The Mount Washington (** (603) 278-1000 TOLL-FREE (800) 258-
0330 FAX (603) 278-3603, Route 302, Bretton
Woods (luxury). In 1944 the Bretton Woods
conference that established an international monetary system for the post-war era
was held here. The same company operates
the Victorian **Bretton Arms Country Inn
(** (603) 278-1000 TOLL-FREE (800) 258-0330
FAX (603) 278-3457, Route 302, Bretton
Woods (expensive); and **The Lodge at
Bretton Woods (** (603) 271-8000 TOLL-
FREE (800) 258-0330, Route 302, Bretton
Woods (moderate). Guests can use Mount
Washington Hotel facilities. You can fax all
three resorts on their mutual reservations
line: (603) 278-3603.

**Waterville Valley** is a four-season vacation resort with inns, luxurious condominiums, spa and fitness programs, free lodging for kids 12 years and under and other facilities. The **Lodging Bureau** ( (603) 236-8371 TOLL-FREE (800) 468-2553 FAX (603) 236-4344, Box LD, Waterville Valley, NH 03215, has many listings and can help make reservations for short or long visits.

In addition to the resorts there are the following:

EXPENSIVE
**The Valley Inn and Tavern** ( (603) 236-8336 TOLL-FREE (800) 343-0969 FAX (603) 236-4294. Tecumseh Road, Waterville Valley; **Christmas Farm Inn** ( (603) 383-4313 TOLL-FREE (800) 443-5837 FAX (603) 383-6495, Route 16B, Jackson; and **Wentworth Resort Hotel** ( (603) 383-9700 TOLL-FREE (800) 637-0013 FAX (603) 383-4265, Route 16A, Jackson.

MODERATE
**Covered Bridge Motel** ( (603) 383-9151 TOLL-FREE (800) 634-2911 FAX (603) 383-4146, Route 16, Jackson; **Dana Place Inn** ( (603) 383-6822 TOLL-FREE (800) 537-9276 FAX (603) 383-6022, Route 16, Jackson; **Eagle Mountain House** ( (603) 383-9111 TOLL-FREE (800) 966-5779 FAX (603) 383-0854, Carter Notch Road, Jackson, an historic 1897 resort; **The Inn at Thorn Hill** ( (603) 383-4242 TOLL-FREE (800) 289-8990 FAX (603) 383-8062, Thorn Hill Road; the seven-room **Nestlenook Inn** ( (603) 383-9443 TOLL-FREE (800) 659-9443 FAX (603) 383-4515, Dinsmore Road, Jackson; and **Wildcat Inn & Tavern** ( (603) 383-4245 TOLL-FREE (800) 228-4245 FAX 603-383-6456, Main Street, Jackson.

**Eating Out**
The **Mount Washington Hotel** has the best dining room (expensive) in the area, serving traditional American cuisine.

**Darby's** in the Lodge at Bretton Woods is fine dining at a moderate to expensive price.

**Fabyan's Station** ( (603) 846-2222, on Route 302, Bretton Woods (moderate), is a restored train depot that serves seafood and steaks.

## THE FAR NORTH

Pittsburg, only six miles (10 km) from the Canadian border, is the heart of New Hampshire's northernmost wilderness. The township comprises 300,000 acres (121,500 hectares) of timberlands, mountains, streams and the Connecticut Lakes (headwaters of the Connecticut River), making it easily the largest township in the United States, as well as one of the most isolated.

This is largely uninhabited country. The roads through this remote area border sections of the **Androscoggin River**, one of the most scenic waterways in the state. You may even catch glimpses of moose grazing in the meadows and swamplands. Waterfalls sparkle down granite cliffs, the stars are bright in the unpolluted night and the hunting and fishing are among the best in the state.

**Where to Stay**
Near **Pittsburg** on U.S. 3 toward the Canadian border is **The Glen** ( (603) 538-6500, on the First Connecticut Lake (moderate to expensive), a fine New Hampshire country inn.

# Vermont

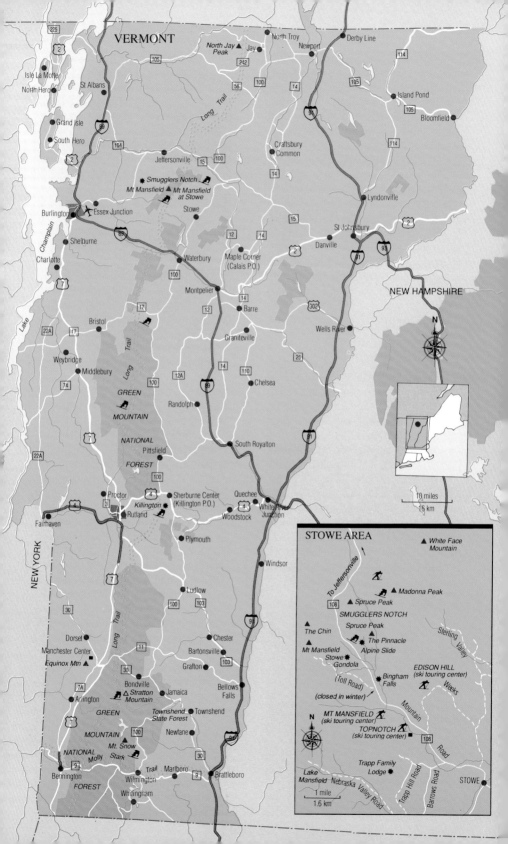

VERMONT is a rural state of farms, gentle hills and mountains with picturesque towns that look as if they were illustrations for storybooks. Its pastoral landscapes are relatively free of sizable cities or centers of industry; Burlington, Vermont's largest community, has a population of less than 40,000.

White steeples dominate the colonial villages, forests and pastures rise above country roads. More than 200 covered bridges add a charm to the countryside as do the maple groves which give rise to the state's claim to be the maple syrup capitol of the world.

Vermont's Green Mountains are the ski center of New England, offering a variety of downhill and cross-country trails at places like the modern complex at Killington or the traditional Stowe. Hikers, as well, can follow the 260-mile (419-km) **Long Trail** that tops the Green Mountain ridge all the way from Massachusetts to Canada and intersects with the Appalachian Trail near Killington.

Vermont's size, only 151 miles (243 km) long and 40 to 90 miles (64 to 145 km) wide, makes it a perfect place to enjoy classic New England at your own pace.

The state is a bicycle-rider's dream with long stretches of back roads dotted with historic inns and lodges. Vermont's fall color extravaganza is a major attraction.

Abraham Lincoln and his family, in the mid-19th century, discovered the state's special qualities. They often vacationed in the Green Mountain resort town of Manchester, in southern Vermont. (In fact Lincoln had reservations at Manchester's historic Equinox Hotel when he was assassinated in 1865.) Noted British historian Lord Bryce was also smitten with Vermont's charm when he called it the "Switzerland of North America."

Vermonters are keen to keep their state's unspoiled, serene image. The state legislature has enacted some of the toughest land use, zoning and environmental protection laws in the nation. Even billboards are prohibited throughout the state.

**General Information**
Both the **Vermont Travel Division** ( (802) 828-3236 TOLL-FREE (800) 837-6668, 134 State Street, Montpelier, VT 05601 and the **Vermont Chamber of Commerce** ( (802) 223-3443, P.O. Box 37, Montpelier, VT 05602, have free maps and travel information.

## BACKGROUND

In 1609 French explorer Samuel de Champlain described what he saw from the lake that now bears his name as *les verts monts* (the green mountains). However, when the French pulled ashore, his Algonquin Indian

guides attacked their enemy, the Iroquois and Champlain was forced to lend aid with his armed troops. *Les verts monts* became a bloody battleground between the French, the Indians and the colonial-minded British for the next 150 years. Only after the English defeated France at Quebec in 1759 did large numbers of colonists begin to settle in the territory.

### THE GREEN MOUNTAIN BOYS

Colonial Vermont was long embroiled in a territorial dispute with neighboring New York over land beyond Vermont's present borders. Ethan Allen's Green Mountain Boys, a self-styled militia, was formed to defend Vermont's position.

The same band of intrepid fighters helped the New World colonists to rid themselves of British rule and proclaim their independence. Vermont then declared itself

Vermont farm near Peacham.

an "independent nation" in 1777 because of continuing land disputes with New York.

Vermont remained independent for 14 years, conducting affairs with the United States as with a "foreign power." Finally, in 1791, it became the 14th state.

During the Civil War, Vermont lost more men proportionately than any other state in the Union. When, during the 19th century, many of its settlers joined the great westward migration, Vermont seemed destined to remain a small, sparsely populated farm state, albeit a beautiful one.

## SOUTHEASTERN VERMONT

### BELLOWS FALLS

Bellows Falls, in southeastern Vermont on the banks of the Connecticut River, is a good place to start a visit to Vermont. The first canal in America was built here in 1802; the **Old Stone Gristmill** (paper mill) museum preserves the town's logging legacy; centuries-old "stone face" petroglyphs attributed to Pennacook Indians are carved into rocks about 50 ft (15 m) downstream from the Vilas Bridge on the Vermont side of the river; and three covered bridges can be found nearby.

### The Green Mountain Flyer

The Green Mountain Flyer ( (802) 463-3069, is a diesel-engine train with authentic 1930s passenger cars that rambles 13 miles (21 km) from Bellows Falls through two scenic river valleys before stopping in **Chester**; it often continues for another 14 miles (23 km) to **Ludlow**. The train crosses the old canal, follows the Connecticut River for a distance, then twists inland up the Williams River Valley; it also traverses the deep Brockway River Gorge and passes both the **Warrel** and **Bartonsville** covered bridges, slowing down here and there for the photographers on board.

### VICTORIAN CHESTER

Fans of Victoriana might make a quick stop at Chester to explore two historic districts, Main Street's stately homes along its village

green and North Street's "Stone Village" which has more than 25 pre-Civil War houses faced with gneiss ledgestone.

### COLONIAL GRAFTON

Grafton, founded in pre-Revolutionary times under George III, has been called the perfect New England village. Historic buildings, high-steepled churches, old inns, specialty shops (most circa 1805) and a little creek meandering through town make it interesting for photographers and browsers alike.

### Where to Stay

**The Old Tavern at Grafton** ( (802) 843-2231 FAX (802) 843-2235, 166 Lake Morey Road, Routes 121 and 35 (expensive), has operated since 1801, hosting such illustrious guests as Daniel Webster, Rudyard Kipling, Woodrow Wilson and Teddy Roosevelt.

### NEWFANE — THE TOWN THAT MOVED

Newfane, south of Bellows Falls on Route 30, is widely recognized for its architecture. The 1825 **Windham County Courthouse**, on the elm-shaded village green, is among the finest Early Republic buildings in the East. In 1825, the entire village moved two miles (three kilometers) south to its present location. Buildings were dismantled timber by timber and moved on ox-drawn sleighs to their new locations.

### Where to Stay and Eating Out

Two historic inns, the **Four Columns Inn** ( (802) 365-7713 TOLL-FREE (800) 787-6633 FAX (802) 365-0022, 230 West Street, on the Village Green (moderate to expensive); and the 10room **Old Newfane Inn** ( (802) 365-4427, Village Green (moderate to expensive), are located on the Green. The Four Columns Inn serves Vermont lamb and veal in its restaurant and the Old Newfane Inn has Louisiana frogs' legs on its menu.

**The Inn at South Newfane** ( (802) 348-7191 FAX (802) 348-9325, Dover Road, South

OPPOSITE TOP: The spacious Common at Townshend. BOTTOM: A colonial-style porch at the Old Tavern.

Newfane (moderate to expensive), features traditional New England specialties.

## TOWNSHEND

About five miles (eight kilometers) north on Route 30 is picturesque and much photographed, Townshend. Especially handsome is the town green surrounded by historic buildings.

Townshend's **Scott Covered Bridge**, just off Route 30, is the longest single-span covered bridge in Vermont; built in

stretches 39 miles (63 km) from Brattleboro to Bennington. It is a two-lane road that is often crowded even during the off-season, but it is an interesting drive that passes through several picturesque villages and reveals some of the most dramatic fall colors in the state.

Molly Stark's husband, Revolutionary War hero General John Stark, led troops against the British at the Battle of Bennington in 1777, one of the campaign's most important clashes. Prior to the battle, Stark told his men, "There stand the redcoats and

1870, it stretches 165 ft (50 m) over the West River.

At **Townshend State Forest**, a very steep hiking trail nearly three miles (four and a half kilometers) long leads to the 1,580-ft (482-m) summit of Bald Mountain. A 10-minute drive north brings you to **Jamaica State Park**, noted for whitewater rafting on the West River.

## ACROSS SOUTHERN VERMONT

### THE MOLLY STARK TRAIL

The main thoroughfare across southern Vermont, the Molly Stark Trail (Route 9),

they are ours, or this night Molly Stark sleeps a widow".

### BRATTLEBORO

You can start the Molly Stark Trail from Brattleboro, in the southeast corner of the state on the Connecticut River. Vermont's first settlement was just south of here at Fort Dummer in 1724. (The Vernon Dam and hydroelectric plant, built in 1907, flooded the site.) Brattleboro is perhaps best known as the one-time residence of Rudyard Kipling, who married a town girl and lived here (actually in Dummerston) during the 1890s. In his unusual boat-shaped mansion, he wrote the *Jungle Books* and *Captain Courageous*.

The **Brattleboro Museum and Art Center** (the old Union Railroad Station at Canal and Bridge Streets) has a fine collection of Estey organs, a 19th-century mainstay in those American homes that could afford one.

South of Brattleboro on the New Hampshire border is Vernon's nuclear power plant, which is open for tours.

The **Creamery Bridge**, west of Brattleboro on Route 9, is a handsome covered bridge built in 1879; from here the Molly Stark Trail leads into high Green Mountain country.

Clinging to the top of the 2,347-ft (715-m) Hogback Mountain is the **Skyline**, a well-known restaurant overlooking **Marlboro** and offering distant views of mountain ranges in New Hampshire and Massachusetts.

The acclaimed **Marlboro Chamber Music Festival** schedules twelve weekend concerts from mid-July to mid-August on the Marlboro College campus ( (215) 569-4690 FAX (215) 569-9497.

**Where to Stay and Eating Out**
**Quality Inn** ( (802) 254-8701 TOLL-FREE (800) 228-5151 FAX (802) 257-4727, Putney Road, U.S. 5 (moderate to expensive); and **Dalem's Chalet** ( (802) 254-4323 FAX (802) 254-3883, 16 South Street (moderate to expensive), which serves excellent Swiss-German meals.

## WILMINGTON AND WHITTINGHAM

Wilmington is the gateway to southern Vermont's ski areas, including **Haystack, Hogback, Dutch Hill, Prospect Mountain, Corinthia** and **Mt. Snow**. Detour south on Route 100 to drive through some remarkable New England scenery, especially during the fall; the tiny hamlet of Whittingham has a monument marking the birthplace of Mormon religious leader Brigham Young.

## BENNINGTON

Back on the Molly Stark Trail, continue west through the high mountain scenery until you reach Bennington, historic headquarters of Ethan Allen's Green Mountain Boys. *Vermont*

The **Bennington Museum** has a collection of Revolutionary War artifacts and Grandma Moses primitives. Anna Mary Robertson "Grandma" Moses started painting simple country scenes at 70 years of age and achieved instant fame; she continued working until her death at 101.

The **Old First Church**, built in 1805 with a three-tiered steeple, is an oft-photographed Bennington landmark. Behind the church, a cemetery contains the graves of soldiers who fell in the Battle of Bennington and that of poet Robert Frost, whose simple

white marble tombstone is engraved with the epitaph: "I had a lover's quarrel with the world."

But the **Bennington Battle Monument** dominates every view of the village. The 306-ft (93-m) blue limestone obelisk was completed in 1889 at a cost of $112,000; it marks the site of an important colonial supply point that was defended in a three-hour clash that was a turning point in the Revolutionary War. From the mountain's observation tower, visitors have superb views of Massachusetts' Berkshires, the Green Mountains and New York.

OPPOSITE and ABOVE: Like much of New England, Vermont has remained largely rural.

Bennington College in North Bennington, situated on a lovely, rambling campus,
is one of the nation's leading non-traditional
or experimental colleges. Emphasizing literature, dance and the other arts, it is known
for its wealthy, non-conformist students and
for innovative approaches to education.

Nearby, surrounded by the Taconic and
Green Mountains, **Old Bennington** offers
lovely village scenes.

**General Information**
The **Bennington Area Chamber of Com-**

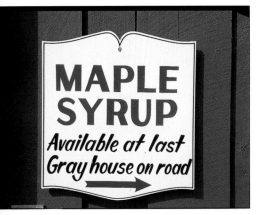

merce ( (802) 447-3311, Veterans Memorial
Drive, Bennington, VT 05201, can provide
any information you might want about the
town and the surrounding area.

**Where to Stay**
Hotels in Bennington are reasonably priced;
many are in the moderate category. Always
reliable are **Best Western New Englander
Motor Inn** ( (802) 442-6311 TOLL-FREE (800)
528-1234 FAX (802) 442-6311, 220 Northside
Drive; **Kirkside Motor Lodge** ( (802) 447-
7596 FAX (802) 447-7596, 250 West Main
Street, next to the Old First Church; and
**Ramada Inn** ( (802) 442-8145 TOLL-FREE
(800) 272-6232 FAX (802) 442-2471, U.S. 7 at
Kocher Drive, which has an indoor pool.

**Eating Out**
For a fine French-style meal, you can dine at
**Four Chimneys Inn and Restaurant** ( (802)
447-3500, Route 9 (expensive). The **Publyk**

ABOVE: There's no substitute for the real thing.
OPPOSITE: The stunning Quechee Gorge and the
Ottauquechee River.

House ( (802) 442-8301, Harwood Hill on
Route 7A, serves inexpensive steak and
seafood dinners.

## NORTH TO DORSET

NEW ENGLAND HERITAGE TRAIL

Route 7 takes the travelers through the
villages and scenic valley of the **Green
Mountains National Forest**. There, in the
tranquil hamlet of **Arlington**, once a
gathering place for the Green Mountain
Boys, artist Norman Rockwell made his
home. The **Norman Rockwell Exhibition
Gallery** in Arlington has hundreds of Saturday Evening Post covers and prints on
display. Often, the models who posed for
his works lead gallery tours.

MANCHESTER

A summer resort since the 1800s, Manchester was enjoyed by Abraham Lincoln,
who was drawn here by its beauty and
serenity. It is a picture-postcard village
nestled in the Valley of Vermont, between
the Taconic and Green Mountains. Mount
Equinox, the tallest peak in the Taconic
Range, rises high above a town where
Federal and colonial Revival mansions line
its shaded streets.

Nearby, Robert Todd Lincoln, the president's son, built a 24-room manor on a large
estate which he called "Hilldene" where he
summered from 1904 until his death in 1926.
**Hilldene** ( (802) 362-1788 FAX (802) 362-1564
(admission $7 adults, $3 children; open
daily, mid-May to October from 9:30 AM to
5:30 PM), commands a splendid view of the
surrounding countryside. Many of the
original family furnishings remain in his
home.

Ernest Hemingway often tried his
luck on the **Battenkill River**, one of New
England's premiere fly-fishing streams. The
**American Museum of Fly Fishing** ( (802)
362-3300, Route 7 and Seminary Avenue
(admission $3 adults, children under 12 are
free; open daily 10 AM to 4 PM, May to October and Monday through Friday the rest of
the year, closed on major holidays), has

books, files, displays and equipment of famous fishermen, including Hemingway, Daniel Webster, Winslow Homer, and Presidents Herbert Hoover and Dwight D. Eisenhower.

The **Southern Vermont Art Center** is located off West Road (admission $3 adults, $.50 students, children under 13 free; open May 26 to October 14, Tuesday through Saturday, 10 AM to 5 PM; Sunday midday to 5 PM).

One of the best views in the area is found along the **Equinox Sky Line Drive**,

five miles (eight kilometers) south of Route 7A. A six-mile (10-km) paved road climbs from 600 to 3,835 ft (183 to 1,169 m) and offers panoramas from the summit of Mt. Equinox.

From the **Lye Brook Wilderness Center**, hikers can follow a two-mile (three-kilometer) trail leading to the Lye Brook Waterfalls, or pick up the Long Trail for a trek among the abandoned marble quarries leading to the 3,186-ft (971-m) Mt. Aeolus. Maps can be

ABOVE: Locals seek recreation in a Woodstock park. OPPOSITE: Union Church and one of New England's famous covered bridges in Stark. Once a common sight in Vermont, few of these bridges now remain.

picked up at the **Manchester-in-the-Mountains Chamber of Commerce** ( (802) 362-2100 in Manchester.

**Where to Stay and Eating Out**

The best accommodations are in the country inns of Manchester, all of which have fine dining rooms.

The **Inn at Manchester** ( (802) 362-1793 TOLL-FREE (800) 273-1793 FAX (802) 362-3218, Route 7A (expensive), is a Victorian inn and converted carriage house. Nearby are the **1811 House** ( (802) 362-1811 TOLL-FREE (800) 432-1811 FAX (802) 362-2443, Route 7 (expensive); and the **Reluctant Panther Inn and Restaurant** ( (802) 362-2568 TOLL-FREE (800) 822-2331 FAX (802) 362-2586, Route 7A, in Manchester Village (expensive), whose chefs create five course dinners that usually include trout and quail.

On a slightly larger scale are the **Manchester View** ( (802) 362-2739 TOLL-FREE (800) 548-4141 FAX (802) 362-2199, U.S. 7, in Manchester Center (moderate to expensive); **Palmer House** (/FAX (802) 362-3600 TOLL-FREE (800) 917-6245, U.S. 7 in Manchester Center (moderate to expensive); and **Willburton Inn** ( (802) 362-2500 FAX (802) 362-1107, off Route 7A (expensive).

For moderately priced meals, **Chantecleer** ( (802) 362-1616, U.S. 7, in East Dorset, has Swiss Provincial dishes and the **Sirloin Saloon** ( (802) 362-2600, Route 11 in Manchester Center, as its name suggests, serves steaks.

## DORSET

Just a few miles north of Manchester, Dorset is an artists' colony in a beautiful mountain setting. Its annual **summer theater festival** offers productions featuring Actors Equity players from June to Labor Day, ( (802) 867-5777.

**Where to Stay and Eating Out**

The **Dorset Inn** ( (802) 867-5500 FAX 867-5542, Church and Main Streets (expensive), located on the green, has been in operation for 200 years.

On the outskirts of town is **Barrows House Inn** ( (802) 867-4455 TOLL-FREE (800) 639-1620 FAX (802) 867-0132, Route 30 (expensive) whose restaurant serves fresh fish and calf's liver and has its own bakery.

**Village Auberge** ( (802) 867-5715, Route 30 (moderate to expensive), offerss a classic French-style menu.

## CENTRAL VERMONT

### RUTLAND

Vermont's second largest city, Rutland has a population of less than 20,000. It was once known as the "Marble City" because of the quarries in the vicinity. The Vermont Marble Company supplied marble from these quarries for construction of the Tomb of the Unknown Soldier and the Kennedy Memorial in Washington, D.C., as well as for the Lincoln Memorial and the Supreme Court Building.

In Rutland, too, along Main and Center Streets and on Merchants Row and Strongs Avenue, buildings of historic significance display marble embellishments. The **Vermont Marble Exhibit** in nearby Proctor has displays of marbles from all over the world, a working sculptor and a sculpture garden with a bas-relief "Gallery of Presidents" (admission $3.50 for adults with reductions for students and children; open daily late May to October, 9 AM to 5:30 PM).

Rutland is also only 10 miles (16 km) from the large **Killington ski resort** (see page 224).

### Where to Stay and Eating Out

Rutland has several good motels, including the **Best Western Hogge Penny Inn** (/FAX (802) 773-3200 TOLL-FREE (800) 828-3334, U.S. 4E (moderate to expensive); and the **Holiday Inn** ( (802) 775-1911 TOLL-FREE (800) 465-4329 FAX (802) 775-0113, South Main Street (moderate to expensive).

You'll find some of the best dining in the area at **Countryman's Pleasure** ( (802) 773-7141, Townline Road in **Mendon** (moderate to expensive), where the veal and lamb dishes are complemented with home-baked goodies.

**Royal's Hearthside** ( (802) 775-0856, junction of U.S. 4 and U.S. 7 (moderate to expensive), serves a traditional New England fare and the Italian sandwiches at **Gill's Deli** on Strongs Avenue are among the best anywhere.

### PLYMOUTH

In the early morning of August 3, 1923, in Plymouth (about 30 miles or 48 km east of Rutland on Route 100A), Vice-President Calvin Coolidge was sworn in as the 30th president of the United States by his father in the parlor of the Coolidge homestead.

These unusual circumstances arose when Coolidge, while visiting his home town, was notified of President Warren Harding's death. Coolidge's father, a notary public, did the honors.

A visit to Plymouth, a typical rural Vermont village nestled among the Green Mountains, should include a walk through the historic district which includes the **Coolidge Homestead** and his birthplace home.

Nearby is the family cheese factory operated by Calvin's son, John. Founded by the president's father, it still specializes in the curd cheese so favored by "Silent Cal." Other Coolidge sites include the steep hillside cemetery where Coolidge and six generations of his family are buried.

### Where to Stay

The **Salt Ash Inn** ( (802) 672-3748 E-MAIL: vermont.vacation.com, at the junction of Routes 100 and 100A (moderate), is an historic country inn.

## WOODSTOCK

Woodstock exudes a peaceful 19th-century charm. The oval town green is surrounded by fine examples of Federal, Greek Revival and Romanesque-style residences.

The Town Crier bulletin board, at Elm and Central Streets, still informs residents of important announcements and events. Of the 87 remaining Paul Revere-made bells, four hang in Woodstock churches; three of these continue to toll as well as ever.

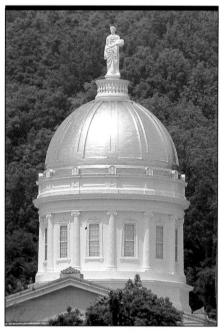

The successful Gold Rush lawyer, Frederick Billings, is credited with generating an interest in village preservation in the 1870s. Sample Woodstock's 19th-century charm during the two-hour guided walking tours of the historic district; for information; call ( (802) 457-1830. Or visit the **Billings Farm & Museum** (admission $6 adults, with reductions for children and senior citizens; open daily May 7 to October, 10 AM to 5 PM), a living history of Vermont farm life a century ago. The last covered bridge built in Vermont (1969) is in the village center.

Skiing is big in Woodstock, with **Suicide Six** and **Sonnenberg** ski areas nearby. The village is credited with the invention of the tow rope (pulling skiers up Mt. Tom, powered by a "Model T" Ford engine) which revolutionized the ski industry.

**Quechee Gorge**, six miles (10 km) east of Woodstock on Route 4, is a sheer 165-ft (50-m) chasm dropping down to the Ottauquechee River; a steep one-mile (over one and a half kilometer)-long hiking trail leads to the bottom of the gorge. An obelisk marks the 1805 birthplace of Mormon Church founder Joseph Smith just outside **South Royalton**, 18 miles (29 km) north and a museum there displays early church artifacts. **Brookfield's floating bridge**, built in 1812, is a structure of weathered timbers floating on 300 barrels spanning tiny **Sunset Lake**, 18 miles (30 km) north of Woodstock.

### Where to Stay and Eating Out

**Woodstock Inn and Resort** ( (802) 457-1100 TOLL-FREE (800) 448-7900 FAX (802) 457-6699, 14 The Green (expensive to luxury), has facilities for almost every sport imaginable. Its restaurant is moderately priced.

The **Braeside Motel** ( (802) 457-1366, U.S. 4 (moderate), situated on a hillside, includes breakfast in the price of its rooms. There is also **The Kedron Valley Inn** ( (802) 457-1473 TOLL-FREE (800) 836-1193 FAX (802) 456-4469, 106 South Woodstock Street (expensive).

**Parker House** ( (802) 295-6077, 16 Main Street in Quechee (expensive); and **Prince and the Pauper** ( (802) 457-1818, 24 Elm Street (expensive), both offer French-style meals.

## MONTPELIER: THE TINIEST CAPITAL

It is the smallest state capital in the nation. Montpelier, with less than 9,000 residents is a pleasant town, set in a valley of the Winooski River. The gold-leaf dome of the **Vermont State House** is resplendent against a backdrop of hills ablaze with fall foliage.

On the State House Lawn is the **Vermont State Museum** (admission free, opening times vary), fashioned to resemble the old Pavilion Hotel, a landmark demolished in 1966. Collections are eclectic and include the last panther shot in Vermont in 1881.

Ice cream lovers should head up Interstate 89 to the Stowe exit, then go about half a mile (800 m) to the headquarters of "the best ice cream in the world," according to *Time* magazine. **Ben & Jerry's** ( (802) 244-5641, all-natural ice cream, offers guided factory tours, and a sample scoop of ice cream before you leave. Ben & Jerry's ice cream is omnipresent in New England, but only in Vermont will you find arguably the world's most sublime "factory rejects": marked-down pints of Ben & Jerry's ice cream with, for example, *too many* chocolate chips. Enjoy.

## AROUND MONTPELIER

### Barre: The Granite Capital
Barre is the center of the country's granite industry. For a better understanding of just how difficult and dangerous granite mining can be, visit **Rock of Ages Quarry** ( (802) 476-3115 (admission $2 adults, $1 children; open June 1 to October 15, Monday through Friday, 9:30 AM to 3:30 PM), four miles (nearly six-and-a-half kilometers) south of Montpelier on Route 14. This is the world's largest granite quarry, 350 ft (107 m) straight down to the bottom of the open rock mine. Huge machines lift 100-ton granite slabs out of the pit, while at the Craftsmen Center, workers cut and polish the rock, then carve it into memorial gravestones or sculptures. A quarry train offers a 20-minute ride through the mining complex.

The town's granite legacy can also be viewed at **Hope Cemetery** on the edge of town, where the headstones are said to rival the finest granite carvings anywhere.

### The Green Mountains
Stretching from Montpelier south to Rutland and north to Underhill State Park, the Green Mountains offer some of the best skiing on the east coast.

## MAJOR SKI RESORTS

### MOUNT MANSFIELD AT STOWE

One of Vermont's two premier ski areas, Mount Mansfield at Stowe, is about an hour's drive east of Burlington. There is always snow at Stowe, is a much-repeated refrain. The Civilian Conservation Corps built Stowe in 1933 when workers carved a trail on Mount Mansfield, Vermont's highest peak (4,393 ft or 1,339 m); since then, Mount Mansfield at Stowe has created more challenging and scenic runs and is often called "the ski capital of the East."

Located at the foot of Mount Mansfield, the village of Stowe is also one of New England's most varied resort communities, with its white-steepled churches, colonial-style buildings and Swiss chalets.

Mount Mansfield's fabled "Front Four" have been called "the toughest expert proving grounds in the East." Beginning at elevations of 4,000 ft (1,339 m), with vertical drops of 2,350 ft (716 m), these slopes challenge a skier's ability with steep, mogul-filled, tree-lined chutes.

Plenty of intermediate slopes provide wide-open touring and a Nordic system meets with three other trails to offer more than 100 miles (161 km) of interconnected backcountry trails.

Stowe has several beginners' trails, so new skiers need not be scared away by its "expert" reputation. For example, the novice run called the Toll Road is more than four miles (six kilometers) long.

### Year-Round Attractions at Stowe
Four-season attractions make Stowe an enjoyable summer resort. The **Mount Mansfield Toll Road** ($12 car and passengers) off

The gold-domed state capital building OPPOSITE and Ben and Jerry's ice cream ABOVE are two of the biggest attractions in the Montpelier region.

Route 108 is a five-mile (eight-kilometer) gravel road leading to a lookout point near the summit; from there you can follow a two-mile (just over three kilometer) hiking path to the top. Mount Mansfield's **gondola ride** (admission $9; open daily June to early September, Saturday and Sunday from September to October) also provides near-summit panoramas. Nearby Spruce Peak has an **alpine slide**, a kind of warm-weather luge with wheels, that barrels down the slopes along an aluminum chute.

It is also renowned for its charming inns and lodges. One of the most famous is the **Trapp Family Lodge**, run by the family whose story the *The Sound of Music* is based upon. The site of their Tyrolean-style lodge is said to remind them of their native Austria.

## SMUGGLERS' NOTCH

At **Smugglers' Notch Ski Area**, about eight miles (13 km) north of Stowe in **Jeffersonville**, the three mountains — Morse, Sterling and Madonna — are connected by winding trails and lifts. Some trails run from the village center.

Smugglers' main attraction is **Madonna**, 3,668ft (1,118m) high with a vertical rise of 2,610 ft (796 m). This is expert skier territory, with giant moguls requiring a high degree of skill. Yet Smugglers' (named after the contraband that was smuggled through the pass during the war of 1812) also has a special children's center which offers day care, ski schools and camps — there is even a Club Med-type program headquartered in the newly completed **Village Center** with a swimming pool.

Smugglers' Notch auto road, open summers only, is a narrow, twisting road that climbs to the scenic notch (mountain pass) between Mount Mansfield and Spruce Peak.

## WHERE TO STAY

### Expensive
The **Trapp Family Lodge** ( (802) 253-8511 TOLL-FREE (800) 826-7000 FAX (802) 253-5740, off Route 108 (93 rooms plus time-share condominiums available for rent on a weekly basis), is the most prestigious of the lodges

in Stowe. Breakfast and dinner are included in the price of rooms.

The **Golden Eagle Resort** ( (802) 253-4811 TOLL-FREE (800) 626-1010 FAX (802) 253-2561, Mountain Road, Route 108, with both rooms and moderately-priced apartments, has every facility imaginable.

Also recommended are: **Topnotch at Stowe Resort and Spa** ( (802) 253-8585, TOLL-FREE (800) 451-8686 FAX (802) 253-9263, 4000 Mountain Road; **The Inn at the Mountain** ( (802) 253-7311 TOLL-FREE (800) 253-4754 FAX (802) 253-3618, 5781 Mountain Road; and **Salzburg Inn** (/FAX (802) 253-8541 TOLL-FREE (800) 448-4554, Route 108.

### Moderate
**Alpine Motor Lodge** ( (802) 253-7700, Mount Mansfield Road; **Stoweflake Inn and Resort** ( (802) 253-7355 TOLL-FREE (800) 253-2232 FAX (802) 253-6858, Route 108, Mountain Road (on the expensive end of the range); and **Stowehof Inn** ( (802) 253-9722 TOLL-FREE (800) 932-7136, Edison Hill Road.

## EATING OUT

### Expensive
The **Trapp Family Lodge** ( (802) 253-8511 TOLL-FREE (800) 826-7000, serves traditional Austrian fixed-price menus. The **Topnotch at Stowe** ( (802) 253-8585 and **Ile de France** ( (820) 253-7751, Route 108 both serve French-style meals.

### Inexpensive
The **Shed** ( (820) 253-4364, Mountain Road, serves hearty hamburgers dubbed "Shedburgers".

## KILLINGTON

Central Vermont's largest ski resort is Killington, 10 miles (16 km) east of Rutland on Route 4. One word describes it: BIG. It has six separate but interconnected mountains (Killington Peak is the highest at 4,241 ft or 1,293 m), with 107 ski trails and moguls the size of small hotels, in all, twice as much skiing as any other Eastern ski resort. And it claims the longest ski lift in the world, stretching more than three miles (nearly five kilometers) over the Green Mountains.

Bear Mountain is expert terrain, with one trail, Outer Limits, at an incline of 62 percent; it is easily the steepest in New England. Beginners should try the 10-mile-(16-km)-long Juggernaut trail, the longest Alpine run in the United States.

Another Killington drawing card is the long ski season. With more than 240 inches (six meters) of snow annually and vast snowmaking capacity, the resort's season often extends from October to June.

Killington's outstanding ski school and Children's Center attract many families. Besides special programs, activities and day care, its "family ski workshop" allows mom, dad and the kids to receive lessons and ski together under the tutelage of a single instructor.

**General Information**
**Killington and Pico Areas Association**
( (802) 773-4181, P.O. Box 114, Killington, VT 05751 and **Killington Lodging Bureau** ( (802) 773-1330 TOLL-FREE (800) 621-6867, are helpful in accommodation and information of recreational facilities in the area.

**Where to Stay**
Specifically recommended accommodations are **Cortina Inn and Resort** ( (802) 773-3333 TOLL-FREE (800) 451-6109 FAX (802) 775-6948, Route 4, Mendon Mountain (expensive); **Grey Bonnet Inn** ( (802) 775-2537 TOLL-FREE (800) 342-2086 FAX (802) 775-3371, Route 100 (moderate); **Killington Village** TOLL-FREE ( (800) 343-0762 FAX (802) 422-6788, 718 Killington Road (96 rooms and more than 600 condominiums, moderate to expensive); **Shelburne-Killington Motel** ( (802) 773-9535 TOLL-FREE (800) 366-0493, U.S. 4 (moderate to expensive); and **The Vermont Inn** ( (802) 775-0708 TOLL-FREE (800) 541-7795 FAX (802) 773-2440, U.S. 4 (expensive).

**Eating Out**
For Vermont country-style food, the restaurant at **The Vermont Inn** (see above) is excellent (moderate to expensive).

The **Cortina Inn** (802) 773-3333, Route 4, Mendon Mountain, serves an excellent breakfast buffet. **Hemingway's** ( (802) 422-3886, U.S. 4 (expensive) is a classic restaurant serving Vermont lamb and fresh trout.

## OTHER SKI RESORTS

Other popular ski areas include **Mt. Snow**, 14 miles (22.5 km) north of Wilmington, which has old New England charm. It offers several open snowfield downhill runs and a five-mile (eight-kilometer)-long Nordic touring trail skirting craggy ridges along six peaks of the Green Mountains, making it the highest-elevation cross-country trail in Vermont.

**Stratton Mountain**, about 15 miles (24 km) north of Mt. Snow, has a European atmosphere and Tyrol-style vaudeville entertainment ("better than Kitzbuhel's.")

**Jay Peak** lies eight miles (13 km) south of North Troy and the Canadian border.

## LAKE CHAMPLAIN

Lake Champlain stretches for 125 miles (201 km) down Vermont's northwest border, separating the state from New York. Nestled in a huge valley with the Adirondacks to the west and the Green Mountains on the east, the lake is one of the most popular resort areas in Vermont.

### MIDDLEBURY

An easy place to begin a Champlain valley tour is at Middlebury (on Route 7, about 46 miles, or 74 km, north of Rutland), a little town whose women's academy, now **Middlebury College**, was founded in 1800; tours of the campus take in the handsome 1806 **Congregational Church** on the Common and the **Starr Library**, with its collection of works by Robert Frost.

Just north of Middlebury in **Weybridge** is the University of Vermont's **Morgan Horse Farm**. You can watch more than 50 Morgans being put through training drills and guided tours will take you into the handsome Victorian barns.

### MAD RIVER VALLEY

**Bristol** is the gateway to the remote Mad River Valley, known for its rolling mountain terrain. Three ski areas and a scenic road leading to the 2,356-ft (718-m) tip of the **Appalachian Gap** are highlights of the valley. Bristol also operates the only freshwater windjammer cruises in America; here you may sail one of these tall-masted ships on Lake Champlain with Vermont's mountains in the background.

At **Charlotte**, an 18-minute ferry ride takes passengers across Lake Champlain to Essex, NY, a charming 19th-century town.

The **Shelburne Museum and Heritage Park** ( (802) 985-3346, is five miles (eight kilometers) south of Burlington. It has been called a collection of collections, with 45 acres (18 hectares) of Americana. The enclave includes 37 buildings: a horseshoe-shaped barn which houses more than 150 horse-drawn carriages and sleighs; the 1783 Stagecoach Inn, with its collection of American folk art; the 1840 Dorset House, featuring more than 1,000 hand carved duck decoys; and even Lake Champlain's historic sidewheeler steamboat *Ticonderoga*, docked alongside the old Colchester Reef Lighthouse.

Another fascinating stop is **Shelburne Farms** ( (802) 985-8686, a beautiful 19th-century agricultural estate on the shores of Lake Champlain. The old farm buildings include Shelburne House, the estate's 110-room mansion with views of both the lake and the Adirondacks in New York. The gorgeous estate grounds are attributed to landscape architect Frederick Law Olmstead. Today it is a working experimental farm and learning center.

---

LAKE CHAMPLAIN'S ISLANDS

The three islands in the northern end of Lake Champlain **Grand Isle**, **North Hero** and **Isle la Motte** are sometimes referred to as "Vermont's Cape Cod." Isle la Motte is the best of the three, with its St. Anne shrine marking the site of a 1666 French fort. All islands can be reached via highway U.S. 2.

There is also "Champ," the Loch Ness monster of Lake Champlain. The humpbacked creature, first "sighted" by Champlain in the 1600s, has been "seen" several times by ferry boats and pleasure craft from both Vermont and New York. However,

much like Scotland's Loch Ness "monster", it has never shown itself to scientific research expeditions.

| BURLINGTON |

On the shore of Lake Champlain, Burlington is the commercial and industrial center of Vermont and its largest city with 38,000 residents. It hosts the annual **Champlain Shakespeare Festival** and the **Vermont Mozart Festival** presented by the University of Vermont (UVM) in July and August.

Some Burlington landmarks are the **University of Vermont** (founded in 1791), located at the top of a hill on the eastern edge of town and the **Old Mill** building, which has a cornerstone laid by Lafayette in 1825. **Battery Park**, on Pearl Street, is where American guns defeated the British during the War of 1812; now it affords great views of the lake. And **Ethan Allen Park** preserves part of the Allen's historic farmstead.

You can sail Lake Champlain on the *Ethan Allen* ( (802) 862-9685, a vintage sternwheeler that takes in the mountain scenery along the shoreline.

---

WHERE TO STAY

**Expensive**

The **Sheraton Burlington Hotel and Conference Center** ( (802) 865-6600 TOLL-FREE (800) 324-3535 FAX (802) 865-6670, 870 Williston Road, Burlington, is built around a central greenhouse.

At the **Radisson Hotel Burlington** ( (802) 658-6500 TOLL-FREE (800) 333-3333 FAX (802) 658-4659, 60 Battery Street, children stay free.

**Moderate**

**Howard Johnson Lodge** ( (802) 863-5541 TOLL-FREE (800) 654-2000 FAX (802)862-2755, 1 Dorset Street, U.S. 2, South Burlington, has an indoor pool and tennis court and children stay free.

Nearby is the **Super 8 Motel** ( (802) 862-6421 TOLL-FREE (800) 800-8000 FAX (802)

---

OPPOSITE: East Orange, Vermont.

862-8009, 1016 Shelburne Road, South Burlington.

## EATING OUT

The best restaurants in Burlington are moderately priced and include the **Thai Parima** ( (802) 864-7917, 185 Pearl Street; **Ice House Restaurant** ( (802) 864-1800, 171 Battery Street, which serves seafood; and **Pauline's** ( (802) 862-1081, 1834 Shelburne Road, which also serves seafood, in home-style cooking.

**Danville**, west of St. Johnsbury, is the headquarters of the American Society of Dowsers, people who use willow wands to find water; their fall convention draws lots of attention. **Lyndonville**, nestled in the green hills of the Passumpsic River valley, has five covered bridges within village limits, the earliest dating from 1795.

Finally, **Derby Line** is one of the most unusual hamlets in America. The United State–Canadian border passes right through the town, resulting in houses sitting astride the border between Vermont and Quebec. In

the town library, the book stacks and checkout desks are in different countries.

## NORTHEASTERN VERMONT

**St. Johnsbury**, on U.S. 2, is the gateway to the northeast, a backwoods region travelers seldom visit. It is a land of lakes, forests, small villages — and few people.

The best time to visit the area is during the fall "color" season in September, when the woods are ablaze with color and villages celebrate with festivals, food and fun.

## AUTUMN FOLIAGE TOURS

Vermont's fall foliage has been called the world's finest, attracting people from all over the world. The leaves usually begin to change in early September at higher elevations in northern Vermont and along the Canadian border. This is the least-populated portion of the state and is noted for its sweeping, panoramic views. The color season moves progressively southward, usually ending in the final weeks of October.

ABOVE: A country-store shopping opportunity in Peacham. OPPOSITE: Cycling in the White Mountains.

The compactness of Vermont (180 miles or 290 km long and about 60 miles or 97 km at its widest point) makes it relatively easy to traverse. Don't be afraid to travel off the main highways where you will often find backroads lined by old stone walls or set off against the brilliant green pastures of rolling countryside.

Scores of small Vermont towns celebrate the season with festivals that might include guided tours, bazaars, live entertainment and homemade, traditional New England foods.

## GENERAL INFORMATION

The **Vermont Travel Division** ( (802) 828-3236 TOLL-FREE (800) 837-6668, operates a foliage hotline and publishes suggested fall color routes covering the entire state. Also remember that overnight accommodation anywhere along popular fall color routes should be made well in advance.

## FALL FOLIAGE ITINERARIES

Some fall color tour suggestions include:
• **Burlington**, surrounded by remarkable scenery, not only offers brilliant autumn colors but also a wide array of cultural activities. Vermont's northern mini-metropolis follows the shore of Lake Champlain and a walk to downtown Battery Park — where American guns turned away British warships during the War of 1812 — reveals a setting that impressed even Rudyard Kipling.
• For color cruising, board *The Spirit of Ethan Allen* ( (802) 862-9685, a recreated paddle-wheel-era boat that offers a 90-minute voyage on Lake Champlain; you will have a magnificent view of Vermont's Green Mountains in the east and New York state's Adirondacks to the west.
• Back on shore, head 20 miles (32 km) southeast on Interstate 89 to reach the **Green Mountain Audubon Nature Center** ( (802) 434-3068, 230 acres (93 hectares) of trails winding around beaver ponds, hemlock swamp and retired farm fields, set in a blaze of color.
• An especially colorful 124-mile (200-km) car tour follows U.S. 7 south from Burling-

ton, skirts **Lake Champlain** and then enters the **Green Mountain National Forest** before reaching Bennington, near the New York/Massachusetts border.
• **Smugglers' Notch State Park**, near Stowe, offers some of the most spectacular color scenery in Vermont, though you may have to fight off the crowds. To get there from Stowe, travel west on Route 108, enter the state park and soon you will be negotiating hairpin curves along sheer cliffs and ledges leading to the 2,162-ft (659-m) "notch," named after19th-century creative

capitalists who smuggled illegal goods from the United States into Canada through the natural pass in the Green Mountains.

## BICYCLING IN VERMONT

Vermont's rolling hills, low-road mountain passes, country back roads, outstanding state parks and light traffic make it a cyclist's paradise. In fact, it has often been rated as the top biking state in America.

Bicycle touring is a great way to enjoy at close range the state's emerald green landscape while discovering interesting villages and historic towns. There are several Vermont cycling groups that conduct tours of varying lengths and degrees of difficulty, from leisurely rides into the countryside to grueling off-road mountain touring. Most not only provide experienced guides who lead the way, explaining state sights and sounds, but also make all the arrangements for overnight lodging and meals.

You can also rent bicycles and strike out on your own, following suggested state cycling routes, or those mapped out by bike clubs that create itineraries to match your interests.

## BICYCLING DIRECTORY

### Guided Tours

• **Back roads** ( (800) 464-2848 FAX (510) 527-1444, 801 Cedar Street, Berkeley, CA 94710, features two itineraries, one in Vermont's Northeast Kingdom, one in its Southern River Valleys. Maximum group size is 26 cyclists with two trip leaders on these well-run trips. Participants choose from a light, medium or challenging route on each of six days cycling from inn to inn. Long-distance custom-designed touring bicycles are available.

• **Bike Vermont** ( (802) 457-3553 TOLL-FREE (800) 257-2226, P.O. Box 207 G, Woodstock, VT 05091, conducts inn-to-inn bicycle tours for cyclists at all skill levels. Groups average 12 to 15 people, with 20 the maximum.

• **Vermont Back Roads Bike Tours** ( (802) 586-7767 TOLL-FREE (800) 720-7751 FAX (802) 586-7768, Box 31, Craftsbury Common, VT 05827, includes three-day and six-day tours on back roads, averaging 10 to 20 miles (26 to 32 km) per day using mountain bikes.

• **Vermont Bicycle Touring** ( (802) 453-4811 TOLL-FREE (800) 245-3868 FAX (802) 453-4806, Box 711-GX, Bristol, VT 05443, offers easy to challenging tours for adults and families, with special emphasis on overnighting at country inns and sampling home-cooked meals. Trips are typically two to five days long, but can be booked for extended periods. A support van assists with luggage transportation, picnic lunches and repairs on the five-day trips. Rentals and customized trips are available.

• **Escape Routes** ( (802) 746-8943, P.O. Box 685, Pittsfield, VT 05762, offers mountain adventures for cyclists who desire an out-of-the-ordinary cycling experience. Only backcountry is traveled, including seldom-used dirt roads, old farm lanes, logging trails and overnights at country inns. Two- to five-day tours, for beginners and intermediate levels. Mountain bikes required; rentals available.

### Self-Guided Tours

• **Country Inns Along the Trail** ( (802) 247-3300 TOLL-FREE (800) 838-3301 FAX (802) 247-6851, Road 3, Brandon, VT 05733, specializes in customized biking itineraries based on length of trip and degree of difficulty desired. Their program includes the partici-

pation of more than 25 country inns in western and central Vermont.

## More Cycing Information

• The **Vermont Travel Division** ( (802) 828-3236 TOLL-FREE (800) 837-6668, 134 State Street, Montpelier, VT 05602, provides up-to-date information about biking in the state, including suggested routes and material on attractions, accommodation and restaurants along the way.

• The **Handbook on American Youth Hostels, Inc.,** provides information on budget accommodation; you must become a member to use the hostels. Send a self-addressed envelope to **Greater Boston Council, American Youth Hostels**

( (617) 731-5430 TOLL-FREE (800) 444-6111, 1020 Commonwealth Avenue, Boston, MA 02215.

• One of the most popular information sources over the years has been *25 Bicycle Tours in Vermont,* available through Vermont Bicycle Touring, listed above.

Weathered wood farm houses along Waits River.

# Connec-
# ticut

FOR MORE THAN three centuries, Connecticut has welcomed travelers. George Washington visited the state a number of times; the bedroom his hosts decorated at Webb House for his visit to Wethersfield in 1781 still looks the same today.

Mark Twain stopped in Connecticut on business in 1873 and stayed for a good portion of his life, writing such classics as *Tom Sawyer* during his time in Hartford. His flamboyant "Steamboat Gothic" home still stands in Hartford.

Even P.T. Barnum, the master of hype who traveled the world with his Greatest Show on Earth, put all that aside when he returned to his home in Bridgeport. The Barnum Museum there provides lots of entertainment courtesy of the master showman.

However, travelers on Interstate 95 often pass straight through Connecticut on their way to holiday spots elsewhere in New England, missing out on a unique part of New England which is best explored along its picturesque back roads.

It is not hard to get around in Connecticut. The state is a rectangle measuring only 90 miles (145 km) by 55 miles (89 km), bordered by New York on the west, Massachusetts to the north and Rhode Island to the east.

Its southern boundary stretches along Long Island Sound; protected by Long Island, New York, these shores have long sandy beaches and historic port towns. Both the Connecticut River, which bisects the state and the Housatonic in the northwest provide spectacular scenery and the Litchfield Hills, which rise in northern Connecticut, are dotted with villages perfect for leisurely touring.

### General Information

Since no two places in the state are more than a two-hour drive apart, it is possible to enjoy the best of what Connecticut has to offer in a few days. The **Connecticut Department of Economic Development** ( (860) 258-4355 TOLL-FREE (800) 282-6863 FAX (860) 258-4275, 865 Brook Street, Rocky Hill, CT 06067, provides free maps and guides to help plan your trip. For **travel information**, call TOLL-FREE (800) CT-BOUND.

## BACKGROUND

Adriaen Block, a Dutch navigator, was the first recorded European explorer to sail along Connecticut's coast in 1614. He traveled up the Connecticut River, where the Dutch later established a trading post near today's Hartford, for dealing in the region's lucrative beaver trade.

By 1635, English settlers from the already crowded Massachusetts Bay Colony, driven by a search for farmland,

were flowing into the Connecticut River valley.

The Massachusetts colonists established three towns along the Connecticut River — Hartford, Wethersfield and Windsor — known jointly as the Hartford Colony. On January 14, 1639, the colony proclaimed the Fundamental Orders of Connecticut which, some historians contend, is the world's first written democratic constitution; hence the state's nickname, "The Constitution State."

Connecticut revolutionaries played important political and military roles in the American Revolution. Among these were General Israel Putnam, who ordered troops on Bunker Hill not to fire "until you see the whites of their eyes," and the revolutionary Nathan Hale, hanged as a spy by the British, who said before he died, "I regret that I have but one life to give for my country."

Southern Connecticut OPPOSITE is more commercial than the northeast "Quiet Corner" ABOVE.

Commerce, trade and manufacturing took root thereafter. Banks were established in Hartford by 1792 and the insurance industry began in Norwich in 1795. Samuel Colt of Hartford developed the Colt .45; Gideon Roberts made Bristol the clock capital of the United States; everyone wore Danbury hats; and Meriden silver services were treasured.

This level of prosperity endures today, as indicated by the state's per capita income which is the highest in the nation.

## HARTFORD

Mark Twain once said, "Of all the beautiful towns it has been my fortune to see, Hartford is chief." The capital of Connecticut, Hartford, can look back on 350 years of history from its setting on the banks of the Connecticut River. The **Center Church burying ground** has gravestones dating from 1640. The **Old State House**, built in 1796, is the oldest in the nation and Mark Twain's eccentric mansion still stands on a small green surrounded by skyscrapers.

The state's second largest city has undergone a boom that has transformed downtown Hartford into a mixture of high-rise architecture, new riverfront developments, restorations such as Pratt Street, sophisticated stores and cafés set into refurbished buildings and Constitution Plaza.

ABOVE: The State Capitol reflects Hartford's wealth, much of which has been amassed by its numerous insurance companies. OPPOSITE: An Alexander Calder sculpture at Wadsworth Athenium.

The national headquarters of 40 insurance companies, Hartford has been an insurance haven since an 18th-century ship owner took out a policy on his boat and cargo. When the tragic fire of 1835 destroyed more than 600 buildings in New York City, many insurance companies could not honor claims and went bankrupt. The Hartford Insurance Company's president visited every New York policyholder, assuring them that their claims would be quickly settled. Since then, its financial stability, despite disasters such as the Great Chicago Fire and the San Francisco earthquake of 1906, have enhanced Hartford's reputation as the insurance capital of the nation.

### THE CHARTER OAK

Hartford's riverside location drew early attention. The "city" began as a Dutch trading post named Fort Good Hope in 1633. Massachusetts Bay Colony puritans settled here two years later and the village eventually formed one-third of the Hartford Colony, its independence guaranteed by the Royal Charter of 1662.

Legend has it that when the royal governor demanded return of the charter 25 years later, it was stolen and hidden in the trunk of a massive oak tree, the famous "Charter Oak," that stood until felled by a storm in the 1850s. (The oak's location is now marked by a plaque.) The governor was recalled and the threat to independence overcome.

### GENERAL INFORMATION

For a quick orientation and free maps and guides of the city, you can stop at the **Tourist Information Center (** (860) 522-6766, 800 Main Street, Hartford, CT 06103, in the Old State House, which is open Monday through Saturday, 10 AM to 5 PM.

### A WALKING TOUR

**The Walk** is a self-guided journey through Hartford's historic sites and new landmarks. Begin at the **Old State House** in the downtown district. Tours of the handsome 1796 Federal structure, the first public

building designed by Charles Bulfinch, include the restored Senate chamber with its Gilbert Stuart portrait of George Washington and original furnishings.

North on Main Street is the **Richardson**, a brownstone designed by Henry Hobson Richardson, one of America's foremost architects of the 19th century. It is considered an architectural landmark, now restored to its original condition, with restaurants, specialty shops and apartments.

Across the street, **Christ Church** is made conspicuous by its elegant spire. Then at State and Market Streets is **Constitution Plaza**, a unique, 12-acre (five-hectare) urban park where on sunny days some of Hartford's 100,000 downtown workers take café-style lunches on the green.

The plaza's two-sided boat-shaped building, home to Phoenix Mutual Life Insurance, is already a Hartford landmark. New employees are greeted with "Welcome aboard!" (The Phoenix company was established in 1851 to insure only teetotalers.)

**Travelers Tower**, off Main Street, has a 527-ft- (161-m)-high observation deck offering splendid views of the city and the Connecticut River Valley. It is home to its namesake company, which started in 1863 by insuring Colonel James Bolter for $5,000 on his trips from the post office to his home. His premium? Two cents.

Just ahead is the **Wadsworth Atheneum** ( (860) 278-2670, one of the country's first public art museums. It holds 165 permanent and visiting exhibits that include 40,000 art objects. Its collections include Egyptian and Roman artifacts, paintings by masters such as Goya and Rembrandt and a large selection of works by American artists of the Hudson Valley School.

By far the most impressive building is the **State Capitol**, near Bushnell Park. The golden-domed capitol, with its many turrets, gables and towers, was built in 1879. The **Hartford Civic Center** (Asylum and Trumbull Streets) is home to the Hartford Whalers, the city's team in the National Hockey League.

Among other "Walk" attractions is **City Place**, the tallest office building in Connecticut, with a high-tech system of sensors, scanners and silicon chips that automatically control most of the building's functions.

## MARK TWAIN'S NOOK FARM

Mark Twain (Samuel Clemens) is perhaps America's most oft-quoted writer. Born and raised in Hannibal, Missouri, on the Mississippi River, he came to Hartford in the 1870s. His home at Nook Farm ( (860) 525-9317, Farmington Avenue and Forest Street, was built in 1874 for $131,000 and reflects the grand style of its owner. The many-gabled, orange-red house caused scandalous comments in its time because of its stylistic excesses.

It is Victoriana and Gothic — a tangle of gingerbread, pointy towers, intricate woodworking, even decorating gems fashioned by Louis Comfort Tiffany. It still contains much of Twain's original furnishings, including the huge hand-carved bed purchased on his travels through Europe. He became so enamored of the delicate headboard hand carvings that he often slept with his head at the foot of the bed to gaze at the headboard.

Upstairs in the billiards room is where Twain did much of his writing and entertaining. He wrote *Tom Sawyer*, *The Adventures of Huckleberry Finn* and other masterpieces here.

Twain left the house in 1891 after bad business investments forced him to embark on a quick European lecture tour to raise money. The modest Victorian home of the novelist **Harriet Beecher Stowe** is just across the lawn.

## WHERE TO STAY

**Expensive**
**Sheraton-Hartford Hotel** ( (860) 728-5151 TOLL-FREE (800) 325-3535 FAX (860) 240-7247, 315 Trumbull Street, frequently offers weekend specials to attract travelers. The weekend specials at the **Holiday Inn Downtown** ( (860) 549-2400 TOLL-FREE (800) HOLIDAY FAX (860) 527-2746, 50 Morgan Street, bring this hotel to the moderate category.

For a touch of Old Hartford, try the **Goodwin Hotel** ( (860) 246-7500 TOLL-

FREE (800) 922-5006 FAX (860) 247-4576, 1 Haynes Street, Hartford, 06103, which serves commendable fare in **Pierpont's Restaurant**.

For excellent accommodations outside the city try the **Marriott Hotel Hartford** ( (860) 678-1000 TOLL-FREE (800) 321-2211 FAX (860) 677-8849, 15 Farm Springs Road, Farmington; and the **Courtyard by Marriott Hartford** ( (860) 683-0022 TOLL-FREE (800) 321-2211 FAX (860) 683-1072, 1 Day Hill Road, Windsor. Both offer lower weekend rates.

## Moderate

On the outskirts of town is the **Super 8 Motel** ( (860) 246-8888 TOLL-FREE (800) 800-8000, 7 West Service Road, that includes breakfast in the price of the rooms.

Close by, in East Hartford, are several smaller, moderately priced motels: **Executive Motor Lodge** ( (860) 569-1100, 490 Main Street, East Hartford; **Holiday Inn** ( (860) 528-9611 TOLL-FREE (800) 465-4329 FAX (860) 289-0270, 363 Roberts Street; and **Ramada Hotel Downtown** ( (860) 528-9703 TOLL-FREE (800) 272-6232 FAX (860) 289-4728, 100 East River Drive.

**Four Seasons International Bed & Breakfast** ( (860) 651-3045, 11 Bridlepath Road, West Simsbury, is a booking service for bed-and-breakfast lodging in the Hartford area. Most of their listings are in nearby small towns.

## Inexpensive

The best bargain in the greater Hartford area is **Motel 6** ( (860) 563-5900, Silas Deane Highway, Wethersfield, CT 06109.

## EATING OUT

### Expensive

**Pierpont's Restaurant** ( (860) 246-7500, 1 Haynes Street, Hartford. in the Goodwin Hotel, accents its traditional fare with unusual side dishes and appetizers.

### Moderate

**Peppercorns Grill** ( (860) 547-1714, 357 Main Street, Hartford. This chic bistro features Continental cuisine, pastas, fresh seafood. Patrons of the **First and Last Tavern** ( (860)

956-6000, 939 Maple Avenue, Hartford, willingly drive a few miles out of the city for some of the best pizza in the state.

In nearby **Glastonbury** you can dine in the Colonial atmosphere of the **Blacksmith's Tavern** ( (860) 659-0366, 2300 Main Street.

## HARTFORD AREA EXCURSIONS

### Farmington

Just 10 miles (16 km) west of Hartford on Route 10, this elegant colonial town is

often referred to as one of New England's museum pieces. Its rich 18th-century architecture includes the **Stanley-Whitman House**, parts of which date from 1663. The village's **Hill-Stead Museum** contains several French Impressionist paintings.

### Wethersfield

In Hartford's suburban south, Wethersfield has more than 150 houses pre-dating the mid-19th century, including the 1752 **Webb House**, where George Washington and French commander Jean Baptiste Donatien de Vimeur, Count of Rochambeau, met in

ABOVE: The Harriet Beecher Stowe house.

1781 to plan the Yorktown campaign that led to America's victory in the Revolutionary War.

## Bristol

In 1790, Gideon Roberts started selling his clocks here, just 18 miles (29 km) west of Hartford. Soon the town became the clock-making center of the United States.

The **American Clock and Watch Museum** ( (860) 583-6070, Maple Street, off Route 6, displays more than 2,000 fine time-pieces made in Connecticut.

## CONNECTICUT RIVER VALLEY

The Connecticut River (from the Indian name Quinnituckett or long tidal river) flows for 410 miles (660 km) from its head-waters near the Canadian border in New Hampshire to Long Island Sound, neatly bisecting Connecticut into east and west. **Essex**, **Ivoryton**, **Old Lyme**, **Chester** and **East Haddam**, a cluster of little towns 10 to 15 miles from Long Island Sound, are within

easy reach of the area's attractions — and an ideal place to sample one of the valley's country inns.

## ESSEX

A gateway to the valley, Essex is also the terminus of the **Valley Railroad** ( (860) 767-0103, which offers 55minute tours of the river valley aboard turn-of-the-century steam trains to **Deep River Gorge** near picturesque **Chester**. From Deep River Gorge, riders take an hour-long **riverboat**

**cruise** up the Connecticut River past some of the valley's best scenery, including Gillette's famous castle and the Goodspeed Opera House, before returning by rail to the Essex Depot.

## GILLETTE CASTLE

A five-minute ride by car ferry from **Chester** brings one to **Hadlyme** and an eccentric hilltop fieldstone mansion dubbed **Gillette Castle** ( (860) 526-2336. Built by actor William Gillette, a Hartford native famous for his portrayal of Sherlock Holmes, the 122-acre (49-hectare) medieval castle commands a sweeping view of the Connecticut River and countryside.

ABOVE LEFT: The Connecticut Valley Railroad.
RIGHT: Gillette Castle. OPPOSITE: Essex.

Construction of the 24-room mansion began in 1914 and took five years to complete. Built to Gillette's design, the castle has granite walls that are four feet (103 cm) thick at the base and interior trim hand hewn from southern white oak. Huge oak doors are fastened by complicated wooden locks; some bedroom furniture is built into the castle's structure and other furnishings slide on metal tracks. Electric light fixtures are decorated with bits of colored glass gathered by his friends. He could even see who was entering the house by a series of angled mirrors. Outside, Gillette built a large railroad, with a "Grand Central" depot starting at the entrance gate and winding to "125th Street" at the property's eastern terminus; he delighted in manning the throttle while treating visitors to rides through his estate. The train was dismantled long ago.

In his will, Gillette instructed his executors "to see to it that the property [does] not fall into the hands of some blithering saphead who has no conception of where he is or with what surrounded." In 1943, Gillette Castle was acquired by the state.

## EAST HADDAM

Just north of Gillette Castle on Route 82, East Haddam is an old riverboat landing and the site of the **Goodspeed Opera House** ( (860) 873-8668. This 1876 building on the banks of the Connecticut River cuts a dashing figure when viewed from the water; inside, the beautifully-restored Victorian auditorium now offers Equity productions of American musicals from mid-April to December.

The Victorian-style town is also the location of the **Nathan Hale Schoolhouse** (where Hale taught in 1773). Also available are afternoon **sightseeing cruises** ( (860) 345-4507 and evening music excursions on the river (board in Haddam).

## WHERE TO STAY AND EATING OUT

Part of the experience of visiting the Connecticut River Valley is staying in one of its many country inns. For centuries New Yorkers have come here to escape the hustle and bustle of America's largest city. In the summer, reservations are essential. Most of these inns are in the expensive category.

### Essex

The **Griswold Inn** ( (860) 767-1776, 36 Main Street, is almost a tourist attraction in itself. Reservations to stay in the 212-year-old country inn are made months in advance. In spite of its popularity, its rates are reasonable, at the high end of the moderate range. They do, however, include breakfast. To dine on its wild game specialties, you will

have to make reservations early. On Sundays from 11 AM to 2:30 PM, you can feast at a Hunt Breakfast for $12.95. Children under six eat free.

### Ivoryton

The **Copper Beach Inn** ( (860) 767-0330, 46 Main Street, Ivoryton, is an excellent alternative to the Griswold. Food critics claim it has the best restaurant in southern Connecticut.

For a change of pace in dining, **Steve's Centerbrook Café** ( (860) 767-1277, 78 Main Street, Centerbrook, a couple of miles out of Ivoryton, serves new American cuisine at about the same price as the Copper Beach Inn.

## Chester

**The Inn at Chester** ( (860) 526-4961, 318 West Main Street, is in a lovely rural setting. This late-18th century farmhouse is adjacent to the state forest and has access to miles of hiking trails.

## Old Lyme

Old Lyme has two excellent inns: The **Old Lyme Inn** ( (860) 434-2600 TOLL-FREE (800) 434-5352 FAX (860) 434-5352, 85 Lyme Street, is a stately 1850s mansion with five rooms in the main building and nine in the new

addition; the **Bee and Thistle Inn** ( (860-434-1667 TOLL-FREE (800) 622-4946 FAX (860) 434-3402, 100 Lyme Street, on the banks of the Lieutenant River, serves seafood and duck specialties in its dining room.

---

## MYSTIC AND NEW LONDON

Facing Long Island Sound and the sea, Mystic and New London attracted restless, venturesome Yankees, who sailed around the world in search of whales, rum, spices and the riches of the China Trade.

---

Fog and sun at Mystic Seaport.

## MYSTIC

Since the 17th century, Mystic has been building boats. Its elegant clipper ships made Mystic one of the country's top whaling centers — with nearly 20 whalers in its fleet. Later, its vessels formed the backbone of America's Navy in World War II.

### Mystic Seaport

This recreated 19th-century seafaring village and living-history museum is at the mouth of the Mystic River and has a whaleboat demonstration, oystering displays and sailors tending the sails aboard an elegant whaler.

The 17-acre (seven-hectare) seaport museum, begun in 1929, contains more than 60 historic waterfront buildings, 300 ships and boats and artifacts of 19th-century maritime America.

America's sole surviving wooden whaling ship, the **Charles W. Morgan**, is the Seaport's master attraction. Visitors may walk the main deck, explore the cargo hold which still smells of whale blubber and see where the crew of more than 90 men lived and worked. The 113-ft- (35-m)-long, three-masted **Morgan**, built in 1841, sailed the seas for nearly 80 years, making 37 whaling voyages, some lasting up to five years. A fascinating 30minute program on 19th-century whaling at the Meeting House includes rare footage of an actual whaling voyage.

You can also explore the decks of the square-rigged **Joseph Conrad**, an iron-hulled Dutch training vessel built in 1882; today it serves as a training ship for the Seaport's special sailing program. The **L.A. Dunton Fishing Schooner** (1921) illustrates the days of Grand Banks fishing aboard a two-masted Gloucester schooner. And the coal-fired **Sabino Passenger Steamboat** (1908) provides pleasant cruises down the Mystic River.

Along Gravel, Clift and High Streets, among others on the west bank of the river, are a number of historic sea captains' homes. Especially interesting is 13 Gravel Street, an 1836 "spite house" built into the street to deliberately block the neighbor's view.

(Ninety-minute self-guided audio-cassette tour tapes are available for rent or sale at Olde Mistick Village shops.)

**Stonington**
Don't leave the area without visiting Stonington, just east of Mystic, off Alternate Route 1A. It is considered by many as one of the prettiest coastal villages in Connecticut.

The **Old Lighthouse** on Stonington Point reminds visitors of Stonington's past as a whaling and sealing port; inside, a small

museum contains seafaring artifacts and the lighthouse tower has a view of three states (Fisher's Island, NY, Rhode Island to the east and Connecticut), as well as breathtaking vistas across the sound.

**Where to Stay**
Overlooking the harbor, atop a hill at the junction of U.S. 1 and Route 27, **The Inn at Mystic** ( (860) 536-9604 TOLL-FREE (800) 237-2415 FAX (860) 572-1635, U.S. 1 and Route 27 (expensive), is an old-style New England inn, housed in a cluster of Victorian buildings. On its spacious grounds are tennis courts, a pool and a boat dock.

In town there is another traditional inn, the **Whaler's Inn** ( (860) 536-1506 TOLL-FREE (800) 243-2588 FAX (860) 572-1250, 20 East Main Street, as well as the larger, more modern **Hilton Mystic** ( (860) 572-

0731 TOLL-FREE (800) 445-8667 FAX (860) 572-0328, 20 Coogan Boulevard. At the Hilton, children stay free in their parents' room and special weekend rates are often available.

**Comfort Inn** ( (860) 572-8531 TOLL-FREE (800) 228-5150 FAX (860) 572-1164, 48 Whitehall Avenue (moderate); and **Days Inn** ( (860) 572-0574 TOLL-FREE (800) 325-2525 FAX (860) 572-1164, 55 Whitehall Avenue, Route 27 (moderate), have simpler rooms at a more modest rate.

Just east of Mystic in **Stonington**, you can find bread-and-breakfast accommodations. **The State of Connecticut Tourism Division Information Center** at the North Stonington southbound exit off Interstate 95 has a listing of these homes and will help make reservations.

**Eating Out**
EXPENSIVE
Even if you don't stay at the Inn at Mystic, you may want to dine at its **Flood Tide Restaurant** ( (860) 536-8140 (U.S. 1 and Route 27), with its specialties of Long Island roast duck and Maine lobster.

For a French-style meal, **J.P. Daniels** ( (860) 572-9564, Route 184, Old Mystic, is the best in the area.

MODERATE
Actually three restaurants in one, **Seamen's Inne** ( (860) 536-9649, Germanville Avenue, caters New England meals to suit your price range. You can have an inexpensive snack at the bar, a moderately-priced meal at the café, or a more expensive, larger meal in the dining room.

Nearby in North Stonington, **Randall's Ordinary Inn** ( (860) 599-4540, Route 2, serves fixed-price meals that feature New England specialties.

INEXPENSIVE
To the south in Noank is **Abbot's Lobster in the Rough** ( (860) 536-7719, 117 Pearl Street, where you get the best buy for your money. There are no waiters; you order at the window, pay the tab and wait for your number to be called. In addition to steamed lobster, the menu includes whatever seafood is in season.

ABOVE: Groton, home port of the U.S. Navy's Atlantic Submarine Fleet and the Submarine Force Library. OPPOSITE: Lobster, the New England seacoast specialty

## NEW LONDON

At one time, New London was the second busiest whaling port on the East Coast. The mansions built by her sea captains testify to their successes. Especially interesting is Huntington Street's **"Whale Oil Row"**, where wealthy seamen built four white-columned Greek Revival mansions in the 1830s. The Pennsylvania oil boom in the late 1850s ended the whaling industry's profitability.

New London is still a seafaring town; its fine deep water port is home to the **United States Coast Guard Academy** ( (860) 444-8270, one of the nation's four service academies that train military officers. You can take a walking tour of the grounds; cadet dress parades are held in spring and fall and the training barge *Eagle*, a three-masted square rigger built in 1936, is open for weekend tours when in port. New London also has several historic buildings, including the 1774 **Nathan Hale School House** and **Monte Cristo Cottage**, boyhood home of Nobel Prize-winning playwright Eugene O'Neill.

### Groton

Across the Thames River from New London is Groton, home port of the **United States Navy's Atlantic Submarine Fleet** ( (860) 449-4779. You can take a one-hour submarine base tour aboard sightseeing buses, with the possibility of seeing docked submarines being repaired along the river.

A better way to immerse yourself in submarine lore is by climbing aboard the *SS Nautilus*, the world's first nuclear-powered submarine, built in 1954 by Groton's Electric Boat Division of General Dynamics. The ship's claustrophobic quarters were crammed with 111 officers and crew during its journeys, which included cruising under the Arctic ice cap, from the Bering Strait to the Greenland Sea, in 1958.

The **Submarine Force Library** ( (860) 449-3174, is filled with interesting displays and exhibits that trace the development of United States submarines from the Revolutionary War, through World War II, to today's sleek nuclear-powered ships.

It's also possible to take a sightseeing cruise on the Thames aboard the *River Queen II* ( (860) 445-9516, 193 Thames Street, (board at The Harbour Inn). You will pass the *SS Nautilus* and other submarines at their riverside berths, sight Trident submarines being constructed at Groton, pass the submarine base and Coast Guard Academy and perhaps even see a submarine or two returning to home port.

### General Information

Maps and guides of the area are available

from the **Connecticut's Mystic and More** ( (860) 444-2206 TOLL-FREE (800) 863-6569, 470 Bank Street, Box 89, New London, CT 06320.

## NORTHWEST CONNECTICUT

Quiet country back roads, peaceful colonial villages, great hiking trails — including part of the Appalachian Trail — make touring in this region quite special. **Canaan**, on Route 7 near the state line with Massachusetts in the north and **Kent**, further south also on Route 7 near the New York State line are the access points to the region. From Hartford, **Litchfield**, 30 miles (50 km) away on U.S. 202, is perhaps the best base for a visit to the region.

## CANAAN TO KENT

At Canaan, just south of the Massachusetts border, you can ride the **Housatonic Railroad** along the Housatonic River through the green hill country. Board at the 1872 **Union Station** ℂ (860) 824-0339, Routes 7 and 44, America's oldest train depot in continuous use. Six miles (10 km) east on U.S. 44 at **Norfolk** is the site of **Indian burial**

**grounds.** Nearby **Haystack Mountain** and the 34-ft- (10-m)-high stone tower at the summit (1,716 ft or 523 m) offers views of Long Island Sound, the Berkshires in Massachusetts and mountain peaks in New York. A road one mile (just over one and a half kilometers) north of Norfolk on Route 272 leads halfway up the mountain; a quick 30 minute hike gets you to the top. The June mountain laurel and fall foliage are spectacular.

Another summit pavilion, in **Dennis Hill State Park** south of Norfolk on Route 272, provides views of Haystack Mountain, the

OPPOSITE: Pig farm in Litchfield county. ABOVE: Norwich Connecticut's Leffingwell Inn preserved as it was in 1735.

Green Mountains and part of New Hampshire; even New Haven Harbor can be seen on the horizon on a clear day.

### West Cornwall

West Cornwall, 13 miles (21 km) south of Canaan, has a **covered bridge** (Route 128) that has been in continuous service since 1837. If you are here at meal time, **Brookside Bistro** ℂ (860) 672-6601, Route 128, West Cornwall, serves moderately-priced meals.

### Housatonic Meadows

South of West Cornwall on Route 7 and located in the heart of the rock-strewn Housatonic valley, Housatonic Meadows lies amid rugged hills. Tall pines shade the banks of the river, which is known for its fly fishing.

### Kent

Another **covered bridge** spanning the Housatonic River is south on Route 7 in Kent, where the **Sloane-Stanley Museum** displays handmade tools used by early settlers. The covered **Bull's Bridge** also spans the Housatonic, stretching into New York state; it is four miles (six kilometers) south of Kent.

### Kent Falls

North of Kent on Route 7, Kent Falls whitewater cascades draw thousands of visitors. A gentle stepped pathway runs parallel to the waterfalls. It is also one of the most photographed natural sites in the state.

### Macedonia Brook

At Macedonia Brook, north of Kent, two 1,400ft (427m) peaks offer stunning views of the Catskills and Taconics.

## LITCHFIELD

Many historians consider Litchfield the finest unrestored colonial town in the country. George Washington and General Lafayette both visited here. In fact, the entire borough of Litchfield has been declared a National Historic District.

The 18th-century, white-clapboard mansions lining its peaceful, wide streets are not museums but homes. Historic buildings on serene South Street include the 1753 **home of Oliver Wolcott**, signer of the Declaration of Independence; the **birthplace of the revolutionary Ethan Allen**; and the **Tapping Reeve House**, the first law school in America, founded in 1774. Tapping Reeve claims as alumni two vice-presidents of the United States (Aaron Burr and John C. Calhoun), 101 members of Congress, 34 Chief Justices of the United States, 28 United States Senators and 14 state governors. The beautiful white-steepled

serve excellent meals and are in the expensive category.

### Black Rock State Park
West of **Thomaston** on Route 6, Black Rock State Park is a hiker's paradise, with the scenery of the Western Highlands dominating the blue-blazed **Mattatuck Trail**.

### Lake Waramaug and New Preston
Five miles (eight kilometers) north of New Preston, is an autumn delight, with bright hues mirrored in the smooth surface of Lake

**Congregational Church** presides over the town's lovely village green.

### General Information
Free information is available from the **Litchfield Hills Travel Council** ( (860) 567-4506, P.O. Box 968, Litchfield, CT 06759.

### Where to Stay and Eating Out
The best accommodations in town are at the **Litchfield Inn** ( (860) 567-4503 TOLL-FREE (800) 499-3444 FAX (860) 567-4503, Route 202; and the **Tollgate Hill Inn** ( (860) 567-4545 FAX (860) 567-8397, Route 202, which was established as a tavern in 1789, but at the time was located on a nearby hill. In 1923 it was moved to its present site. Both inns

Waramaug. **Mt. Tom**, near Bantam, boasts hiking trails leading to a summit tower. Overlooking the lake is the **Hopkin's Inn** ( (860) 868-7295, Hopkins Road, New Preston, with 10 rooms (moderate), famous for its restaurant which serves Austrian and Swiss specialties.

### HIKING AND CANOEING

Hikers might want to trek part of the **Appalachian Trail** that stretches from Kent to Canaan, while canoeists can look forward to flat-water or **whitewater adventures** on the Housatonic. For information, contact **Clarke Outdoors** ( (860) 672-6365), West Cornwall.

## THE SOUTHWEST COAST

For those entering Connecticut from New York on Interstate 95, it will be hard to tell just when the Empire State ends and the Constitution State begins. That's because coastal cities and villages, such as affluent **Greenwich**, **Stamford**, **Riverside** and **Darien**, are as much suburbs of New York City as Connecticut towns.

An endless number of New Yorkers talk about owning a little farmhouse in

Darien, to get away from the Big Apple's problems at the end of the workday. Only 50 to 90 minutes from Manhattan, some of these towns have evolved into "bedroom" communities.

## BRIDGEPORT

Farther up the coast is Bridgeport, an important manufacturing city with a population of 150,000. P.T. Barnum, the circus impresario and creator of the "Greatest Show on Earth", wintered in

The city **Summer Music Festival** hosts the New York Philharmonic.

**Stratford**, just east up the Sound, is the home of the **American Shakespeare Theater**, which offers the Bard's plays all summer and pre- and post-Broadway productions the rest of the year.

**Where to Stay**

As this area is just across the state line from New York, many visitors to New York city elect to stay in Connecticut where rates are more reasonable and train service to Manhattan is good.

EXPENSIVE

At the top of the line is the **Hyatt Regency Greenwich** ( (203) 637-1234 TOLL-FREE (800) 233-1234 FAX (203) 637-2940, 1800 East Putnam Avenue, Old Greenwich. Also in this category are the **Holiday Inn** ( (203) 358-8400 TOLL-FREE (800) 465-4329 FAX (203) 358-8872, 700 Main Street; and the **Stamford Marriott Hotel** ( (203) 357-9555 TOLL-FREE (800) 228-9290 FAX (203) 324-6897, 2 Stamford Forum.

The **Greenwich Harbor Inn** ( (203) 661-9800 TOLL-FREE (800) 243-8511 FAX (203) 629-4431, 500 Steamboat Road, Greenwich, is a good medium-sized hotel.

MODERATE

**Holiday Inn Hotel and Conference Center** ( (203) 334-1234 TOLL-FREE (800) 465-4329 FAX (203) 367-1985, 1070 Main Street, Bridgeport; **Howard Johnson Lodge** ( (203) 655-3933 TOLL-FREE (800) 654-2000 FAX (203) 655-3084, 150 Ledge Road, Darien. The most economical lodging in the area is **Super 8 Motel** ( (203) 324-8887 TOLL-FREE (800) 843-1991 FAX (203) 964-8465, 32 Greenhard Road, Stamford.

**Eating Out**

Greenwich has quite a few good French restaurants such as the **Cinquante-cinq** ( (203) 869-5641, 55 Arch Street (expensive); and the **Jean-Louis** ( (203) 622-8450, at 61 Lewis Street (moderate to expensive). The **64 Greenwich Avenue Restaurant** ( (203) 861-6400, Greenwich (moderate), serves nouvelle American cuisine and delicious homemade desserts.

Bridgeport. He also discovered one of his greatest acts here, namely the 28-in-(71-cm)-tall General Tom Thumb, a Bridgeport native.

The **P.T. Barnum Museum** ( (203) 331-1104, located on the Main Street, underwent a $6 million renovation. It boasts much circus lore and has on display many curiosities that made Barnum famous, including personal memorabilia of Thumb and others.

The **Beardsley Zoological Gardens** in Bridgeport is the only zoo in Connecticut.

## NEW HAVEN

Founded in 1638 on the Connecticut coast, New Haven began as a Puritan settlement at the end of a harbor four miles (six and a half kilometers) from Long Island Sound.

Three rivers flow into the sound here — the Quinnipiac, the Mill and the West. Around the village, low meadows give way to gently sloped hills. The prominent landmarks then, as now, were two

a manufacturing center; that tradition continues today.

In 1716, the Collegiate School of Saybrook, established 15 years earlier, moved to New Haven and changed its name to **Yale University** to honor a generous donor, Elihu Yale.

The earliest Yale buildings were built just west of the Green; the campus now covers 160 acres (65 hectares) in the central city and dominates New Haven. The distinguished Ivy League school has nearly 12,000 students divided among its 12 col-

isolated peaks known as East Rock and West Rock.

The town was planned in classic fashion with nine squares. The center square today is New Haven's public Green, once a marketplace and pastureland. It is surrounded by three historic churches built between 1812 and 1815, all exhibiting distinctive architectural styles: Federal, Georgian and Gothic Revival.

In the 19th century, worn out farmlands forced people into cities and towns; by the end of the Civil War, more than half of Connecticut's population lived in urban areas. After Eli Whitney created a mass-production line for manufacturing his cotton gin, New Haven gradually became

leges — each with its own library, dormitories and dining halls. Historically, about 15 graduates each year eventually become United States Congressmen. Renowned alumni include Nathan Hale, William Howard Taft, Noah Webster and George Bush.

Guided one-hour walking tours of the historic campus start at **Phelps Gateway** ( (203) 432-2300, on College Street, across from the New Haven Green. One of the most interesting areas is the **Old Campus**, containing Yale's oldest buildings, including Connecticut Hall, where Nathan Hale studied. One of the most unusual campus buildings among those designed by famous architects is the **Ingalls Hockey Rink** by

Eero Saarinen, inspired by the shape of a whale.

The **Yale University Art Gallery**, on Chapel Street, is one of the finest small galleries in the country. In addition to a collection of French Impressionist paintings, it has on show many works by patriot painter John Trumbull, including the original "Bunker Hill" and "Declaration of Independence".

New Haven's **Shubert Performing Arts Center** features Broadway-bound productions and road shows. The New Haven

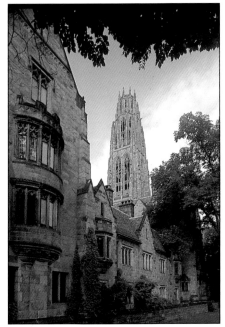

Symphony Orchestra performs at Yale's **Woolsey Hall**.

**Where to Stay**

At graduation and matriculation (May and September), hotels in New Haven can be completely booked. If your trip takes you here during these times, you will have to make your reservations well in advance.

EXPENSIVE

**The Inn at Chapel West** ( (203) 777-1201, 1201 Chapel Street. Excellent service here raises this inn above the category of expensive to luxury.

Also in the heart of downtown is **Park Plaza** ( (203) 772-1700 FAX (203) 624-2683,

155 Temple Street, which has a rooftop restaurant.

Less expensive and close to Yale is **The Colony** ( (203) 776-1234 TOLL-FREE (800) 458-8810 FAX (203) 772-3929, 1157 Chapel Street.

MODERATE

Children stay free with their parents at the **Holiday Inn Downtown at Yale University** ( (203) 777-6221 TOLL-FREE (800) 465-4329 FAX (203) 772-1089, 30 Whalley Avenue.

The **Howard Johnson Lodge** ( (203) 288-3831 TOLL-FREE (800) 654-2000 FAX (203) 281-6032, 2260 Whitney Avenue; **Hamden**, north of New Haven, is more expensive than the more centrally located **Susse Chalet** ( (203) 562-1111 FAX (203) 865-7440, 400 Sargent Drive, New Haven.

**Eating Out**

The best restaurants in New Haven serve ethnic dishes.

**Saigon City** ( (203) 865-5033, corner of Chapel and Park Streets, prepares Vietnamese cuisine in fine style, while **Blessings** ( (203) 624-3557, 45 Howe Street, serves tasty northern Chinese specialties. **Delmonaco's** ( (203) 865-1109, 232 Wooster Street, prepares northern Italian-style meals. For excellent pizzas try **Frank Pepe's** ( (203) 865-5762, 157 Wooster Street.

Perhaps as much an attraction as a place to eat is **Atticus Bookstore-Café** ( (203) 776-4040, 1082 Chapel Street, where they serve coffee and pastries (for breakfast), or tea and cakes (for afternoon tea) surrounded by of one of the best selections of books in the state.

New Haven's Yale University, among the nation's most distinctive in learning and architecture.

# Rhode
# Island

A CASUAL GLANCE at a map of the United States reveals that Rhode Island at 1,212 sq miles (3,144 sq km), even with the many islands of Narragansett Bay, is the smallest state in the nation. But the "Ocean State," as it calls itself, with its 400 miles (664 km) of shoreline, has a variety of coastal land and undeveloped beaches. It also claims the longest official name of any state — "Rhode Island and Providence Plantations."

It was the seacoast that brought the blue bloods of America to Newport, a harbor town transformed into a haven for the millionaires of the "Gilded Age." They built magnificent estates (referred to as "summer cottages") along the cliffs and ledges that border the ocean. Many of these structures remain today as a testament of Newport's affluent past.

## BACKGROUND

The Florentine navigator Giovanni da Verrazano explored Narragansett Bay in 1524 under commission from the King of France. He is said to have named the area Rhode Island because of its resemblance to the island of that name in the Aegean Sea. One hundred years were to pass before the first colonists would arrive — from England, not from France. Among the first of these was Reverend William Blackstone, a nomadic preacher who came to Rhode Island when his lands on the Shawmut Peninsula, near Boston, were taken over by Puritan settlers.

Roger Williams, who founded Providence Plantations in 1636, had been driven out of Salem, Massachusetts, for advocating religious freedom and tolerance. His convictions were to have a benign and continuing effect on the development of the new colony. Ann Hutchinson, who helped to establish Portsmouth in 1638, soon followed, as did others anxious to be free of the rigors of Boston Puritanism. By the 19th century, immigrants in large numbers were coming to Rhode Island to seek a new life.

Religious freedom, rich farmlands and sheltered harbors provided, for Rhode Island, an environment in which tolerance and liberty could prosper.

### THE TRIANGLE TRADE

Providence and Newport became leading seaports and centers of the infamous, "Triangle Trade" in the New World. Their merchants sent ships loaded with rum to Africa, traded the rum for slaves, then sailed to the West Indies where they traded slaves for sugar and molasses, the ingredients from which, in home ports, rum could again be distilled. By 1760, Newport had become New England's major port for

slave-trading ships — a dubious distinction in a colony founded on tenets of religious and individual freedom.

In the same century, Rhode Island's craggy coastline, islands and coves sheltered pirates and privateers who raided ships far out in the Atlantic; later in life, these scoundrels and their crews returned, often, to reside ashore in respectable affluence. The search for legendary pirate treasure, said to be buried somewhere in Jamestown, continues today.

### STATEHOOD AND THE TWENTIETH CENTURY

In 1772, the resistance of Rhode Islanders to British rule became increasingly overt, as witnessed by the burning of the British ship, *Gaspee*. After the Revolutionary War broke out, the colony joined wholeheartedly in the long struggle for independence that

Boating and fishing: holiday pastimes on Rhode Island's rugged coast.

culminated in the final American-French victory at Yorktown.

Despite its passion for independence, Rhode Island was the last of the original 13 states to ratify the United States Constitution. Subsequently, the state enjoyed rapid growth and prosperity, becoming in time a major industrial center. By 1793, a large-scale textile industry had been established in Pawtucket and, by the mid-19th century, it was producing almost 20 percent of the nation's cloth. By the turn of the century, immigrant workers and their families accounted for almost 70 percent of the state's population. When textile factories were drawn to the south by cheaper labor after World War II, the state was forced to diversify its economy.

## GENERAL INFORMATION

Today, with nearly 950,000 people squeezed into 1,214 sq miles (3,144 sq km), Rhode Island is a bustling, energetic state and a popular summer resort in which Newport continues to enjoy preeminence. The state's compactness — only 48 miles (77 km) long and 37 miles (60 km) wide — makes it easy for visitors to enjoy its quiet coves and beaches, wildlife-filled salt marshes, open meadows and big cities. The **Rhode Island Division of Tourism** ( (401) 277-2601 TOLL-FREE (800) 556-2484, 7 Jackson Walkway, Providence, RI 02903, has prepared numerous maps and brochures to help you enjoy your stay in Rhode Island.

## NEWPORT

Dramatic cliffs rising out of the ocean, elegant mansions, expansive lawns and baronial gardens are to be seen in Newport. The rich transformed this harbor town into their own summer resort, commissioning America's finest architects to recreate gaudy palaces, mansions and ersatz châteaux along Ocean Drive and Bellevue Avenue.

Pre-Revolutionary southern plantation owners were the first to discover Newport's summer pleasures as they exchanged the intense heat of the south for refreshing ocean

breezes. Following the Civil War, such scions of American wealth as the Astors and the Vanderbilts flocked to the town, entertaining their friends with picnics and parties, caviar and champagne, in keeping with the excesses of what came to be known as the Gilded Age.

Today, no visit to Newport is complete without a tour of a few of these mansions abandoned when income and property taxes and the Great Depression made their upkeep too expensive.

An option is a bus tour of Newport, a 22-mile (35-km) ride through the historic Colonial section, Ocean Drive and its spectacular coastline, Bellevue Avenue with its millionaire "cottages," and guided tours through two of the mansions, conducted by

Viking Tours of Newport ( (401) 847-6921, 101 Swinburne Row, Brick Market Place. Or you can rent a 90-minute guided auto-tour cassette tape which covers more than 300 years of Newport history and local anecdotes. Cassettes can be purchased at local gift shops or rented at The Paper Lion on America's Cup Avenue in the Long Wharf Mall.

## GENERAL INFORMATION

Visit the **Newport County Convention and Visitors Bureau** ( (401) 849-8048 TOLL-FREE (800) 326-6030, Gateway Center, 23 America's Cup Avenue, from May to September for a viewing of an orientation film, cassette tours, brochures and maps. Open year round, the **Newport County Chamber of Commerce** ( (401) 847-1600, 45 Valley Road, Newport RI 028441, can recommend lodging and information on festivals and special events.

## THE MANSIONS OF THE GILDED AGE

Although scores of mansions existed during the Gilded Age, only 50 or so remain, of which eight, owned by the **Preservation Society of Newport County** ( (401) 847-1000, are open to tours.

It is a good idea to purchase a combination ticket that allows you to visit a number

One of the sumptuous "summer" cottages on Bellevue Avenue, Newport, Rhode Island.

of mansions at your leisure; each tour takes less than two hours.

**The Breakers**, on Ochre Point Avenue, is the most spectacular of the Newport mansions and largest of the grand summer cottages. Built in 1895 for Cornelius Vanderbilt and designed by architect Richard Morris Hunt, it replicates a 16th-century northern Italian palace. Seventy rooms (tended by 40 servants in its heyday) are graced with imported blue marble, alabaster pillars, gold gilt, mosaics and stained glass, with magnificent grounds overlooking the Atlantic Ocean — all enclosed by immense wrought iron fences and gates.

**Marble House**, on Bellevue Avenue, was built in 1892 as a gift for the wife of William K. Vanderbilt. Another Hunt design, it is one of the most sumptuous of Newport's cottages, featuring a dazzling gold ballroom in the French style. (The house is thought to have been styled after the Petit Trianon in Versailles.)

**The Elms**, on Bellevue Avenue, was completed in 1901 for Pennsylvania coal king Edward Julius Berwind. Modeled after the Chateau d'Asnieres near Paris, it features large rooms and an awesome entrance hall, with its own fountains and formal gardens. It is perhaps the most gracefully-styled of the mansions.

**Rosecliff**, on Bellevue Avenue, is a 40room mansion designed by Stanford White and inspired by the Grand Trianon in Versailles. Completed in 1902 for the daughter of the man who discovered Nevada's Comstock Lode, it was the scene of brilliant society balls and galas.

**Hammersmith Farm**, on Ocean Drive, was the site for the wedding reception of John F. Kennedy and Jacqueline Bouvier after their Newport marriage in 1953. The rambling 1887, 28room shingled mansion, with gardens designed by Frederick Law Olmstead, was often used as a summer White House by President Kennedy and now houses mementos from those years. The farm itself was established in 1640 by William Brenton of England and remains the only working farm in the city.

The Cliff Walk OPPOSITE in Newport has been the home of New England's nouveau riche since the Civil War.

## CLIFF WALK

To enjoy the grandeur of the mansions and the sea in a more natural setting, take the **Cliff Walk**, a three and a half mile (five and a half kilometer) coastal path that hugs the craggy shoreline along Rhode Island Sound. From its starting point just off Memorial Boulevard (near Newport Beach) to its terminus at Ocean Avenue, the walk is a narrow strip of public land that separates great estates such as The Breakers, Rosecliff, Marble House and Salve Regina College from the sea.

In the 19th century, wealthy residents attempted to close the path to the public. But the locals protested and eventually the state backed them. Proceed to the end of Narragansett Avenue; there the "Forty Steps" enable you to reach the water without following the entire length of the walk.

## COLONIAL NEWPORT

Among Newport's great treasures is its colonial architecture, especially evident in the Point and Historic Hill neighborhoods. The 1748 **Hunter House**, considered "one of the 10 best examples of residential colonial architecture in America," was also the headquarters of the French Navy during the American Revolution. **Trinity Church** (1726), with its tall white colonial spire, is based on a Christopher Wren design and is a landmark visible for miles. The **Touro Synagogue** (1759) was the first ever built in America. **Old Colony House**, an 18th-century structure, was headquarters for General George Washington as he planned the battle of Yorktown in 1781; it also became the seat of Rhode Island's colonial government. The 1699 **Quaker Meeting House** is the oldest religious building in Newport. And the **White Horse Tavern**, built before 1673, is America's oldest operating tavern.

The **Old Stone Tower**, a "mysterious" structure variously attributed to the Phoenicians, Celts, Vikings and the Portuguese, is more probably the remains of a colonial windmill built by then-governor

Benedict Arnold. **Green Animals** on Cory's Lane in nearby Portsmouth, dating from 1880, is considered the best topiary garden in America, with 80 trees and shrubs sculpted in every animal shape imaginable.

Visitors who wish to take home a memento of Newport history should head to "**Antique Alley**," a cluster of antique shops grouped on Thames and Spring Streets; especially good antique hunting is found on Franklin Street in the Historic Hill section of town.

1851; the last Cup race held here, in 1983, saw the Australians become the first foreign country to wrestle the trophy from the United States.

### Fort Adams State Park

America's Cup memorabilia is housed at the **Museum of Yachting**, worth a visit just for its spectacular waterfront location at Fort Adams State Park on Ocean Drive. It is a display of Newport's rich yachting heritage, with small craft, ship models, costumes and photographs. The America's

### THE WATERFRONT

It is not unusual to see million-dollar yachts anchored in **Brenton Cove** or sailing the waters of Narragansett Bay. Of the bay it has been written, "It is big and scenically lovely, surrounded by wooded countryside, colonial towns, big cities and history-packed shores, with sightseeing opportunities matched by few cruising grounds."

Newport and yachting are inseparable; in fact, it has often been called the yachting capital of the world, harboring countless yacht clubs, boatyards and sailmaking shops. Twenty-four America's Cup races were held in Newport waters beginning in

Cup section includes the 1930 Cup challenger, *Shamrock V*, one of the largest sailing sloops in the world at 127 ft (38.7 m) long and 160 ft (48.8 m) high. The museum also sponsors the Classic Yacht Regatta each Labor Day weekend.

Sightseeing cruises set sail daily (May to October) from Goat Island Marina, off Washington Street and other dock areas. Cruises take you past the mansion-dotted coastline of Newport, the once pirate-infested shores of Jamestown, towering Newport Bridge and Fort Adams, guardian of the harbor; some include a visit to Hammersmith Farm.

Another major attraction is shore surfcasting and bottom fishing in protected bay and shoreline areas and offshore big-game fishing for white marlin and tuna. Numerous charters are available and license is required; for information call ( (401) 789-3094.

## TENNIS HALL OF FAME

The **Newport Casino**, facing Bellevue Avenue, was America's most exclusive country club in the 1880s. Now it houses the **International Tennis Hall of Fame**. American lawn tennis started at the Casino some 100 years ago and the first national championships were held on its grassy courts from 1881 until 1915, when the tournament moved to Forest Hills, New York.

Hall of Fame exhibits include Davis Cup memorabilia, historical displays and equipment exhibits. Outside the main building, the Casino's dozen grass courts stretch across to the restored "court tennis" court, where you can see how the "sport of kings" was played in England and Europe during the 13th century. Each summer, a Grand Prix tennis tournament lures top international players; it is one of the few professional tennis championships played on grass in the United States.

## WHERE TO STAY

**Luxury**
The luxury **Inn at Castle Hill** ( (401) 849-3800 TOLL-FREE (800) 466-1355 FAX (401) 849-3838, on Ocean Drive has 10 rooms and a beautiful view. This handsome retreat rests on 32 acres (13 hectares) of shoreline hugging Narragansett Bay and the Atlantic Ocean. Reservations should be made well in advance.

**Expensive**
If you prefer to stay in one of the old Newport homes, the **Guest House Association of Newport** ( (401) 846-5444, P.O. Box 981, Newport, RI 02840, will help you find rooms.

Offering standard hotel and motel accommodations are **Newport Harbor Hotel and Marina** ( (401) 847-9000 TOLL-FREE (800) 955-2558 FAX (401) 849-6380, 49 America's Cup Avenue; and **Doubletree Hotel New-**

port ( (401) 849-2600 TOLL-FREE (800) 222-8733 FAX (401) 846-7210, Goat Island.

**Moderate**
There are many bed-and-breakfast establishments in the area. For a list of them, contact the **Bed & Breakfast of Rhode Island** ( (401) 849-1298, P.O. Box 3291, Newport, RI 02840, which also helps in making reservations.

Other accommodations include **Best Western The Mainstay Inn** ( (401) 849-9880 TOLL-FREE (800) 528-1234 FAX (401) 849-4391, 151 Admiral Kalbfas Road; **Mill Street Inn** ( (401) 849-9500 TOLL-FREE (888) 645-5784 FAX (401) 848-5131, 75 Mill Street.

## EATING OUT

Newport presents a variety of dining choices.

**Expensive**
One of New England's most appealing French-style restaurants is **La Petite Auberge** ( (401) 849-6669, 19 Charles Street, with its French classic and nouvelle cuisine.

The **ISS Newport** ( (401) 846-1200, is a restored fishing-boat-turned-restaurant moored offshore at Waite's Wharf; it specializes in lobster.

French-style provincial fare is the mainstay at **Le Bistro** ( (401) 849-7778, Bowen's Wharf.

Interesting colonial dishes are served at the **White Horse Tavern** ( (401) 849-3600, Marlborough and Farewell Streets, the nation's oldest operating tavern.

**The Inn at Castle Hill** ( (401) 849-3800; **The Black Pearl** ( (401) 864-5264, Bannister's Wharf; and **Clark Cooke House** ( (401) 849-2900, Bannister's Wharf, are also fine restaurants.

**Moderate**
Choices include plain and exotic seafood at the **Scales and Shells** ( (401) 846-3474, 527 Thames Street; **The Mooring** ( (401) 846-2260, Sawyer's Wharf, which serves great clam chowder; and **Puerini's** ( (401) 847-5506, 24 Memorial Boulevard West, where excellent pasta dishes are served.

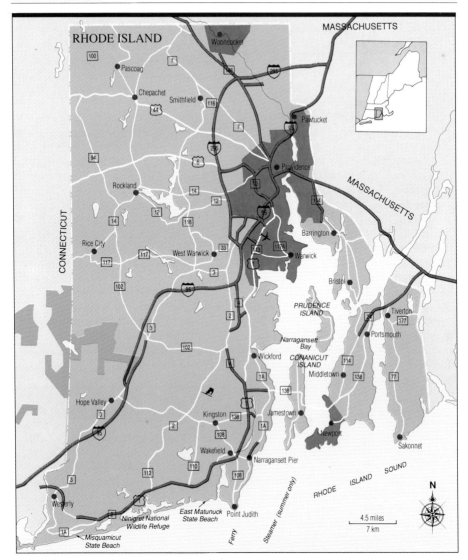

For more restaurant suggestions, pick up a free *Newport Guide* from the town's Information Center at the Brick Market Place.

## NEWPORT AREA EXCURSIONS

A side trip to **Jamestown**, three miles (five kilometers) west of Newport on Conanicut Island, should include a drive along its southern tip; there are superb views across Narragansett Bay from Beaver Trail Lighthouse, including **Fort Wetherhill** — built on 100-ft- (30-m)-tall granite cliffs — and Mackerel Cove.

## BLOCK ISLAND

Where do Rhode Islanders go during the summer to get away from it all? Small, Block Island, 11 sq miles (28 sq km), situated about 12 miles (19 km) south of the mainland off Point Judith.

A relatively unspoiled retreat of oceanside cliffs, shifting sand dunes and spectacular annual spring and fall bird migrations, Block Island has cooler summer temperatures than on the mainland and great beachcombing and biking. The beaches are almost deserted even at the height of the tourist season and some of the best deep-sea fishing can be had in the island's waters.

## GETTING THERE

Most visitors to the island arrive by ferry from Port Galilee, Providence, or New London, Connecticut. However, **New England Airlines** operate regular 12 minute chartered flights from **Westerly**, Rhode Island, ( (401) 596-2460 TOLL-FREE (800) 243-2460 and from Block Island ( (401) 466-5881.

Before (or after) your trip to Block Island, you can stay in Westerly at the **Pine Lodge Motel** ( (401) 322-0333 TOLL-FREE (800) 838-0333, 92 Old Post Road, Westerly which has 22 cottages rented weekly in summer and 11 motel rooms (moderate), reservations are recommended; and dine on New England cuisine at **Shelter Harbor Inn** ( (401) 833-8883 TOLL-FREE (800) 468-8883, 10 Wagner Street, Westerly (moderate). On Block Island try the **Olympia Tea Room** ( (401) 348-8211, Bay Street, in the center of town, an authentic early-American soda fountain transformed into a great little bistro (moderate).

## AROUND THE ISLAND

**Cycling** is one of the most popular ways to get around Block Island. Bicycle rentals are near the Old Harbor and Great Salt Pond ferry docks. By bike or car, head to **Mohegan Bluffs** on the island's south shore; multicolored clay cliffs 200 ft (61 m) in height stretch for several miles along the shore, offering a spectacular ocean vista, with the steep walking paths to the beaches that rim the coastline below.

Not far away is **Palatine Graves**, east off Dickens Point, said to be the burial grounds of 18th-century Dutch immigrants. **Settlers' Rock**, resting on the shore of Cow Cove, is the island's own Plymouth Rock, commemorating the arrival of the first pioneers on the island in 1661.

Much of the north shore is a bird and wildlife refuge and an old stone lighthouse on Sandy Point can be reached along a sandy path. **North Light** is a prime spot for birdwatching and sunsets.

**New Harbor** is great for surf fishing and water sports. The best swimming is along the eastern shore, especially at **Crescent Beach**, but the deserted beaches along the windswept western shore can also be very appealing. (Be cautious of strong undertows and rugged surf.) You can also explore some of the 365 freshwater ponds in the island's interior.

Taxi island tours (pick them up near Old Harbor ferry) are gaining popularity with visitors who prefer to leave the driving to someone else. A round trip lasts little more than an hour and drivers will usually let you stop for photographs.

The island's folklore is rich in stories of 18th century pirates and in tales of undiscovered treasure buried on the island by Captain Kidd and others.

Even more infamous than pirates is the island's reputation for shipwrecks. More than 1,000 ships have gone down off its fog bound coast. Folk tales tell of unscrupulous islanders who lured boats to the treacherous waters, then looted, wrecked and sank the ships. Tourists today receive a friendlier welcome.

## WHERE TO STAY

### Expensive
The **1661 Inn and Guesthouse** ( (401) 466-2421 or (401) 466-2063 TOLL-FREE (800) MANISSES FAX (401) 466-2858, Old Harbor, Spring Street, is a luxurious Victorian hotel with ocean views. There is also the **Samuel Peckham Inn** ( (401) 466-2439 or 466-2567, New Harbor.

### Moderate
Historic **Spring House** ( (401) 466-5844 FAX (401) 466-2633, 52 Spring Street, one of the island's best known hotels, has been greeting visitors since 1852; its verandah offers a fine view of the Atlantic. Block Island has several other moderately priced inns and bed-and-breakfast accommodation.

## EATING OUT

Block Island has several fine, moderately-priced restaurants: **Ballard's Inn** ( (401) 466-2231, Old Harbor, serves Italian and American cuisine; **Harborside Inn** ( (401)

466-5504, Old Harbor, has good steaks and seafood and **Samuel Peckham Tavern** ( (401) 466-2439, New Harbor, has lobster specialties.

## PROVIDENCE

This handsome city, set like Rome on seven hills and bisected by the Providence River, was founded in 1636 by Roger Williams after clashes with the Puritans forced him out of Massachusetts. Williams' open, spirited

offers guided tours with 18th-century machine demonstrations.)

Textile manufacture brought the city into the 19th century and Providence became an important industrial center. However, with the Great Depression and the southward shift of industry after World War II, the city fell on harder times.

Today Providence, the capital of Rhode Island and the second largest city in New England, has a revitalized downtown district and streets of Federal-style homes that haven't changed much since the 19th century.

humanity has endured in Providence's sunny streets and lovely homes and in the liberal character that gave rise to two of the nations finest schools, Brown University and the Rhode Island School of Design.

### BACKGROUND

Early Providence earned its reputation as a seaport in the Triangle Trade (rum, slaves and sugar). When the China Trade opened in 1781, many Providence merchants made a fortune. By 1793, with maritime fortunes declining, Slater Mill (in suburban Pawtucket) became the first American mill to harness water power to spin cotton. (Now an historic site, the Roosevelt Street mill

### GENERAL INFORMATION

Providence is an ideal city for walking, given its one-way streets, narrow roadways and snarled traffic.

The **Preservation Society** ( (401) 831-7440, offers several guided walking tours of various city districts. If you prefer to stroll at your own pace, contact the **Convention and Visitors Bureau** ( (401) 274-1636, 30 Exchange Terrace, RI 02903, for its pamphlets on self-guided walking tours.

Providence, Rhode Island's state capital and New England's second-largest city.

## TOURING THE CITY

**City Hall**, at Kennedy Plaza in the revitalized downtown district, is designed in the manner of the Louvre and the Tuileries in Paris. The **Providence Biltmore Hotel** a 1920s showplace is now transformed into a first-class hostelry, with a grand marble staircase in the lobby.

South of Kennedy Plaza is the ornate Majestic Theatre (now called the **Lederer Theater**), a 1917 movie house that is all terra cotta and arches; it is home to the Tony Award-winning Trinity Square Repertory Company, one of the finest in the country. East of the plaza, between Westminster and Weybosset Streets, is **The Arcade**, the country's oldest indoor shopping "mall" (1828) and sole survivor of several Greek Revival-style "temples of trade," built in America in the early 1800s. Today, it is a lively marketplace with shops and eateries.

Across the Providence River at the foot of College Hill (South Water and College Streets) is **Market House**, a red brick building built in 1773 that served as the political and commercial center of colonial Providence. It is also the site of the Providence Tea Party, where on March 2, 1775, revolutionaries burned hundreds of pounds of British tea in an act of defiance against the Crown. The house is part of the prestigious **Rhode Island School of Design**. The school maintains a museum, part of which is the elegant, mahogany-paneled Pendleton House and its collection of 18th-century American furniture.

North on Main Street is the **Meeting House of the First Baptist Church** in America, a preserved 1775 colonial church designed by Joseph Brown; it is a tribute to Roger Williams, founder of Providence, who established the church in 1638. Continue north on Main and you come to the **Roger Williams National Memorial**, a park that is the site of the original Providence settlement in 1636.

Opposite is the **Cathedral of St. John**, established in 1722, one of four original colonial parishes in the state. Its box pews and communion silver date to the Queen Anne period.

You are now approaching the beginnings of Benefit Street.

## BENEFIT STREET — A MILE OF HISTORY

Benefit Street area is an impressive concentration of original colonial buildings. Beautifully restored 18th- and 19th-century Federal houses, churches and museums overlook the city's historic waterfront. The Providence Preservation Society (headquarters at 24 Meeting Street) offers guided tours and pamphlets that describe some of the 100 historic homes (built largely by early sea captains and colonial merchants) that line Benefit and adjoining streets.

The street itself has a curious history. Once a meandering dirt path that led to informal graveyards behind family homes, it was straightened and "improved for the benefit" of the people, so the official proclamation reads.

Walking south, you will see several Federal homes and the **Old State House**, where the Rhode Island General Assembly renounced allegiance to King George III and signed their Declaration of Independence on May 4, 1776, more than two months before the 13 colonies gave their assent to liberty in Philadelphia.

Farther south is the **Providence Athenaeum**, an 1838 building that resembles a Greek temple and is one of America's oldest libraries. The modest clapboard, 1707 Quaker-style **house of Governor Stephen Hopkins**, a signatory of the Declaration of Independence (Benefit and Hopkins Streets) is open to visitors. It is said that he nudged other delegates at the Continental Congress into supporting that document. Next is the **First Unitarian Church**, built in 1816, whose steeple holds the largest and heaviest bell cast by Paul Revere & Sons.

The **John Brown House**, on Power Street just east of Benefit Street, was described by John Quincy Adams as "the most magnificent and elegant mansion that I have ever seen on this continent." Built in 1786, the three-story Georgian mansion once belonged to John Brown, one of four Brown brothers. Another brother, Moses, developed the Slater Mill; Joseph was a noted architect who designed some of Providence's most enduring landmarks; and Nicholas was the founder of Rhode Island College, now Brown University. All of the brothers played important roles in shaping the future of Providence.

The Brown family collections include a display of early Rhode Island furniture. One of the best pieces, a block-front secretary, has been described as "one of the finest examples of American colonial furniture existent."

North of the Brown House, at Prospect and Cottage Streets, is the 133-acre (54-hectare) College Hill campus of **Brown University**. Chartered in 1764, it is the seventh oldest college in the United States. The university's **John Carter Brown Library** holds the world's premier collection of early and colonial Americana.

---

## CONSTITUTION HILL

Across the river and west on Interstate 44 is the summit of Constitution Hill, upon which rests the **State Capitol**, its white marble glistening in the sun. The capitol was built in 1891 and its cupola is the second largest unsupported dome in the world, after St. Peter's in Rome. The building houses an historic full-length portrait of George Washington by Gilbert Stuart, the original royal Charter of 1663 and of course, legislative chambers and the governor's office. One-hour guided tours are offered weekdays from 9 AM to 3:30 PM.

---

## WHERE TO STAY

The **Providence Biltmore** ( (401) 421-0700 TOLL-FREE (800) 437-4824 FAX (401) 455-3050, Kennedy Plaza (expensive to luxury) was built in the 1920s and beautifully transformed into a modern hotel. It is in a class all its own.

The city's newest, **The Westin Hotel** ( (401) 598-8000 TOLL-FREE (800) 228-3000 FAX (401) 598-8200, is located at One West Exchange Street (expensive to luxury). It overlooks the state capitol and downtown and includes a full-service health spa, lounges, two restaurants. Special packages are available.

*Rhode Island*

In the moderate to expensive range are the 13story **Holiday Inn Downtown** ( (401) 831-3900 TOLL-FREE (800) 465-4329 FAX (401) 751-0007, 21 Atwells Avenue; and **Marriott Providence** ( (401) 272-2400 TOLL-FREE (800) 228-9290 FAX (401) 273-2686, Charles and Orms Streets. In nearby **Pawtucket** is the moderately-priced **Comfort Inn-Providence** ( (401) 723-6700 TOLL-FREE (800) 228-5150 FAX (401) 726-6380, 2 George Street, where children stay free.

---

## EATING OUT

### Expensive

The best seafood in town is found at the **Bluepoint Oyster Bar** ( (401) 272-6145, 99 North Main Street. For excellent Italian cuisine, try **Camille's Roman Garden** ( (401) 751-4812, 71 Bradford Street. **Pot au Feu** ( (401) 273-8953, 44 Custom House Street, serves excellent continental cuisine.

### Moderate

**Wes's Rib House** ( (401) 421-9090, 1 Robar Plaza, serves hearty meals of Missouri-style barbecue ribs, chicken, pork chops, or cured ham. **Alforno** ( (401) 273-9760, 577 South Main Street, features northern Italian cuisine.

### Inexpensive

**Little Chopsticks** ( (401) 351-4290, 495 Smith Street, specializes in Hunan and Szechuan dishes.

# Travelers'
# Tips

## GETTING THERE

New England is accessible by air, rail and road. Major entry points are Boston, New York (only minutes away from Connecticut, the southernmost New England state) and Montreal, Canada.

### By Air

Most major international airlines provide service to Boston, but fares are often cheaper to New York. Some United States carriers offer in-country flight coupons at substantial savings to foreign travelers. These programs change from year to year, so check with you travel agent when planning your trip. In 1997, for example, a **Visit USA Pass**, for travel within the continental United States is available from US Air for foreign travelers. The coupons could only be purchased outside the United States by foreigners or United States citizens working abroad.

**International Airlines**
The following are telephone numbers of international carriers who maintain an office in Boston or at Boston's Logan International Airport:
**Aer Lingus** ( TOLL-FREE (800) 223-6537
**Air Alliance** ( TOLL-FREE (800)778-3000
**Air Atlantic/Canadian Air** ( TOLL-FREE (800) 426-7000
**Air Canada** TOLL-FREE ( (800) 422-6232
**Air Nova** TOLL-FREE ( (800) 776-3000
**Air France** TOLL-FREE ( (800) 237-2747
**Air New Zealand** TOLL-FREE ( (800) 262-1234
**Alitalia Airlines** TOLL-FREE ( (800) 223-5730
**American Airlines** TOLL-FREE ( (800) 433-7300
**ATA** ( TOLL-FREE (800) 225-2995
**British Airways** TOLL-FREE ( (800) 247-9297
**Continental Airlines** ( (617) 569-8400
**El Al Israel** TOLL-FREE ( (800) 223-6700
**Icelandair** TOLL-FREE ( (800) 223-5500
**Finnair** TOLL-FREE ( (800) 223-5700
**Japan Airlines** ( (617) 262-8800
**KLM** TOLL-FREE ( (800) 374-7747
**Korean Air** TOLL-FREE ( (800) 438-5000
**Lufthansa** TOLL-FREE ( (800) 645-3880
**Northwest** TOLL-FREE ( (800) 225-2525
**Olympic** TOLL-FREE ( (800)223-1226

**Qantas** TOLL-FREE ( (800) 227-4500
**Sabena** ( (617) 542-4296 TOLL-FREE ( (800) 955-2000
**Swissair** ( (617) 423-7778 TOLL-FREE (800) 221-4750
**TAP Air Portugal** TOLL-FREE ( (800) 428-4322
**TWA** ( (617) 367-2800 TOLL-FREE (800) 221-2000
**United** ( (617) 482-7900 TOLL-FREE (800) 241-6522
**US Airways** TOLL-FREE ( (800) 429-4322
**Virgin Atlantic Airways** TOLL-FREE ( (800) 862-8621

**Domestic Airlines**
Most domestic carriers fly to Boston and the other large New England cities (Hartford, Providence, Portland, etc.) To find economy flights to New England, you will have to consult your travel agent. Fares are variable. Competition among companies can cause sudden price wars that can make flying to New England quite reasonable. During the summer, it is advisable to avoid any discount packages that require you to fly standby. Flights are not only full but also overbooked. Make your seat reservations a week in advance to be assured of not being bumped off your flight and do your fellow travelers a favor and cancel any unwanted reservations.

The following are the toll-free numbers of domestic airlines who fly to New England and have offices in the Boston area:
**American Airlines** TOLL-FREE ( (800) 433-7300.
**American Eagle** TOLL-FREE ( (800) 433-7300
**America West** TOLL-FREE ( (800) 235-9292
**Eastwind Airlines** TOLL-FREE ( (800) 644-3592
**Midwest Express** TOLL-FREE ( (800) 452-2002
**Spirit Airlines** TOLL-FREE ( (800) 772-7117
**Continental Airlines,** TOLL-FREE ( (800) 525-0280
**Delta Airlines** TOLL-FREE ( (800) 221-1212
**Northwest Orient** TOLL-FREE ( (800) 225-2525
**TWA** TOLL-FREE ( (800) 221-2000
**United Airlines** TOLL-FREE ( (800) 241-6522
**US Airways** TOLL-FREE ( (800) 428-4322

### By Rail

Amtrak, the only passenger carrier in the United States, connects a few New England cities and offers frequent service to Boston from Montreal and New York. Intermediate stops in Connecticut are scheduled on the New York–Boston line. From mid-May to mid-October, you can hop off the train from Montreal at Port Kent, New York and take the ferry across Lake Champlain to Burlington, Vermont. For prices and schedules, call **Amtrak** ( TOLL-FREE (800) 872-7245. For a free travel planner, write to Amtrak Distribution Center, P.O. Box 7717, Itasca, IL 60143.

## By Greyhound Bus

Greyhound Lines can get you to New England from within the United States or Canada. Its routes will usually take you into Boston or New York with connections to Maine, New Hampshire and Vermont. Your travel agent or local Greyhound agent can provide information on schedules and fares, or contact Greyhound ( TOLL-FREE (800) 231-2222, in **New York** ( (212) 971-6300 and in **Boston** ( (617) 526-1800.

## By Road

Although most New Englanders consider New England a country unto itself, there are no border crossings when driving within the Unites States.

When entering from Canada, even United States citizens need to have appropriate identification (see TRAVEL DOCUMENTS below).

## TRAVEL DOCUMENTS

When arriving in the United States, Canadian and Mexican citizens need only show proof of identification and residence (a driver's license will do). British need only a valid passport. Other visitors need a valid passport and a United States visa. Contact the United States embassy or consulate in your country for the exact details for obtaining a visa.

Your travel agent can also help in obtaining a visa. Allow 28 days for processing.

Vaccinations may or may not be required for entry into the United States. (Country of origin or recently-visited countries could alter your situation; check before you depart.)

*Travelers' Tips*

## CONSULATES

### In Boston

AUSTRALIAN ( (617) 248-8655, 20 Park Plaza, Boston, MA 02166
BRITISH ( (617) 248-9555, 600 Atlantic Avenue, Boston, MA 02166
CANADIAN ( (617) 262-3760, 3 Copley Place, Boston, MA 02116
FRENCH ( (617) 542-7374, 21 St. James Avenue, MA 02116
GERMAN ( (617) 536-4414, 3 Copley Place, Suite 500, Boston, MA 02116
IRISH ( (617) 267-9330, 535 Boylston, Boston, MA 02116
ITALIAN ( (617) 542-0483, 100 Boylston Street, Boston, MA 02116
NETHERLANDS ( (617) 542-8452, 6 St. James Avenue, Boston, MA 02116
SPANISH ( (617) 536-2506, 545 Boylston Street, Boston, MA 02116
SWEDISH ( (617) 350-0111, 286 Congress Street, 6th Floor, Boston, MA 02116

### In New York

AUSTRALIAN ( (212)408-8400, 630 Fifth Avenue, New York, NY 10021
BRITISH ( (212) 745-0200, 845 Third Avenue, New York, NY 10022
CANADIAN ( (212) 596-1600, 1251 Avenue of the Americas, New York, NY 10020-1175
DANISH ( (212) 223-4545, 825 Third Avenue, 32nd floor, New York, NY 10022
FRENCH ( (212) 606-3621, 934 Fifth Avenue, New York, NY 10021
GERMAN ( (212) 308-8700, 400 Park Avenue, New York, NY 10022
IRISH ( (212) 319-2555, 345 Park Avenue, 17th Floor, New York, NY 10022
ITALIAN ( (212) 739-9100, 690 Park Avenue, New York, NY 10022
NETHERLANDS ( (212) 246-1429, One Rockefeller Plaza, 11th Floor, New York, NY 10020
NORWEGIAN ( (212) 421-7333, 825 Third Avenue, 38th Floor, New York, NY 10022-7584
SPANISH ( (212) 355-4091, 150 East 58th Street, 30th Floor, New York, NY 10015
SWEDISH ( (212) 583-2250, 885 Second Avenue, New York, 45th Floor, One Dag Hammarskjold Plaza, NY 10017

## CUSTOMS

Customs allows you to bring in duty-free gifts valued up to $100. For more specific information, including shopping restrictions, contact your local American embassy or consulate branch. Carrying non-prescription narcotic drugs into the country may well result in a long prison sentence. When entering the United States, foreign visitors should allow a minimum of an hour to clear customs at Boston or New York. For Euro-

pean travelers, the close scrutiny of customs and immigration officers is sometimes shocking and annoying. During the peak summer season, foreign passport holders have had to wait up to two hours before even reaching passport control at New York's Kennedy International Airport. At Boston this rarely happens.

## WHEN TO GO

There is no best time to come to New England. Summer, fall, winter and spring all have something to offer. However, New England has a season all its own — "Colors." This arrives in early fall when the leaves change to crimson, gold and orange. Days are warm and evenings cool. The countryside is at its best then.

New England summers are traditionally glorious and comfortable, with lots of sun

ABOVE: Moped rental on Martha's Vineyard.
OPPOSITE: Boston's MTA subway, made famous by the Kingston Trio's lyrics in the 1950s.

and gentle cooling breezes off the ocean, although hot and humid conditions are not altogether unfamiliar to the region. Summer is the height of the tourist season, with most attractions open from late May to October.

Winters can be bitterly cold, with snow and cutting winds. But it is rarely too severe for skiers. New England has more than 100 ski areas throughout its six states. It is neither the Alps nor the Rockies, but the slopes are good and fast, the cross-country runs Olympic class and the hospitality, warm and friendly.

Spring is often referred to as the mud season: lots of rain, with warm days and cool nights. However, several airlines offer special low fares during this traditional off-season period. Your reward is the freshness of spring with its new growth and blooming flowering wild flowers and fruit trees.

## WHAT TO TAKE

New England styles tend to be casual, especially in Maine, Vermont and New Hampshire. More traditional styles rule preppy Connecticut and Rhode Island; Massachusetts has a little bit of everything. Big cities, especially Boston, may require very formal wear, especially for business meetings and restaurant dining. Men should pack a jacket and tie and women should bring a dress or suit.

While season dictates other clothing needs, summer visitors should bring along a warm sweater or jacket in case of cool evening temperatures — especially when visiting the coast.

Regardless of season, rain gear is appropriate.

## GETTING AROUND

Rail travel is the most limited means of getting around New England (see GETTING THERE page 260).

### AIRLINES

Airplanes can get you from city to city. In addition to the domestic carriers listed under GETTING THERE page 268, there are small domestic airlines that provide flights within New England:

**Cape Air and Nantucket Airlines** TOLL-FREE ( (800) 272-5488, from Boston's Logan Airport to Provincetown, Martha's Vineyard and Nantucket.

**Colgan Airlines** TOLL-FREE ( (800) 272-5488, from Boston's Logan Airport to Rockland, Augusta and Bar Harbor, Maine.

## BUS SERVICES

Reasonable bus services are available throughout New England, provided by the following three major companies with central offices in Boston:

**Bonanza** ( (617) 423-5810 TOLL-FREE (800) 556-3815.

**Greyhound** ( (617) 526-1800 TOLL-FREE (800) 231-2222.

**Peter Pan Bus Lines Inc**. ( (617) 426-7838 TOLL-FREE (800) 628-8468 outside Massachusetts; in-state TOLL-FREE (800) 332-8995.

Bus travel is more time-consuming than air, but it does offer the advantage of allowing you to see the countryside at a relaxed pace.

## TAXIS AND LIMOUSINES

Taxis operate throughout New England, although they are most often found in big cities rather than the small towns. Rates vary; ask if there are standard rates for airport routes.

Limousines are another way to get conveniently from airports to major cities; rates are often comparable to taxi fares. In Boston, contact:

**Carey of Boston Limousine** ( (617) 623-8700

**Commonwealth Limousine** ( (617) 787-5575

**Boston Cab** ( (617) 536-5010

**Checker Cab** ( (617) 536-7000

**Red Cab** ( (617) 734-5000

## AUTOMOBILE RENTAL

By far the best way to see New England is at your own pace and schedule by automobile. Exploring the small country roads is to find the best New England has to offer.

Most airports, major hotels, or tourist centers have offices (or can provide information) for car rentals. Renters must have a valid driver's license and a credit card (used for deposit), be at least 21 years of age, though, in certain circumstances some companies set the minimum age at 25 years. Foreign drivers may need an international driver's license. Be sure to check out liability clauses in the rental agreement; they are not automatically included and your personal automobile insurance or credit card may cover none, part, or all of your liability risks.

Check if your airline offers car rental packages with airfare. Car rental agency telephone numbers include:

**Alamo** TOLL-FREE ( (800) 329-9633

**Avis** TOLL-FREE ( (800) 331-1212

**Budget** TOLL-FREE ( (800) 527-0700

**Dollar** TOLL-FREE ( (800) 800-4000

**Hertz** TOLL-FREE ( (800) 654-3131

**National** TOLL-FREE ( (800) 227-7368

Foreign travelers can often get better rates when booking from abroad. "Fly and Drive" packages are often better buys than booking flights and car rentals separately.

For the most adventurous travelers, consider renting a camper. Throughout New England, in state and national forests, there are well-maintained and equipped campgrounds, some of the best in the United States. There are also many private campgrounds that have luxury camping facilities — hot water, showers, pool, playground, electrical hook-ups, etc. Listings of camping facilities can be obtained from the individual state offices of tourism, whose addresses are included in the opening section of each chapter.

## ACCOMMODATION

Throughout New England, many hotels and motels provide the standard room with one or two double or queen-sized beds, private bath, telephone and television. As rates often change without notice, specific prices are not noted in this guide. Hotels and motels are classified in the following categories and prices assume a double room, two-person occupancy:

- inexpensive, less than $50
- moderate, $50 to $100
- expensive, $100 to $200
- luxury, over $200

Also listed are the traditional New England country inns and bed and breakfasts that are growing in popularity. Rates at the country inns are generally in the expensive category. However, if you book for a week-long stay or mid-week and off season, you can sometimes negotiate a price in the moderate range.

Bed and breakfast accommodations are in the moderate category and bring you in more individual contact with New Englanders. The bed-and-breakfast operators have a closely knit organization and will usually be more than happy to help you arrange a bed and breakfast at your next destination.

The lists of accommodations are included at the end of each destination and are not all-inclusive. State and local tourism agencies will gladly supply you with further information and help in booking rooms. On New England's back roads, many small motels offer good accommodations at reasonable prices. It is always best to examine the rooms before making a decision.

You may want to contact **Vacation Exchange Club** ( (305) 294-7766 TOLL-FREE (800) 638-3841 FAX (305) 294-1448, P.O. Box 650, Key West, FL 33041.

## EATING OUT

The most difficult thing about eating out in New England is deciding which of the many

excellent restaurants to choose. Needless to say, the lists of restaurants included with each destination are far from exhaustive. Ownership, prices, chefs and specialties do change. However, those recommended are established houses that have provided a tradition of good food over the years. Price guidelines for full meals (without liquor) are as follows: inexpensive, under $15 per person; moderate, $15 to $30; expensive, over $30. Reservations are always recommended.

## TIPPING

Tips are not included on your tab. Fifteen percent is the standard. Don't hesitate to leave more if the service has been exceptional, but never leave less unless the waiter or waitress has been surly.

## SHOPPING

For general shopping information see SHOP TILL YOU DROP on page 46. Below is some advice for specialty shopping.

### ANTIQUES

"Antique" is generally a term bandied about in a rather casual manner. In the United States, it has often become interchangeable with the word "old." Therefore, it is best to look to United States Customs for some kind of workable definition.

In 1930, the federal government ruled that objects must be at least 100 years old to be classified as antiques and admitted into the country duty-free and in 1966, a tariff act further ruled that there would be duty-free admission into the country of all objects 100 years old before the date of entry.

Therefore, anything at least 100 years old is "officially" given antique status, although many objects less than a century old are generally included under that term. It is wise to be aware of the official government distinction.

OPPOSITE: Second-hand clothing and bric-a-brac in rural Northeast Connecticut.

## Buying Antiques

Like anything else, antique prices reflect the free enterprise marketplace. In other words, things are worth whatever someone will pay for them. You should therefore consider all antique price tags as general starting points for negotiation. You should not have to pay the asking price for an antique unless there is heavy demand or competition for the particular piece or style. (Then you might even be forced to pay more, if your heart is set on it and your wallet deep enough.)

## Furniture Styles

Colonists who settled in New England in the 17th century tried to duplicate those styles which were popular vack home in England. But very few had the skills or services of a master carpenter or furniture maker. Thus, you will find that the earliest "early American" antiques might be rudimentary pieces of furniture — often large, squared-off pine and oak cupboards, broad flat tables, and smaller boxy furnishing.

After the wilderness was ruined and great cities sprang up along the eastern

Always attempt to bring down the price, even if you are normally a timid negotiator. Antique dealers expect you to do it; besides, the asking price probably reflects this realization.

As an educated consumer, you might want to pick up an antique price/guide book that offers background on history, styles and general prices. One of the most consistent and respected guides is Kovel's, which can be purchased at most major bookstores.

Also bear in mind that almost all types of Americana — whether or not they are listed in official antique guidebooks — have become sought-after collector's items.

seaboard in the 18th century, colonial furniture took on its distinctive, elegant style. Some antiques are recognized art forms. Typical of certain time periods and much sought after today, they include the following:

**Queen Anne** (1702–1714) — walnut furniture distinguished by curved contours, often with ball and claw feet and shell carvings.

**Early Georgian** (1714–1745) — the Queen Anne style was elaborated with paw feet and eagles' or lions' head carvings; a heavy baroque style came into vogue after 1735. Most of the furniture makers continued to use walnut, but mahogany was becoming increasingly popular.

Chippendale (1745–1765) — perhaps the most renowned period in American furniture styling, with the works of master cabinet maker Thomas Chippendale most prominent. Straight square legs, but a great freedom of design, with many Gothic, Chinese and French touches, including lavish fretwork and rococo flourishes. Almost exclusive use of mahogany.

**Adam Style** (1760–1785) — classical, delicate with much painted decoration. This period also saw the introduction of oval and sideboard tables and wheel back chairs. Mahogany dominated, although sycamore and other light woods were also used.

**Hepplewhite Style** (1780–1795) — light and graceful with much painted decorations, inlay and delicate carving that often used Prince of Wales feathers, ears of wheat and honeysuckle motifs. Also Anglicized versions of contemporary French styles; continued use of mahogany.

**Sheraton Style** (1790–1810) — Thomas Sheraton was a gifted furniture designer, not a cabinet maker. His style is dominated by square back chairs, tapered legs, bow front chests and sideboards, pedestal dining tables and much use of inlay in mahogany.

### Dealer's Directory

In Massachusetts, contact the **State Tourism Department** for a list of the antique dealers in the area.

Watch for those who belong to the Berkshire County Massachusetts Antiques Dealers Association and guarantee antique authenticity.

### Cautions

Be very careful about what you buy when purchasing expensive or valuable pieces. Always ask for antique authentication, or frequent dealers who take pride in their merchandise and guarantee authenticity. A simple tag description should not necessarily satisfy you unless you are knowledgeable about antiques. In fact, stories abound about how unscrupulous dealers fabricating entire case histories for antiques in order to impress — and con — buyers. It is *caveat emptor* — "let the buyer beware."

### HANDICRAFTS

Throughout New England are many specialty shops that sell only regionally or locally crafted merchandise. Particularly appealing are the wooden and fabric items. You can find a variety of children's pull toys and puzzles that are as durable as they are attractive. These are not bargains because many are one of a kind, more works of art than toys.

Handmade cotton clothing, stuffed animals and kitchen items are also plentiful. These are usually products of cottage industries that each year play a larger role in the economies of the small New England towns.

### OUTLET STORES

Until a quarter of a century ago, all the New England factory towns had stores that sold their "accidented" products. The careful, clever shopper could save enormous amounts. A family could be dressed and shod for a fraction of retail cost and household linens were likewise cheaper. Now most of these factories are closed, but outlet stores remain. They are not the great sources of bargains they once were, but the discounts are generally 20 to 30 percent which include seconds, remaindered stock, samples, overruns of almost every name brand sold in the United States: Fieldcrest, Dior, Barbizon, Levi, Bass, Arrow, Haynes, White Stag, Nike, Adidas, New Balance, etc.

Freeport, Maine, is the best known of the outlet store shopping areas, but there are others throughout New England. Each spring new guides to the outlet stores appear on the New England newsstands to help visitors and residents alike find the best bargains.

### MONEY

United States dollar rates have fluctuated so wildly of late it is pointless to include any specific comparative guidelines. Trends have slightly decreased the home currency value of many European and Asian visitors.

It is advisable to purchase travelers' checks in United States dollars for your money use because many banks do not offer foreign currency exchange services. Travelers' checks can be easily replaced if stolen or lost. Most hotels, shops and restaurants accept major credit cards — Mastercard and Visa are the most common; only very large establishments and travel related agencies accept American Express. You can also apply for a PIN number and use your credit card, debit card, or ATM card to obtain money from cash dispensers just about everywhere in New England. There may be a withdrawal fee of the equivalent of US$1.

## WEIGHTS AND MEASURES

The United States does not use the metric system. Conversions to US standard measures are as follows:

**Length, Distance & Area**
| | |
|---|---|
| inches to centimeters | multiply by 2.54 |
| centimeters to inches | multiply by 0.39 |
| feet to meters | multiply by 0.30 |
| meters to feet | multiply by 3.28 |
| yards to meters | multiply by 0.91 |
| meters to yards | multiply by 1.09 |
| miles to kilometers | multiply by 1.61 |
| kilometers to miles | multiply by 0.62 |
| km sq to miles sq | multiply by 0.38 |
| acres to hectares | multiply by 0.40 |
| hectares to acres | multiply by 2.47 |

**Weight**
| | |
|---|---|
| ounces to grams | multiply by 28.35 |
| grams to ounces | multiply by 0.035 |
| pounds to kilograms | multiply by 0.45 |
| kilograms to pounds | multiply by 2.21 |

**Volume**
| | |
|---|---|
| gallons to liters | multiply by 3.79 |
| liters to gallons | multiply by 0.26 |

## COMMUNICATIONS

### NEWSPAPERS

Pick up any local daily newspaper for the latest overview of local and national news. The *Boston Globe* is New England's leading regional newspaper. *USA Today*, a national daily, provides national news capsules. The *New York Times* is widely read in New England and available in major cities. When in Boston and Cambridge, those aching for news of home can find comfort at the Harvard Square institution, **Out of Town News**. Look for the kiosk smack in the middle of the square. Out of Town has dailies from all over the world. They also sell a wide assortment of magazines and journals.

### TELEVISION

America has four major television networks and thousands of local affiliate stations. Devotees of public television will find excellent programming on Boston's public network. Add cable and pay TV to the selections and the country becomes a TV-junkie's paradise, with scores of choices.

### MAIL

Most post offices are open Monday through Friday from 9 AM to 5 PM. At the time of publication, first-class letters require a 32-cent stamp and postcards 20 cents. International rates vary with destination, but are generally about twice the domestic tariff.

### TELEPHONE

The breakup of AT&T has played havoc with phone users throughout the country. Now several kinds of pay phones are in operation, all requiring different steps of operation; read the directions carefully before depositing your coins. A local call is $.20 at most pay phones. To use international calling cards, you'll need to dial 0 to get the operator.

Major hotels have fax services, at a price, as do office services stores in the larger cities.

For the electronically equipped traveler, CCITT and Bell approved modems that will work in the United States.

## PUBLIC HOLIDAYS

National public holidays include:
New Year's Day — January 1

Martin Luther King, Jr.'s Birthday — January 15
Lincoln's Birthday — February 12
Washington's Birthday — February 22
Memorial Day — last Monday in May
Independence Day — July 4
Labor Day — first Monday in September
Columbus Day — second Monday in October
Thanksgiving Day — fourth Thursday in November
Christmas Day — December 25

During those holidays, federal, state and city offices close and more importantly the banks. In cities and towns, stores and many restaurants are closed on Sundays, but shopping malls are usually open seven days a week.

Other holidays such as St. Patrick's Day (March 17), Easter Sunday (April), Mother's Day (May), Father's Day (June) and Halloween (October 31) may be celebrated in various ways by different states and communities.

Also, state holidays vary widely. For a calendar of state events, contact the appropriate state tourism agencies.

## TIME ZONES

New England is in the Eastern Time Zone, the same time of day as New York, one hour ahead of Chicago, three hours ahead of California, normally five hours behind Great Britain and six hours behind western Europe. There is a five hour time differential between New England and Europe for a few weeks in October and April when the Europeans switch to daylight saving time before the Americans.

## Further Reading

ALCOTT, LOUISA MAY, *Little Women*
EMERSON, RALPH WALDO, *Essays*
FALLIN, CATHERINE & ELIZABETH TALBOT, *Martha's Vineyard Gardens & Houses* New York, Simon and Schuster, 1992
*Fifty Hikes* (series; one book for each New England state), Woodstock, Vermont, Backcountry Publications, 1983
HALE, JUDSON, *Inside New England*, New York, Harper & Row Publishers, 1982
HARRIS, JOHN, *The Boston Globe Historic Walks in Old Boston*, Old Saybrook, Connecticut, The Globe Pequot Press, 1995
HAWTHORNE, NATHANIEL, *The Scarlet Letter*, *The House of the Seven Gables*
HAZLEGROVE, CARY, *Nantucket, Seasons on the Island*, San Francisco, Chronicle Books, 1995
JAMES, HENRY, *The Bostonians*
MARTIN, TOVAH, *Tasha Tudor's Garden*, New York, Houghton Mifflin, 1994
MELVILLE, HERMAN, *Moby Dick*
PEIRCE, NEAL, *The New England States*, New York, W.W. Norton and Company, Inc. 1976
PENNYPINCHER, A & A MISER, *Outlet Guide to New England 9th Edition*, Old Saybrook, Connecticut, Globe Pequot Press, 1995
SCHUMAN, MICHAEL, *Favorite Daytrips in New England*, Emmaus PA, Yankee Books Imprint, Rodale Press, 1987
SQUIRE, ELIZABETH, *Guide to the Recommended Country Inns of New England*, Old Saybrook, Connecticut, The Globe Pequot Press, 1996
THOREAU, HENRY DAVID, *Walden*
WOODWORTH, NANCY & RICHARD, *Getaways for Gourmets*, West Hartford, Connecticut, Wood Pond Press, 1997.

## Photo Credits

Ellis Klarenbeek: pages 5 *right*, 63 *right*, 70, 71, 77, 80, 89, 90 *top*, 98, 99, 113, 114–115, 120, 152–153, 163, 164 *left*, 168, 176, 190, 197 *right*, 202, 215 *top and bottom*, 222, 252, 253, 255, 259, 267, 271. Marcia Schneldler: pages 40 *bottom*, 59, 61. Westin Hotel: page 37.

Publisher's note: *Traveler's Companion* is the series title under which the international series of Kümmerly+Frey *Insider's Guides* is published in North America. The content of all editions are identical.

# Quick Reference A–Z Guide
## to Places and Topics of Interest with Listed Accommodation, Restaurants and Useful Telephone Numbers